Uncle John's BATHROOM READER®

EXTRAORDINARY BOOK OF FACTS

AND BIZARRE INFORMATION

Bathroom Readers' Institute

San Diego, California

**Uncle John's Extraordinary
Book of Facts and Bizarre Information**
is a compilation of running feet and selected feature
articles from the following eight previously
published Bathroom Reader titles:

Uncle John's Unstoppable Bathroom Reader, 2003
Uncle John's Ahh-Inspiring Bathroom Reader, 2002
Uncle John's Bathroom Reader Plunges Into the Universe, 2002
Uncle John's Supremely Satisfying Bathroom Reader, 2001
Uncle John's All-Purpose Extra Strength Bathroom Reader, 2000
Uncle John's Absolutely Absorbing Bathroom Reader, 1999
Uncle John's Giant 10th Anniversary Bathroom Reader, 1997
The Best of Uncle John's Bathroom Reader, 1995

For information, write: The Bathroom Readers' Hysterical Society
Portable Press, 5880 Oberlin Drive, San Diego, CA 92121
E-mail: unclejohn@advmkt.com

ISBN 10: 1–59223–605–7
ISBN 13: 978–1–59223–605–3

Printed in the U.S.A.
First printing: March 2006

06 07 08 09 10   10 9 8 7 6 5 4 3 2 1

The Team

This compilation of intriguing
information was put together by:

Allen Orso, Publisher, Portable Press
JoAnn Padgett, Director, Editorial & Production
Jennifer Browning Payne, Production Editor
Jennifer Thornton, Managing Editor
Stephanie Spadaccini, Copy Editor
Angela Kern, Research Assistant
Connie Vazquez, Product Manager
Cynthia Francisco, Executive Assistant
Robin Kilrain, Proofreader
Michael Brunsfeld, Cover Designer
Christine Factor, Editorial Intern

Thank you

The Bathroom Readers' Institute sincerely
thanks the following people whose advice
and assistance made this book possible.

Kaelin Chappell

Lynn Christel

John Dollison

Mary Lou Goforth

Kristine Hemp

Gordon Javna

Amy Miller

Bruce Myers

Jay Newman

Quynh Nguyen

Ellen O'Brien

Julia Papps

Kris Payne

Sydney Stanley

Nancy Toeppler

Contents

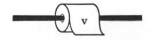

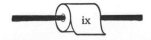

Introduction

Once again, it's time for the fat lady to sing . . . and for me to write the introduction.

Over the years our fans have sent us countless letters in which there seemed to be a recurring theme—other than that they love our books. They really enjoyed reading the little factoids on the bottom of the pages. (We call them "running feet.") We even had numerous requests for a collection of just the running feet—and we aim to please.

So about six months ago, in my blissful ignorance, we began the task of creating a unique book of running feet. In the beginning the project seemed relatively simple. The very capable Jennifer Browning Payne was elected to be my copilot (and, as it turned out, intellectual sparring partner). We proceeded to make sense of thousands of unrelated but very interesting bits of information. There were differing points of view as to how to organize the information and how to make it interesting and entertaining at the same time. We consulted numerous Bathroom Reader experts and sought the advice of many editors and writers we trust.

What you hold in your hands is the product of our labors: 390 pages of solid-gold facts and trivia, mined from eight of Uncle John's finest Bathroom Readers. It's taken many hours of hard work. It was tough, but we like what we see. We hope you do, too.

Now, if you're still reading this, it's really time to move on to the many varied pages of our new book. Just remember: it's a factoid-rich read. Take your time. And as always, go with the flow . . .

—Uncle Al

P.S. We've done our best to make sure that the facts in this book are accurate and updated, but we may have missed a few. Please let us know if we've made an error, and we'll be sure to correct it.

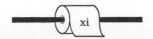

That's Ironic

Alexander Graham Bell refused to have a phone in his study—the ringing drove him nuts.

Al Capone's older brother Vince was a policeman in Nebraska.

Buzz Aldrin's mother's maiden name: Moon.

Cyndi Lauper's 1984 hit "Girls Just Want to Have Fun" was written by a man.

Fish can get seasick.

Pierre Michelin, inventor of super-safe Michelin tires, died in a car accident.

French and African marigolds both come from North America.

Pigs can catch swine flu from humans.

Kodak founder George Eastman hated to have his picture taken.

There is no rice in rice paper.

According to a Gallup Poll, one in seven Americans can't locate the United States on a map.

A check of 62 police cars in Atlanta, Georgia, found that 27 had expired tags.

John Wilkes Booth's brother once saved the life of Abraham Lincoln's son.

P. J. Tierney, father of the modern diner, died of indigestion in 1917 after eating at a diner.

The day Judy Garland died, a tornado touched down in Kansas.

Animal Briefs

Fish cough.

Walrus burp.

Snails have teeth.

Whales stampede.

Termites are blind.

Rabbits can't walk.

Jellyfish eat other jellyfish.

Snakes and armadillos can get malaria.

Camels are born without humps.

Rabbits and horses can't vomit.

Frogs drink through their skin.

Shrimp only swim backward.

Armadillos can get leprosy.

Kangaroos can't walk.

Ducks can get the flu.

Bathroom Break

If you live an average life span, you'll spend about six months on the toilet.

Rumor has it that whenever actress Joan Crawford remarried (she had five husbands), she replaced all the toilet seats in her house.

There are 34 bathrooms in the White House.

Seventy-six percent of bathroom readers prefer their toilet paper to hang over the top.

Toilet Rock, a natural rock formation shaped like a flush toilet, is in City of Rocks, New Mexico.

Favorite Barbie accessory: a pink toilet with real flushing action.

Americans use more than 4.8 billion gallons of water flushing toilets each day.

The average toilet will last about 50 years before it has to be replaced.

Alaska has more outhouses than any other state.

The first stall in a public restroom is usually the cleanest. Seeking privacy, most people skip it.

The first American to have plumbing installed in his home: Henry Wadsworth Longfellow, in 1840.

The average public swimming pool contains more urine than fluoride.

An estimated 976,000 U.S. homes have no flush toilets.

Most toilets flush in E flat.

Farting contests were held in ancient Japan. Prizes were awarded for loudness and duration.

Academy Awards

During World War II, the Oscar statue was made of plaster. Metal was an essential wartime material.

Alfred Hitchcock never won an Academy Award.

Tweety Pie won an Oscar in 1948.

Shortest film role to win an Oscar: Sylvia Miles, on-screen for six minutes in *Midnight Cowboy*.

Julie Andrews didn't get to play Eliza in the film version of *My Fair Lady* because she wasn't a "big enough star." So she starred in *Mary Poppins* and won the Oscar for Best Actress the same year, 1964.

Composer Irving Berlin is the only Academy Award presenter to give an Oscar to himself.

"Oscar" is a registered trademark of the Academy of Motion Picture Arts and Sciences, as are "Oscars," "Academy Awards," "Oscar Night," and "A.M.P.A.S."

Shirley Temple won an honorary Oscar in 1934 at the age of five.

The Oscar statue weighs 8 pounds, 13 ounces.

Edith Head won eight Oscars out of 35 nominations, making her both the top Oscar winner among costume designers and women.

The award's official title is "The Academy Award of Merit."

Cost, in parts and labor, for an Academy Award Oscar statuette: about $300.

World Population

By the year 2050 the world's elderly will outnumber the young for the first time.

In the next 60 seconds, 101 people will die and 261 babies will be born.

The world's youngest-ever parents were eight and nine years old, respectively, and lived in China in 1910.

One in five people alive today is Chinese.

Country with the longest life expectancy: Japan (78.6 years for men, 85.6 years for women).

There is no leading cause of death for people who live past the age of 100.

It is estimated that in A.D. 1000, the world population was about 300 million.

Your odds of living to age 116: one in 2 billion.

Since 1850 world population has increased by 500 percent.

Of all the people who have ever lived, only 5 to 10 percent are alive today.

By the time you reach age 60, your eyes will have been exposed to more light than would be released by detonating a nuclear bomb.

In 2006 the world's population will reach 6.5 billion. About 30 percent will be under age 15.

Today more people live in the United States (298 million) than lived in the entire world in A.D. 1000.

Baby boomers now say that "old age" begins at 79.

Ah, Caffeine

Caffeine has been scientifically proven to temporarily increase alertness, comprehension, memory, reflexes, and even the rate of learning. It also helps increase clarity of thought.

Too much caffeine can cause hand tremors, loss of coordination or appetite, insomnia—and in extreme cases, trembling, nausea, heart palpitations, and diarrhea.

Widely varying the amount of caffeine you ingest can put a strain on your liver, pancreas, heart, and nervous system. And if you're prone to ulcers, caffeine can make your situation worse.

The average American drinks 210 milligrams of caffeine a day. That's equal to two or three cups of coffee, depending on how strong it is.

How you make your coffee has a lot to do with how much caffeine you get. Instant coffee contains 65 milligrams of caffeine per serving; coffee brewed in a percolator has 80 milligrams; and coffee made using the drip method has 155 milligrams.

Top four sources of caffeine in the American diet: coffee, soft drinks, tea, and chocolate, in that order. The average American gets 75 percent of their caffeine from coffee. Other sources include over-the-counter pain killers, appetite suppressants, cold remedies, and some prescription drugs.

Pound for pound, kids often get as much caffeine from chocolate and soft drinks as their parents get from coffee, tea, and other sources.

Games & Gambling

How do you know when you're playing with an Italian deck of cards? No queens.

The ancient Greeks played cards. In those days aces were known as "dogs."

There are 635,013,559,599 possible hands in a game of bridge.

How many bedrooms are there on the board game Clue? None.

Longest recorded Monopoly game: 1,680 hours, the equivalent of 70 days of uninterrupted play.

What do you call the spots on dice and dominoes? The pips.

Seventy-six percent of Americans say they have never participated in illegal gambling.

The game Simon Says was originally called Do This, Do That.

If you add up all the numbers of the roulette wheel (1 to 36), the sum is 666.

In a standard deck of cards, the king of hearts is the only king without a mustache.

Most frequently landed-on squares in Monopoly: Illinois Ave., GO, B&O Railroad.

There is one slot machine in Las Vegas for every eight inhabitants.

One in four compulsive gamblers is a woman.

First prize in the 1850 French national lottery: a one-way ticket to the San Francisco gold rush.

That Was Then

Besides human sacrifices, Aztecs offered the gods tamales.

In the 1500s England's Queen Elizabeth I outlawed wife beating after 10 p.m.

In the Middle Ages having ants in the house was a sign of good luck.

Only pharaohs were allowed to eat mushrooms in ancient Egypt.

The Chinese used to scatter firecrackers around the house—as fire alarms.

First kitchen utensils: the ladle and the apple corer, in that order.

The low man on a totem pole is the most important man in the tribe.

In medieval England jurors weren't fed until they reached a decision.

In England in 1558, beards were taxed according to their length.

When a cat died in ancient Egypt, its owners shaved off their eyebrows as a sign of mourning.

* * *

5 MOST-READ U.S. NEWSPAPERS

1. *Wall Street Journal*
2. *USA Today*
3. *Los Angeles Times*
4. *New York Times*
5. *Washington Post*

American Potpourri

U.S. organization with the most members: American Automobile Association (AAA), with 48 million.

One out of five pieces of the world's garbage was generated in the United States.

Americans stand about 14 inches apart when they converse. Russians stand about 10 inches apart.

The United States is first in the world in gun ownership per capita. Finland is second.

Today, 25 percent of American men are 6 feet or taller, compared to only 4 percent in 1900.

Most popular reason for not voting in elections, according to the U.S. Census: "Too busy."

The average American buys 17 yards of dental floss each year.

Floods cause more death and destruction in the United States than any other natural disaster.

Number of real haunted houses in the United States, according to the Ghost Research Society: 789.

Two percent of Americans always tip a waiter. Seventy percent say it depends on service.

Only 30 percent of U.S. adults actually have dandruff, but nearly 50 percent say they're "self-conscious about it."

The average American spends two years of his or her life waiting for meals to be served.

According to the real estate industry, the average American looks at eight houses before buying one.

A Fishy Tale

Goldfish were originally green. The Chinese bred them to be many different colors. Gold stuck.

Sea urchins reproduce by splitting themselves in two.

Goldfish have a memory span of three seconds.

The skin of a tiger shark is 10 times as strong as ox hide.

Oysters can change gender according to the temperature of the water they live in.

A group of jellyfish is known as a "smack."

Jellyfish are 99 percent water.

The man-of-war jellyfish can have tentacles up to 60 feet long.

The Anableps fish has four eyes: two to see underwater, two to see above the surface.

Starfish have anywhere from three to 50 arms—and one eye at the end of each arm.

Fish with forked tails swim faster than fish with straight tails.

The dolphins that live in the Amazon River are pink.

If you have a backbone, there's about a 50 percent chance you're a fish.

Clams can live as long as 150 years.

If an octopus is hungry enough, it will eat its own arms.

* * *

STATE WITH THE MOST POLLUTION
Texas

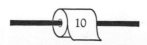

Bagel Bits

CLASSIC COMBO
Cream cheese was invented in 1872; Philadelphia Cream Cheese hit the market in 1880. But it wasn't until Joseph and Isaac Breakstone began selling their Breakstone Cream Cheese brand in 1920 that New York bagel eaters discovered it—and cream cheese became *the* bagel spread.

BAGEL AMMO
In 2000 several rioters at a Fourth of July celebration in Morristown, New Jersey, were arrested for throwing "dangerous" projectiles into the crowd and at police. The projectiles: "batteries, golf balls, and stale bagels."

BIG BAGEL
According to *Guinness World Records*, the world's largest bagel was made by Bruegger's in Syracuse, New York. Weight: 868 pounds. Diameter: 6 feet. Thickness: 20 inches. Flavor: blueberry.

BAGEL BET
During the 2002 American League Championship Series between the New York Yankees and Anaheim Angels, Anaheim mayor Tom Daly bet New York mayor Michael Bloomberg a crate of oranges and chilies that the Angels would win. Bloomberg's bet: a crate of Nathan's hot dogs and 48 H&H bagels. (Daly won.)

LITIGATED BAGEL
In 2002 John and Cecelia O'Hare sued a McDonald's restaurant in Panama City Beach, Florida, claiming that an improperly cooked bagel damaged Mr. O'Hare's teeth . . . and somehow ruined their marriage as well. They sued for $15,000 in damages.

Creepy Crawlers

Frogs use their eyeballs to push food down their throat.

An adult crocodile can go two years without eating.

Wood frogs freeze solid in winter and thaw back to life in spring.

In its lifetime an alligator will go through as many as 3,000 teeth.

The bite of a king cobra can kill a full-grown elephant in less than three hours.

The jaws of a decapitated snapping turtle can keep snapping for about a day.

The Carthaginians fought off Roman ships in 300 B.C. by catapulting live snakes at them.

Toads don't have teeth. Frogs do.

All toads are frogs, but not all frogs are toads.

Some snakes can go an entire year without eating.

Australia is the only continent where poisonous snakes outnumber nonpoisonous kinds.

The smallest known frog is the size of a dime.

South Florida is the only place in the world where crocodiles and alligators coexist in the wild.

An alligator has a brain the size of your thumb.

The bullfrog is the only animal that never sleeps.

Crocodiles can't move their tongues.

If a frog keeps its mouth open too long, it will suffocate.

If a chameleon loses a fight, it turns gray. If it wins, it turns green.

Making Music

In 2004 Congress passed a $388 billion spending bill that included $25,000 for the study of mariachi music.

Deborah Harry of Blondie worked briefly as a Playboy bunny. And in case you didn't suspect, she's really a brunette.

Even in the post-Taliban era, it's still against the law in Afghanistan for a woman to sing on TV.

The last reel-to-reel tape manufacturer in America closed its doors in January 2005.

According to *Billboard* magazine, the number one single of the 1960s was "Hey Jude," by the Beatles.

Best-selling posthumous hit of all-time: "(Just Like) Starting Over," by John Lennon.

Music videos were originally known as tele-records.

Mick Jagger had the emerald filling on his front tooth replaced with a diamond because people kept telling him he had spinach in his teeth.

Jimi Hendrix made 26 jumps with the 101st Airborne Paratroopers in 1961. Who finally killed him? Find some possibilities on page 375.

Word Roots

Dr. Seuss coined the word *nerd* in his 1950 book *If I Ran the Zoo*.

How did grocers get their name? They sold goods by the gross.

In the 1700s trappers could get a dollar for a buckskin. Hence the term *buck*.

People used to say "will I, nil I?" when they couldn't make up their minds. Thus the expression *willy-nilly*.

How did hammocks get their name? They were first made from the fibers of the hamack tree.

Theater spotlights used to burn lime for light. Thus the term *limelight*.

The lollipop was named after Lolly Pop, one of the most famous racehorses of the early 1900s.

The slang term for an emergency room patient who isn't sick enough to justify being there: *Gomer* (Get out of my emergency room).

Princeton professor John W. Tukey coined the term *software* in 1958.

When you do something "on the q.t.," you are using an abbreviation of the word *quiet*.

Police are sometimes called the fuzz because London police once wore fuzzy helmets.

Why did Thomas Henry Huxley invent the word *agnostic* in 1869? He got tired of being called an atheist.

Pet Me

Sir Isaac Newton invented the swinging door . . . for the convenience of his cats.

Most dogs run an average of 19 mph.

Ancient Egyptians could be put to death for mistreating a cat.

Does your dog seem wary of going out in the rain? It's not because it's afraid to get wet. Rain amplifies sound and hurts dogs' ears.

Toy-breed dogs live an average of seven years longer than large breeds.

In ancient Rome it wasn't "officially" dark until you could no longer tell the difference between a dog and a wolf howling in the distance.

Average cat bill at the veterinarian: $80 per year for life.

Most popular dog names in Russia: Ugoljok (Blackie) and Veterok (Breezy).

In Japan you can rent a dog as a companion for $20 an hour.

In 1997 a member of Australia's parliament proposed that all cats be eradicated from the country by 2002.

A Persian cat named Precious survived for 18 days without food. She was found when rescue crews heard her cries— across the street from the site of the World Trade Center.

The heaviest (and longest) dog ever recorded was an Old English Mastiff named Zorba: 343 pounds (and 8 feet 3 inches from nose to tail).

They're Canadian

On August 30, 1995, Sean Shannon of Canada recited Hamlet's "To be or not to be" soliloquy in 23.8 seconds—an average of 655 words a minute.

On August 17, 1991, 512 dancers of the Royal Scottish Dance Society (Toronto branch) set the record for the largest genuine Scottish country dance (a reel).

In 1988 Palm Dairies of Edmonton created the world's largest ice cream sundae— 24,900 kg. (54,895 lbs.).

In 1993 the Kitchener-Waterloo Hospital Auxiliary filled a bowl with 2,390 kg (5,269 lbs.) of strawberries.

Four hundred mothers in Vancouver broke the record for mass breast feeding in 2002.

In February 2000, 1,588 couples at the Sarnia Sports Centre broke the record for most kissing in one place at one time.

Dave Pearson holds the record for clearing all 15 balls from a standard pool table in 26.5 seconds at Pepper's Bar in Windsor, Ontario, in 1997.

In 1998, 1,000 University of Guelph students formed the longest human conveyor belt, laying down in a row and rolling a surfboard over their bodies. In 1999 they set the record for simultaneous soap-bubble blowing.

* * *

PHRASES COINED BY SHAKESPEARE

green-eyed monster
into thin air
kill with kindness
milk of human kindness
neither rhyme nor reason

one fell swoop
primrose path
star-cross'd lovers
sweets for the sweet
tower of strength

Merry Christmas

Who still believes in Santa? Studies say more four-year-olds do than any other age group.

Only 10 percent of U.S. households put cookies out for Santa on Christmas Eve.

U.S. kids leave an estimated 812 million cookies out for Santa on Christmas Eve.

Odds that a battery was bought during the Christmas season: 40 percent.

More than 25 million kids visit Santa in malls nationwide each year.

Worldwide, Christmas has been celebrated on 135 different days of the year.

Americans send about 2 billion Christmas cards every year.

Ninety-eight percent of Christmas trees are grown on tree farms.

Every year, 1.76 billion candy canes are made.

The tradition of sending Christmas cards originated in England in 1843.

CB radio users don't like to get Christmas cards—that's a code name for speeding tickets.

About 83 percent of U.S. families put up a Christmas tree. Fifty-eight percent of the trees are artificial.

Fake Christmas trees have outsold real ones every year since 1991.

The average shopping-center Santa weighs 218 pounds and has a 43-inch waist.

The holiday song played most often in malls in 2004 was "Jingle Bells."

Top five holiday pies in the United States: pumpkin, apple, cherry, lemon meringue, and pecan.

Assuming Rudolph's in front, there are 40,320 ways to arrange the eight other reindeer.

Super Glue

Superglue is so strong that a single square-inch bond can lift a ton of weight.

Superglue doesn't stick to the bottle because it needs moisture to set, and there is no moisture in the bottle.

Cyanoacrylate products are a $325-million-a-year industry. Approximately 90 percent of U.S. homes have at least one tube.

During the Vietnam War tubes of superglue were put in U.S. soldiers' first-aid kits to help seal wounds. Special kinds of superglue are now used in hospitals worldwide, reducing the need for sutures, stitches, and staples. (It doesn't work on deep wounds or on wounds where the skin does a lot of stretching, such as over joints.)

Superglue is now used in forensic detection. When investigators open a foil packet of ethyl-gel cyanoacrylate, the fumes settle on skin oils left behind in human fingerprints, turning the invisible smears into visible marks.

TIPS FOR USING SUPERGLUE

A little dab'll do ya. Superglue bonds best when it's used at the rate of one drop per square inch. More than that requires a much longer bonding period, which may result in a weaker bond.

If you're gluing two flat surfaces together, rough them up with sandpaper first. That'll give the glue more surface area to bond to. But make sure you blow off any dusty residue first.

Glued your fingers together? Use nail polish remover. Don't have any? Try warm, soapy water and a little patience. Your sweat and natural skin oils will soon loosen the bond.

Music & Musicians

Marcel Marceau's greatest-hits album consisted of 40 minutes of silence, followed by applause.

More than 2.2 million Americans play the accordion.

There are more bagpipe bands in the United States than there are in Scotland.

When he needed inspiration, Ludwig van Beethoven poured water on himself.

Mozart wrote a piano piece that required the player to use both hands and his nose.

J. S. Bach played the cathedral organ. So did 100 of his descendants.

Sixty-one percent of Americans like to hear music when put on hold. Twenty-two percent prefer silence.

The "five golden rings" in "The Twelve Days of Christmas" weren't originally rings. They were ringed pheasants.

The original jukeboxes came with earphones—only one person could listen at a time.

Artists who have recorded the most songs: the Mills Brothers (about 2,250).

The musical *Cats* ran on Broadway for 18 years.

Traditionally it isn't a "big band" unless it has 10 different instrumentalists.

There are 158 verses in the Greek national anthem.

Singer Wayne Newton is a descendant of Pocahontas.

No one knows exactly where Mozart is buried in Vienna.

It's Mind-Boggling

111,111,111 x 111,111,111 =
12,345,678,987,654,321

If you tried to count off a billion seconds, it would take you 31.7 years.

One speck of dust contains a quadrillion atoms.

Take a century and divide it into 50 million. You get about a minute.

Experts say time is getting shorter: 280 million years ago a year lasted 390 days.

The average drinking glass holds 50 teaspoons of water.

There are 31,557,600 seconds in a year.

It takes seven shuffles to thoroughly mix a 52-card deck.

The official definition of a "jiffy" is 1/100 of a second.

The Gregorian calendar is accurate to within half a day per 1,000 years.

Number of toothpicks you can make from one cord of wood: 75 million.

The word *million* was invented sometime around the year A.D. 1300

The Chinese were the first to use a decimal system, in the 6th century B.C.

There are 3 x 10 to the 33rd power (3,000 quintillion) individual living things on earth. (Of these, 75 percent are bacteria.)

The odds of someone winning a lottery twice in four months is about one in 17 trillion. But Evelyn Marie Adams won the New Jersey lottery in both 1985 and 1986.

And the Wiener Is ...

Known as the Animal, Ed Krachie is America's wiener-eating champion. His best: 22.5 wieners (including buns) in 12 minutes.

Wieners are an economical buy. With virtually no weight loss during preparation, a pound of wieners yields a pound of edible food.

In 1970, at Camp David, the presidential retreat, wieners were served to Great Britain's Prince Charles and Princess Anne.

More hot dogs—2 million a year—are sold at Chicago's O'Hare International Airport than at any other single location in the world.

NASA included the hot dog as a regular menu item on its Apollo moon flights, *Skylab* missions, and the space shuttle.

The U.S. Department of Agriculture "officially recognizes" the following as legitimate names for the hot dog: 1) wiener, 2) frankfurter, 3) frank, 4) furter, 5) hot dog.

The favorite meal of acclaimed actress Marlene Dietrich was hot dogs and champagne.

Lucky dog: In May 2000 Larry Ross stopped for a hot dog at Mr. K's Party Shoppe in Utica, Michigan. He had a $100 bill and bought lotto tickets with the change. One ticket was a $181.5 million winner.

"Some people don't salivate when they walk by a hot dog stand and smell that great symbol of American cuisine, bursting with grease and salt. But they are a very, very small group."
—*New York Times*

Brand Names

ACE BANDAGES

When World War I broke out in 1914, the Becton Dickinson Company had to stop importing German elastic bandages and start making them in the United States. They held a contest to give the new product a name. The winners: a group of doctors who called it ACE, for All Cotton Elastic.

DIAL SOAP

The name refers to a clock or watch dial. The reason: it was the first deodorant soap, and Lever Brothers wanted to suggest that it would prevent body odor "all around the clock."

WD-40

In the 1950s the Rocket Chemical Company was working on a product for the aerospace industry that would reduce rust and corrosion by removing moisture from metals. It took them 40 tries to come up with a workable Water Displacement formula.

SARA LEE

Charles Lubin and his brother-in-law owned three bakeries in the Chicago area. But Lubin dreamed of bigger things. He wanted a product that would be distributed nationally. In 1949 he created a cheesecake that he could sell through supermarkets, and named it after his daughter, Sara Lee Lubin. Within five years the company had developed a way to quick-freeze Sara Lee cakes and was selling them all over the United States.

ADIDAS

Adolph and Rudi Dassler formed Dassler Brothers Shoes in Germany in 1925. After World War II the partnership broke up, but each brother kept a piece of the shoe business. Rudi called his new company Puma; Adolph, whose nickname was Adi, renamed the old company after himself—Adi Dassler.

Word Origins

BOO
Meaning: An exclamation used to frighten or surprise someone
Origin: "The word *boh!*, used to frighten children, was the name of Boh, a great general, the son of the Norse god, Odin, whose very appellation struck immediate panic in his enemies." (*Pulleyn's Etymological Compendium*, by M. A. Thomas)

HANGNAIL
Meaning: A small piece of skin that's partially detached from the side or root of the fingernail
Origin: "Had nothing to do with a hanging nail—the original word was angnail. The ang referred to the pain it caused—as in ang/uish." (*Take My Words*, by Howard Richler)

GYPSY
Meaning: A nomad, or a member of a nomadic tribe
Origin: "In the early 16th century members of a wandering race who called themselves Romany appeared in Britain. They were actually of Hindu origin, but the British believed that they came from Egypt, and called them Egipcyans. This soon became shortened to Gipcyan, and by the year 1600, to Gipsy or Gypsey." (*Webster's Word Histories*)

PEDIGREE
Meaning: A register recording a line of ancestors
Origin: The term comes from the French words *pied de grue*, which mean "foot of a crane." French families of old kept family trees, but that's not what they called them. They thought the look of a genealogy chart—small at the top and branching out at the bottom—looked more like the webbed foot of a bird than the roots of a tree. Any Frenchman who came from a family prominent enough to have a family tree was said to have a *pied de grue*.

TROPHY

Meaning: Something gained or given in victory or conquest
Origin: From the old Greek word *trope*, which meant the turning point in a battle. The Greeks used to erect monuments at the exact spot on a battlefield where the tide had turned in their favor. Over the centuries the word evolved to represent any battle monument, whether or not it was on a battlefield . . . and even if it just commemorated a sporting victory.

CASTLE

Meaning: A large building, usually of the medieval period, fortified as a stronghold
Origin: "Castle was one of the earliest words adopted by the British from their Norman conquerors. Originally hailing from the Latin *castellum* (diminutive of castrum, 'fort'), it reminds us that Old English also acquired castrum, still present in such place-names as Doncaster and Winchester. From Old French's chastel (a version of castel) came the word château (circumflex accent marking the lost 's')." (*The Secret Lives of Words,* by Paul West)

MIGRAINE

Meaning: A severe recurring headache
Origin: "Migraine had its beginning as a word in the Greco-Latin parts hemi-, 'half,' and cranium, 'skull,' which is descriptive of the violent headache that attacks one-half of the head." (*Word Origins,* by Wilfred Funk)

BOULEVARD

Meaning: A broad avenue, often with one or more strips of plantings (grass, trees, flower beds) on both sides or down the center
Origin: "The name originally came from the Middle Low German Bolwerk, the top of the wide rampart—often 20 or more feet wide—that served as the defensive wall of medieval towns. As more sophisticated weaponry rendered such structures obsolete, they sometimes were razed to ground level and used as a wide street on the town's perimeter. Vienna has such a broad boulevard, called the Ring, circling the old town on the site of its original city walls." (*Fighting Words,* by Christine Ammer)

Americans at Home

Seventy-two percent of Americans don't know the people who live next door.

Eleven percent of Americans have thrown out a dish just because they don't want to wash it.

Researchers say one in four people admits to snooping in their host's medicine cabinet.

If you're an average adult, you spend 11 to 13 minutes in the shower.

Every 45 seconds, a house catches fire in the United States.

More than 50 percent of Americans get out of bed before 7 a.m.

Americans recycle more than 60 percent of their soft-drink containers.

Seventy-four percent of Americans say they make their beds every day. Five percent say they never do.

Fifty-seven percent of American households have three or more telephones.

Half of all Americans live within 50 miles of where they grew up.

Do you alphabetize your spice rack? Only one in 12 Americans does.

Experts say the average person spends 30 years mad at a family member.

According to the U.S. Census Bureau, the average American marriage lasts 9.4 years.

In 71 percent of baby boomer households, both spouses work.

According to a Tupperware study, you'll wind up throwing out about three fourths of your leftovers.

Forty percent of Americans who move to a new address switch toothpaste brands at the same time.

Everyday Origins

SCOTCH TAPE

Believe it or not, the sticky stuff gets its name from an ethnic slur. When two-toned paint jobs became popular in the 1920s, Detroit carmakers asked the 3-M Company for an alternative to masking tape that would provide a smooth, sharp edge where the two colors met. 3-M came up with two-inch-wide cellophane tape, but auto companies said it was too expensive. So 3-M lowered the price by applying adhesive only along the sides of the strip. That caused a problem: The new tape didn't stick—and company painters complained to the 3-M sales reps, "Take this tape back to your stingy 'Scotch' bosses and tell them to put more adhesive on it!" The name—and the new tape—stuck.

BRASSIERES

Mary Phelps Jacob, a teenage debutante in 1913, wanted to wear a rose-garlanded dress to a party one evening. But as she later explained, her corset cover "kept peeping through the roses around my bosom." So she took it off, pinned two handkerchiefs together, and tied them behind her back with some ribbon. "The result was delicious," she later recalled. "I could move much more freely, a nearly naked feeling." The contraption eventually became known as a brassiere—French for "arm protector"—a name borrowed from the corset cover it replaced. (Jacob later became famous for riding naked through the streets of Paris on an elephant.)

TOOTHPASTE TUBES

Toothpaste wasn't packaged in collapsible tubes until 1892, when Dr. Washington Wentworth Sheffield, a Connecticut dentist, copied the idea from a tube of oil-based paint. Increased interest in sanitation and hygiene made it more popular than jars of toothpaste, which mingled germs from different brushes. Toothpaste tubes quickly became the standard.

WRISTWATCHES
Several Swiss watchmakers began attaching small watches to bracelets in 1790. Those early watches weren't considered serious timepieces and remained strictly a women's item until World War I, when armies recognized their usefulness in battle and began issuing them to servicemen instead of the traditional pocket watch.

FORKS
Before forks became popular, the difference between refined and common people was the number of fingers they ate with. The upper classes used three; everyone else used five. This began to change in the 11th century, when tiny, two-pronged forks became fashionable in Italian high society. But they didn't catch on; the Catholic Church opposed them as unnatural (it was an insult to imply that the fingers God gave us weren't good enough for food), and people who used them were ridiculed as effeminate or pretentious. Forks weren't generally considered polite until the 18th century—some 800 years after they were first introduced.

PULL-TOP BEER CANS
In 1959 a mechanical engineer named Ermal Cleon Fraze was at a picnic when he realized he'd forgotten a can opener. No one else had one either, so he had to use the bumper of his car to open a can of soda. It took half an hour, and he vowed he'd never get stuck like that again. He patented the world's first practical pull-top can later that year, and three years later, the Pittsburgh Brewing Company tried using it on its Iron City Beer. Now every beer company does.

CASH REGISTERS
In 1879 a Dayton, Ohio, saloon keeper named James J. Ritty was vacationing on a transatlantic steamer when he took a tour of the engine room and saw a machine that counted the number of revolutions of the ship's propeller. He figured a similar machine might help him keep track of his saloon sales, and prevent dishonest bartenders from looting the till. When he got home, he and his brother invented Ritty's Incorruptible Cashier—a machine with two rows of keys with amounts printed on them, a clocklike face that added up the amount of money collected, and a bell that rang after every transaction. It was the first product from the business that would become the National Cash Register Company (NCR).

Smoking

A nonsmoking bartender inhales the equivalent of 36 cigarettes during an eight-hour shift.

Smokers need to ingest 40 percent more vitamin C than nonsmokers just to stay even.

In an average day 3,000 Americans take up smoking. Most of them are kids under age 18.

Twenty-one percent of U.S. smokers say they don't believe nicotine is addictive.

Nearly 8,000 children each year are poisoned by eating cigarette butts.

Each puff of smoke inhaled from a cigarette contains 4 billion particles of dust.

The U.S. government approves 599 additives for use in the manufacture of cigarettes.

About 10 million cigarettes are sold every minute.

During London's Great Plague of 1665, smoking tobacco was thought to have a protective effect.

Nonsmokers dream more at night than smokers do.

Christopher Columbus introduced the smoking of tobacco to Europe after discovering the "strange leaves" on the island of Cuba.

Nicotine is named for Jean Nicot de Villemain, France's ambassador to Portugal, who wrote of tobacco's medicinal properties, describing it as a panacea.

According to the American Heart Association, an estimated 47 million Americans smoke: 25.5 million men and 24.1 million women.

Miss Liberty

Emma Lazarus's *The New Colossus* was inspired by the Colossus of Rhodes, one of the Seven Wonders of the Ancient World.

Sculptor Frédéric-Auguste Bartholdi modeled the statue after his mother. When she got tired, his mistress stepped in for the final touches.

Lady Liberty stands looking eastward, across the Atlantic, to the Old World.

Winds of 50 miles per hour cause the statue to sway as much as three inches. Her torch sways five inches.

The 25 windows in the crown symbolize gemstones found on the earth and the heavens' rays shining over the world.

The seven rays on her crown represent the seven seas and continents of the world.

The tablet that Lady Liberty holds in her left hand reads "July 4, 1776" in (mostly) Roman numerals.

Total weight of the concrete foundation: 54 million pounds (27,000 tons).

The statue's two-layer gown would take about 4,000 square yards of cloth to duplicate.

The Statue of Liberty's waist size is 35 (feet).

The Statue of Liberty's mouth is three feet wide.

The Statue of Liberty's index finger is eight feet long.

On average, the fingernails of the Statue of Liberty weigh 100 pounds each.

The Statue of Liberty is patented.

On Mirrors

In the 1600s the Dutch used to cover their mirrors with curtains when not in use, lest the reflectiveness be used up!

In ancient China reflective pieces of polished brass were placed over doorknobs so that evil spirits would scare themselves away.

Ben Franklin mounted mirrors outside his second-story window so he could secretly see who was knocking at his front door.

The word *mirror* comes from the Latin *mirari*, meaning "to wonder at." It's also the root word for *miracle* and *admire*.

The world's largest mirrors sit inside the twin Keck Telescopes—the world's largest telescopes—at the W. M. Keck Observatory in Hawaii. Each mirror is made of 36 hexagonal segments that work together as a single piece. Diameter: ten meters (32 feet) across.

In olden days some thought that the reflection of the body in a shiny surface or mirror was an expression of the spiritual self, and therefore if anything happened to disturb that reflection, injury would follow. This was the origin of the superstition that breaking a mirror would bring seven years of bad luck.

Trade secret: building managers install mirrors in lobbies because people complain less about waiting for slow elevators when they're occupied looking at themselves.

In 1994 Russian astronauts orbiting in the *Mir* spacecraft tried using mirrors to reflect sunlight into northern areas of their country, in an attempt to lengthen the short growing season. It didn't work.

That's Rich!

Where was the first U.S. gold rush? Not California—North Carolina, in 1803. (Started when a boy found a 17-pound nugget on his father's farm.) It supplied all the gold for the nation's mints until 1829.

It is estimated that only about 100,000 tons of gold have been mined during all of recorded history.

The word *garnet* comes from the Latin word for pomegranate. (Garnets were thought to resemble pomegranate seeds.)

From 330 B.C. to A.D. 1237, most of the world's emeralds came from Cleopatra's mine in Egypt.

The chemical formula for lapis lazuli: (Na,Ca)8(Al,Si)12O24-(S,SO4). The chemical formula for diamond: C.

The name "turquoise" comes from the fact that it was first brought to Europe from the Mediterranean by Levantine traders, also known as Turks.

The California gold rush yielded 125 million ounces of gold from 1850 to 1875—more than had been mined in the previous 350 years and worth more than $50 billion today.

Ancient Greeks named amber from the word *electron*, because rubbing amber gives off static electricity.

Legend says that one day Cupid cut Venus's fingernails while she was sleeping and left the clippings scattered on the ground. So that no part of Venus would ever disappear, the Fates turned them into stone. The stone: onyx, Greek for "fingernail."

Rarest gem: Painite, discovered in Burma. Fewer than 10 specimens exist in the world.

The Plant World

Fastest-growing plant on earth: bamboo,
which can grow as much as 35 inches a day.

About 45 percent of all prescription drugs
contain ingredients originating in the rain
forest.

The seed cones of the cycad tree can weigh
up to 90 pounds.

The bark of the giant sequoia can be up to
two feet thick.

If a plant is native to the Arctic Circle, it
doesn't have thorns.

The potato and the tomato are more closely
related than the potato and the sweet potato.

Onions are members of the lily family.

Herbicide use has created at least 48 "super-
weeds" that are resistant to chemicals.

Coconut shells can absorb more impact than
most crash helmets.

The pineapple is neither a pine nor an apple.
It's actually a very big berry.

Seventy-five percent of the trees in Australia
are eucalyptus.

That's Disgusting!

The average human foot has about 20,000 sweat glands and can produce as much as half a cup of sweat each day.

Most people generally fart between 10 and 20 times a day, expelling enough gas to inflate a small balloon.

Cockroaches can flatten themselves almost to the thinness of a piece of paper in order to slide into tiny cracks; they can be frozen for weeks and then thawed with no ill effect; and they can withstand 126 g's of pressure with no problem (people get squished at 18 g's).

Most of the dust in your house is made up of dead human skin cells—every day, millions of them float off your body and settle on furniture and floors.

The average municipal water treatment plant processes enough human waste every day to fill 72 Olympic-size swimming pools.

In a survey, 2.1 percent of nose pickers said they did so "for enjoyment."

According to a survey, over 10 percent of Americans have picked someone else's nose.

Tears are made up of almost the same ingredients as urine.

Your mouth slows production of bacteria-fighting saliva when you sleep, which allows the 10 billion bacteria in your mouth to reproduce all night; "morning breath" is actually bacterial B.O.

A tapeworm can grow to a length of 30 feet inside human intestines.

The crusty goop you find in your eyes when you wake up is the exact same mucus you find in your nose—boogers.

Spiders don't eat their prey; they paralyze the victim with venom, vomit a wad of acidic liquid onto them, and then drink the dissolved body.

Safe & Sound

Eighty percent of the deaths that occur in U.S. casinos are caused by "sudden heart attack."

Murders claimed more American lives during the 20th century than wars did.

The odds of being killed by a bolt of lightning are about the same as those of being killed by falling out of bed.

More people are killed by donkeys every year than are killed in plane crashes.

Top five causes of household accidents: stairs, glass doors, cutlery, jars, power tools (in that order).

Over 2,500 lefties die each year "using products meant for right-handed people."

In the next seven days, roughly 800 Americans will be injured by their jewelry.

Odds that you'll be killed by a plane falling from the sky: one in 25 million. Odds that it will happen today: one in 7 trillion.

The four most dangerous steps on most staircases: the two at the top and the two at the bottom.

Since 1950, more than 700 people have been killed by avalanches in the United States.

In 1992, 2,421 people checked into U.S. emergency rooms with injuries involving house plants.

Number of documented deaths-by-piranha in human history: not even one.

You're more likely to be struck by lightning than to be eaten by a shark.

Down on the Farm

If you pet your pig, it will have a larger litter.
Pigs, like people, respond to kindness.

New Zealand sheep outnumber New Zealanders
13 to one.

If a pig is sick it stops curling its tail.

The average cow produces 70,000 glasses of milk
in her lifetime.

An adult horse eats 15 pounds of hay and nine
pounds of grain every day.

A horse will win a sprint against a camel, but a
camel will win a marathon against a horse.

Pound for pound, sheep outeat cows seven
to one.

Name for a suckling calf: a bob.

Black sheep have a better sense of smell than
white sheep.

Horses can only breathe through their nostrils.

Dumbest farm animal, according to farmers: the
turkey.

Elemental Questions

WHAT ELEMENTS MAKE UP A HUMAN BEING? As a child you were told that girls were made of sugar and spice and everything nice, and that boys were made of snips and snails and puppy dog tails, but let's just say that this list of primary components was, well, a little off. Actually, just six elements comprise 99 percent of the mass of every boy and girl. They are (in order of weight): oxygen, carbon, hydrogen, nitrogen, calcium, and phosphorus. Coincidentally, these same elements are major players in snails, spices, sugars, and puppy dog tails. But it's not so much the ingredients as the way they're put together.

WHAT'S THE MOST COMMON ELEMENT ON EARTH? Oxygen. It makes up nearly half the weight of the earth's crust and 62 percent of the total by sheer number of atoms. In the earth's crust, after oxygen, the most abundant elements are (in order of weight): silicon, aluminum, iron, calcium, and sodium. However, in terms of elements in the atmosphere, oxygen ranks a paltry second to nitrogen. Nitrogen is 78 percent of the earth's atmosphere, while oxygen is just 21 percent.

WHAT'S THE MOST COMMON ELEMENT IN THE UNIVERSE? Roughly three quarters of the universe is nothing more than hydrogen, the simplest element there is, and most of the rest of it is helium. The rest of the naturally occurring elements, from lithium to uranium, make up less than 1 percent of the universe.

CAN YOU NAME THE PLACE ON EARTH THAT HAS FOUR ELEMENTS NAMED AFTER IT? This is one to stump your friends at the next chemistry department mixer you go to. The answer: Ytterby, Sweden, which gave its name to ytterium, erbium, terbium, and ytterbium. The first three of these were found in a quarry near the town, which seems reason enough for their naming;

ytterbium, however, was discovered in Switzerland by Jean de Marignac. He named the element after the town because it was a "rare earth" element, and the first rare earth elements discovered were in that quarry outside Ytterby.

WHAT ELEMENT ARE YOU LEAST LIKELY TO FIND IN YOUR EVERYDAY LIFE? That would probably be francium, the most highly unstable naturally occurring element. Less than an ounce is present on the face of the earth at any one time, and none of that in any measurable amounts; it had to be discovered through the decay of actinium, another element entirely.

WHICH ELEMENT IS THE MOST EXPENSIVE? Among the naturally occurring elements, protactinium is likely to be the most expensive, not just because it's rare but also because it's so hard to isolate. In 1961 the British government extracted 125 grams of the stuff from over 60 tons of material at a cost of half a million bucks; in today's money, that works out to $24,000 a gram. But don't start flashing that jewel-encrusted protactinium ring to your friends just yet: it's radioactive and highly toxic.

WHY IS THE CHEMICAL SYMBOL FOR GOLD "AU"? There's neither an *a* nor a *u* in *gold*. Well, not in English. There is both an *a* and a *u* in *aurum*, the Latin word for gold (*gold*, incidentally, comes from the Old English *geolo*, meaning "yellow"). Other elements whose chemical symbols don't match their English names include silver (Ag, *argentum*, Latin), lead (Pb, *plumbum*, Latin), potassium (K, *kalium*, Latin), tungsten (W, *wolfram*, German), and tin (Sn, *stannum*, Latin).

WHAT'S THE DUMBEST NAME FOR AN ELEMENT? Take your pick: unnnilium, unununium, or ununbium. These names were given to recently discovered elements after chemists and physicists couldn't play nice and agree on the names these new elements ought to have. So the International Union for Pure and Applied Chemistry devised a naming system based on the Latin names for numbers and the atomic weight of the element. Unnnilium, for example, has an atomic weight of 110; so, one-one-zero. The Latin word for one is *un*, and for zero it's *nil*—therefore: un-un-nil-ium.

Sounds Familiar

Sarah Josepha Hale's 1830 poem "Mary Had a Little Lamb" was inspired by a little girl named Mary Tyler. Her pet lamb used to follow her to school.

Australian soldiers used "We're Off to See the Wizard" as a marching song during World War II.

The song "You're a Grand Old Flag" was originally called "You're a Grand Old Rag."

"Battle Hymn of the Republic" was written by Julia Ward Howe. She sold the rights for five dollars.

"The Alphabet Song," "Twinkle, Twinkle Little Star," and "Baa, Baa Black Sheep" are all sung to the same music: a 1765 French song titled "Ah! Vous dirais-je, Maman."

The third verse of "For He's a Jolly Good Fellow" is "The bear went over the mountain . . ."

There are 364 gifts in "The Twelve Days of Christmas."

First song ever sung in space: "Happy Birthday," performed by the *Apollo* astronauts on March 8, 1969.

Pete Seeger, who wrote "Turn, Turn, Turn" and "We Shall Overcome" (among others), was born into a musical family: both his parents were teachers at Juilliard School in New York.

"Dixie," the anthem of the South, was written by a Yankee: Dan Emmett of Ohio. Emmett also wrote "Polly Wolly Doodle."

A rough translation of "Auld Lang Syne" is "times gone by."

Charles Wesley wrote the words to "Hark! The Herald Angels Sing" in 1739. More than 100 years later composer Felix Mendelssohn put the song to music.

Ask the Experts

Q: HOW DO PARROTS TALK?
A: Exactly why parrots can change their calls to make them sound like words is still not understood. Their ability to mimic may possibly be linked with the fact that they are highly social birds. A young parrot in captivity learns the sounds it hears around it and quickly realizes that repeating these sounds brings attention and companionship. This is perhaps a substitute for its normal social life. Although they are such good mimics in captivity, parrots do not imitate other sounds in the wild. There are, however, many other species that do: mynah birds and lyrebirds, for example, do mimic the sounds they hear in their everyday lives. (*What Makes the World Go Round?*, edited by Jinny Johnson)

Q: IS THERE SOUND IN SPACE? IF SO, WHAT'S THE SPEED OF SOUND THERE?
A: No, there is no sound in space. That's because sound has to travel as a vibration in some material such as air or water or even stone. Since space is essentially empty, it cannot carry sound, at least not the sorts of sound that we are used to. (*How Things Work,* by Louis A. Bloomfield)

Q: HOW DO WOODPECKERS AVOID BRAIN DAMAGE AFTER HITTING THEIR HEADS AGAINST TREES ALL DAY?
A: The force generated by the woodpecker pecking does not pass through its braincase—it travels along the bird's upper jaw, which connects below the brain and allows shock to dissipate throughout the bird's entire body. Naturally, some of the blow does reverberate back into the cranium, but since the woodpecker's brain surface area is relatively large, the impact is absorbed as a slap, not a punch. And because the avian skull fits tightly around its bird brain—like a bicycle helmet—it prevents internal bruising. Every bit of cushioning

helps: according to experts, the acceleration force felt by a common acorn woodpecker measures between 600 and 1,200 g's—enough that its eyeballs would literally pop out on impact if it didn't blink. (*The Wild File*, by Brad Wetzler)

Q: DOES THE FOURTH SPATIAL DIMENSION REALLY EXIST?

A: That depends on what you mean by space. There are only three dimensions to our everyday, commonsense kind of space, the space we can perceive and move in. But physicists have developed persuasive theories using an extra six spatial dimensions. These higher dimensions are curled up into tiny circles, or similar closed surfaces. This curling up of dimensions is like our observing, say, a piece of string from a distance and seeing it as a line, then moving closer and observing that it actually has an extra, circular dimension. If we could observe any point (say a subatomic particle) at a large enough magnification, we would similarly see that it is not a point, but has further dimensions in unexplored directions. (*The Best Ever Queries*, by Joseph Harker)

* * *

IRONIC DEATH

Thomas Parr was thought to be England's oldest living man in the 17th century. He was supposedly 152 years old in 1635, when King Charles invited him to a royal banquet in hopes of learning the secret to his longevity. Parr's answer: "Simple meals of grains and meats."

Final Irony: According to one account: "'Marvelous,' said the King as he offered Parr goose livers and baby eels basted in butter and onions, followed by fried sheep's eyeballs. Throughout the banquet, Parr regaled the King with stories while the King saw to it that Parr's plate and glass were always full. Unfortunately, Parr, overwhelmed by the food, expired during the meal. The distraught King, feeling responsible, had him buried in Westminster Abbey."

More Animal Briefs

Kangaroos are lactose-intolerant.

Crab-eating seals don't eat crabs.

Elephants adopt orphans.

Foxes pollinate plants.

Otters can get herpes.

Gophers are hermits.

Cows get hair balls.

Horses can't sit.

Sheep snore.

Squirrels can't see red.

Armadillos can be housebroken.

Elephants breathe 12 times a minute.

Latin America

Not only is Lake Titicaca the highest navigable lake in the world, it's also the most fun to say.

Angel Falls in Venezuela is 15 times higher than Niagara Falls. It was named after U.S. pilot Jimmy Angel.

The Mayan Empire lasted six times as long as the Roman Empire.

The Caribbean island of St. Bart's is named for Bartolomeo Columbus, Christopher's brother.

North America uses over eight times as much energy per person as does Latin America.

Quetzal is the name of Guatemala's national bird and its national currency.

The Bahamas are made up of of more than 700 islands.

Panama hats originally came from Ecuador. They got the name Panama from the gold rush prospectors who bought them in Panama on their way to California.

Women in Guatemala work longer days than any other women in the world: an average of 11 hours a day.

Odds are that the next cherry you eat will come from Chile. It's the leading exporter of cherries to the United States.

El Salvador leads the world in deaths per capita from contact with centipedes and venomous millipedes.

There are only two landlocked countries in South America: Bolivia and Paraguay.

Lake Nicaragua in Nicaragua is the only freshwater lake with sharks in the world.

The Time It Takes

.05 seconds for a human muscle to respond to stimulus

.06 seconds for an automotive air bag to fully inflate

.2 seconds for the International Space Station to travel one mile

.46 seconds for a 90-mph fastball to reach home plate

.6 seconds for an adult to walk one step

One second for a hummingbird's wings to beat 70 times

1.25 seconds for light to travel from the moon to Earth

Three seconds for 475 lawsuits to be filed around the world

Four seconds for 3,000,000 gallons of water to flow over Niagara Falls

Ten seconds for 50 people to be born

Twenty seconds for a fast talker to say 100 words

On Vegetables

CORN. The most versatile of all food plants, it can be eaten at every stage of development. You can find it in more than 3,000 grocery items. In fact, according to *The Great Food Almanac*, "the average American eats the equivalent of three pounds of corn each day in the form of meat, poultry, and dairy products."

GARLIC. One of the first foods ever cultivated. First written reference: 5,000 years ago, in Sanskrit. At banquets ancient Greeks served each guest a bowl of parsley, believing it would mask "garlic breath." A vestige of this custom survives. Many restaurants still drop a sprig of parsley on every plate.

LETTUCE. The name comes from the Latin *lactuca* (milk) because of the white liquid that oozes from broken stalks. The Romans prized it so highly that any slave caught eating lettuce was given 30 lashes.

EGGPLANT. Originated in China, where it was grown as a decoration. The Chinese called eggplants mad apples, believing they caused insanity. It was accepted as a food only after it was brought to the Mediterranean.

LEEKS. These members of the onion family originated in Egypt, then spread to Rome. (Emperor Nero drank a quart of leek soup every day, thinking it improved his singing voice.) The Romans introduced the leek to Wales, and it became the Welsh national symbol in 640, when Saxons invaded from England. With no uniforms, it was hard to tell friend from foe in the battlefield, so each Welsh soldier pinned a leek on his cap to identify himself. They won, and every March 1, St. David's Day, the Welsh pin a leek to their hats or lapels to commemorate the victory.

What the #!&%?

?

QUESTION MARK

When early scholars wrote in Latin, they would place the word *questio*—meaning "question"—at the end of a sentence to indicate a query. To conserve valuable space, writing it was soon shortened to *qo*, which caused another problem—readers might mistake it for the ending of a word. So they squashed the letters into a symbol: a lowercase *q* on top of an *o*. Over time the *o* shrank to a dot and the *q* to a squiggle, giving us our current question mark.

!

EXCLAMATION POINT

Like the question mark, the exclamation point was invented by stacking letters. The mark comes from the Latin word *io*, meaning "exclamation of joy." Written vertically, with the *i* above the *o*, it forms the exclamation point we use today.

=

EQUAL SIGN

Invented by English mathematician Robert Recorde in 1557, with this rationale: "I will sette as I doe often in woorke use, a paire of paralleles, or Gemowe [i.e., twin] lines of one length, thus:====, bicause noe 2 thynges, can be more equalle." His equal signs were about five times as long as the current ones, and it took more than a century for his sign to be accepted over its rival: a strange curly symbol invented by Descartes.

&

AMPERSAND

This symbol is a stylized *et*, Latin for "and." Although it was invented by the Roman scribe Marcus Tullius Tiro in the 1st century B.C., it didn't get its strange name until centuries later. In the early 1800s schoolchildren learned this symbol as the 27th letter of the alphabet: X, Y, Z, &, but the symbol had no name. So they ended their ABCs with "and, per se, and" meaning "&, which means 'and.'" This phrase was slurred into one garbled word that eventually caught on with everyone: *ampersand*.

OCTOTHORPE

The odd name for this ancient sign for numbering derives from *thorpe*, the Old Norse word for a village or farm that is often seen in British place names. The symbol was originally used in mapmaking, representing a village surrounded by eight fields, so it was named the octothorpe.

DOLLAR SIGN

When the U.S. government began issuing its own money in 1794, it used the common world currency: the peso—also called the Spanish dollar. The first American silver dollars were identical to Spanish pesos in weight and value, so they took the same written abbreviation: Ps. That evolved into a *P* with an *S* written right on top of it, and when people began to omit the circular part of the *P*, the sign simply became an *S* with a vertical line through it.

* * *

HOLY BAT FACTS, BATMAN!

Most species of bats live 12 to 15 years, but some live as long as 30 years. Some species can fly as fast as 60 miles per hour and as high as 10,000 feet.

Bats are social animals and live in colonies, in caves. The colonies can get huge: Bracken Cave in Texas contains an estimated 20 million Mexican free-tailed bats.

Vampire bats drink blood through a "drinking straw" that the bat makes with its tongue and lower lip. Their saliva contains an anticoagulant that keeps blood flowing by impeding the formation of blood clots.

It's not uncommon for a vampire bat to return to the same animal night after night, weakening and eventually killing its prey.

Big Government

In 1990 the U.S. government tested 29,000 federal employees for drugs. Cost: $11.7 million. Positive tests: 153. Cost per positive test: $76,470.

The CIA once called an assassination team the Health Alteration Committee.

Green Cards (the permanent resident IDs for the United States) are yellow.

The only crime defined in the U.S. Constitution is treason.

Congress has proposed over 10,000 amendments to the U.S. Constitution since 1789. Twenty-seven have passed.

The city of Chicago has hosted more major national political conventions than any other city in the United States.

Republican and Democrat are both towns in North Carolina.

The Oval Office in the White House is 22 feet long.

The U.S. government called the invasion of Grenada a "predawn vertical insertion."

Thirty-two percent of all land in the United States is owned by the federal government.

In 2005 there were 281 ships in the U.S. Navy, fewer than in any year since 1939.

U.S. law requires that Yankee bean soup be served in the congressional dining room at all times.

Strom Thurmond was the only person ever elected to a U.S. Senate seat as a write-in candidate (in 1954).

Percent of the cost of a 12-ounce bottle of beer that goes to federal and state taxes: 43.

Nose & Ears

Medical term for earwax: cerumen.

Your ears secrete more earwax when you're afraid than when you aren't.

The easiest sound for the human ear to hear is "ah."

The smell in your right nostril is more pleasant, but your left nostril is more accurate.

According to research, you'll blow your nose about 250 times this year.

The droplets in a sneeze can travel 12 feet and remain in the air for as long as three hours.

Can you flare your nostrils? Only 30 percent of people can.

Vertigo is most commonly caused by a problem with the balancing mechanism in the inner ear.

If saliva can't dissolve it, you can't taste it.

The ability to taste sweets decreases with age.

There are nine muscles in your ear.

According to Pickle Packers International, the crunch of a pickle should be audible from 10 paces.

On average, people who have asthma hear better than people who don't. Nobody knows why.

It's possible to sneeze so hard that you break your ribs.

The sensors in your nose can detect as many as 10,000 different odors.

Studies show that familiar odors revive old memories more easily than familiar sights or sounds do.

The Sporting Life

The 1900 Olympic Games included croquet, fishing, billiards, and checkers. Tug-of-war was an Olympic event between 1900 and 1920.

In a 1936 Ping-Pong tournament, the players volleyed for over two hours on the opening serve.

Polo players are not allowed to play left-handed—it's too dangerous.

Half of the members of the Rodeo Cowboys Association have never worked on a ranch.

Kayaking is a required subject in Greenland's schools.

The first tennis balls were stuffed with human hair.

Karate was invented in India. It was not introduced to Japan until about 1917.

In the 1880s waterskiing was known as plankgliding.

Boxing rings are called rings because they used to be round.

Average number of days each year when no major league sports are played: five.

According to the California Medical Association, 87 percent of pro boxers have brain damage.

Twenty-seven people in the United States were killed by falling soccer goalposts between 1979 and 1993.

Sport played on the largest playing field (300 yards by 200 yards): polo.

In 1970, 127 runners ran the New York Marathon. In 2005, 36,562 did.

Mental Health

Neuroscientists have determined that motherhood makes female rats smarter, calmer, and more courageous.

On average, people between the ages of 24 and 35 worry less than adults of any other age group.

Scientists say that women are more caring than men, and old women are smarter than old men.

Only 2 percent of Americans say they're in a good mood every day.

A study in December 2004 found that parents enjoy a visit with Santa more than their children do.

In a *Newsweek* poll, 48 percent of those surveyed thought that UFOs were real; among *National Enquirer* readers, it was 83 percent.

Thirteen percent of adults say the last day of summer is the occasion they dread the most.

Washington, D.C., has more psychiatrists per capita than any other city in the country.

Buenos Aires has more psychoanalysts per capita than any other city in the world.

Ninety percent of Americans describe themselves as shy.

Sigmund Freud charged the equivalent of $8.10 an hour for his therapy sessions.

Australian researchers found that the brain really does experience pain when a person's heart is "breaking."

People laugh least in the first hour after waking up in the morning.

Transportation

Oldest vehicle in human history: a floating log. Second oldest: a sled.

In 1904 a cruise from New York to Great Britain was $10 (third class).

Motor vehicle with the best safety record in Europe? The moped.

How did the kerosene fungus get its name? It eats kerosene and lives in jet fuel tanks.

Why does NASA send small animals into space? Among other things, to see if they throw up.

The last U.S. train robbery took place in 1933.

In 2001 Indian railroads cited 14 million people for riding without a ticket.

Longest railway in the world: the Trans-Siberian Railway in Russia. It's nearly 6,000 miles long.

Trying to call a ship in the eastern Atlantic? Use area code 871. Western Atlantic? Try 874.

Adolf Hitler had his own private train, complete with 15 railcars. It was named the *Amerika.*

Ancient Rome had rent-a-chariot businesses.

* * *

THE COST OF THINGS: 1900

Men's leather belt: 19¢
Seven-shot revolver $1.25
Alligator bag: $5
Bicycle: $20
Grand piano: $175

A Food Is Born

GIRL SCOUT COOKIES
The Girl Scouts were founded in 1912. For 20 years they raised money by selling knitted clothes, baked goods, and chickens. Then, in 1934, a Philadelphia Girl Scout leader (who was also a press agent) came up with the idea of selling a vanilla cookie in the shape of the Girl Scout seal. She contracted with a local bakery to make them.

One day she heard that reporters would be interviewing actresses at a local flower show. Figuring her Girl Scout troop would get free publicity if they showed up selling cookies, she sent a contingent to the show. The troop got so much publicity and sold so many cookies that Girl Scout troops all over the country began emulating them. Within three years, more than a hundred local councils were selling the same professionally baked cookies. It was the beginning of an American institution.

MAYONNAISE
Originally brought to France by Duc de Richelieu, who tasted it while visiting Mahon, a city on the island of Minorca. It was eventually dubbed Mahonaisse by French chefs, and was considered a delicacy in Europe. In America it became known as mayonnaise, but for over a century was still regarded as suitable for only the most elegant meals. Finally, in 1912, Richard Hellman, a German immigrant, began packing it and selling it in jars from his New York deli. This transformed mayonnaise to a mass-merchandised condiment.

MACARONI AND CHEESE
During the Depression, the Kraft Company tried.to market a low-priced cheddar cheese powder—but the public wouldn't buy it. One St. Louis sales rep, looking for a way to unload his allotment of the stuff, tied individual packages of the cheese to macaroni boxes and talked grocers on his route into selling them as one item, which he called Kraft Dinners. When the company found out how well they were selling, it made the dinners an official part of its product line.

CAESAR SALAD

The name of this salad doesn't refer to the Roman conqueror, but to the man who created it: a Tijuana restaurateur named Caesar Cardini. Here's one account of its origin: "Cardini started several restaurants in Tijuana, Mexico, in the early 20s. He devised the salad in 1924 during the Fourth of July weekend at Caesar's Place. He served it as finger food, arranging the garlic-scented lettuce leaves on platters. Later, he shredded the leaves into bite-sized pieces. The salad became a hit with the Hollywood movie stars who visited Tijuana, and soon was a specialty of such prestigious restaurants as Chasen's and Romanoffs."

KETCHUP

The Chinese invented ke-tsiap, a concoction of pickled fish and spices (but no tomatoes), in the 1690s. By the early 1700s its popularity had spread to Malaysia, where British explorers first encountered it, and by 1740 the sauce—renamed ketchup—was an English staple. But it wasn't until the 1790s that New England colonists first mixed tomatoes into the sauce. The reason: until then, it was widely believed that tomatoes (a close relative of the toxic belladonna and nightshade plants) were poisonous.

Making tomato ketchup at home is a tedious all-day project, and American housewives hated the process. So when Henry J. Heinz introduced bottled ketchup in 1875, he promoted it as a laborsaving device. His first slogan was: "Blessed relief for Mother and the other women of the household." By the 1980s Heinz ketchup was in one of every two households in the United States.

WHEATIES

Invented in 1921 by a Minneapolis health spa owner who fed his patients homemade bran gruel to keep them regular and help them lose weight. One day he spilled some on the stove, and it hardened into a crust. He was going to throw it out, but tasted it first. To his surprise, the flakes he scraped off the stove were better than the stuff in the pot. He made more and showed them to a friend at the Washburn Crosby Company (predecessor of General Mills). People at the company liked the flakes, too, but didn't like the way they crumbled. So they came up with a better flake—using wheat. Then they held a company-wide contest to name the product. Jane Bausman, the wife of a company executive, suggested Wheaties.

Man's Best Friend

The average American dog will cost its owner approximately $14,600 over its lifetime.

Three percent of Americans shower with their dogs.

Sixty-three percent of pet owners sleep with their pets.

In their first year of life, puppies grow 10 times faster than human infants do.

Sixty percent of pets in Great Britain have some form of health insurance.

One in three dog owners say they've talked to their pets on the phone.

A dog can't hear the lowest key on a piano.

Houdini trained his dog to escape from a pair of miniature handcuffs.

In 2003, U.S. postal workers were bitten by dogs 3,423 times.

The heaviest dog on record: a Saint Bernard that weighed 310 pounds.

The basenji is the only dog breed that doesn't bark.

Even bloodhounds can't smell the difference between two identical twins.

Top four biting dogs: German shepherd, chow chow, collie, and Akita.

Least likely biters: Chihuahua, golden retriever, poodle, Scottish terrier, and Shetland sheepdog.

Border collies are the most intelligent breed. Afghan hounds are the dumbest.

Ten percent of all dalmatians are born deaf.

Bloodhounds are the only animals whose evidence is admissible in U.S. courts.

Dog with the best eyesight: the greyhound.

Bug Off!

A Goliath beetle weighs about the same as a hamster.

Centipedes are carnivores, millipedes are vegetarians.

Earthworms have five hearts.

A snail breathes through its foot.

The housefly's taste buds are in its feet.

The muscles that power a dragonfly's wings make up 23 percent of its body weight.

Wasps kill more people in the United States every year than snakes, spiders, and scorpions combined.

Bees are born fully grown.

Termites eat wood twice as fast when listening to heavy metal music.

Water freezes before a cockroach's blood will.

Pound for pound, spiders, flies, and grasshoppers all contain more protein than beef.

World's fastest flying insect: the deer botfly, capable of flying 36 miles per hour.

A hive of honeybees eats up to 30 pounds of honey over the winter.

The mayfly's eggs take three years to hatch. Life span: about six hours.

Houseflies prefer to breed in the middle of a room.

* * *

CHIQUITA BANANA

To let the public know that bananas should be allowed to ripen at room temperature, not in the refrigerator, in 1944 United Fruit commissioned a song and a character: Chiquita Banana. The song was so popular that it was once played on the radio 376 times in one day.

Salt of the Earth

We each have about eight ounces of salt inside us. It's vital for regulating muscle contraction, heartbeat, nerve impulse transmission, protein digestion, and the exchange of water between cells, so as to bring food in and waste out. Deprived of salt, the body goes into convulsion, paralysis, and death.

It's healthy to eat about 1/3 ounce of salt a day, but if you eat more than four ounces at once, you'll die.

We can never run out of salt. There's enough in the oceans to cover the world 14 inches deep.

Salt is hygroscopic, which means it absorbs water. That's why you can't drink seawater; it will dehydrate you.

Only 5 percent of the salt we mine goes into food. The rest goes into making chemicals.

When salt is made by vigorous boiling, it forms cubic crystals, but when it's naturally dried, it makes pyramid-shaped crystals. The pyramid-shaped crystals are particularly sought after for kosher use and in fine cooking.

It takes four gallons of seawater to make a pound of salt.

Salt is often found with oil and is often used by oil companies as an indicator of where to drill.

For centuries salt was served in a bowl, not a shaker. It couldn't be shaken, since it absorbs water and sticks together. The Morton Salt Co. changed that in 1910 by covering every grain with chemicals that keep water out—thus its famous slogan, "When it rains, it pours."

The water in our bodies (we're 70 percent water) has the same saltiness as the seas.

Familiar Phrases

CAUGHT RED-HANDED
Meaning: Caught in the act
Origin: For hundreds of years, stealing and butchering another person's livestock was a common crime. But it was hard to prove unless the thief was caught with a dead animal . . . and blood on his hands.

GIVE SOMEONE "THE BIRD"
Meaning: Make a nasty gesture at someone (usually with the middle finger uplifted)
Origin: There are many versions. The "cleanest": Originally "the bird" referred to the hissing sound that audiences made when they didn't like a performance. Hissing is the sound that a goose makes when it's threatened or angry.

MAKE MONEY HAND OVER FIST
Meaning: Rapid success in a business venture
Origin: Sailors through the ages have used the same hand-over-hand motion when climbing up ropes, hauling in nets, and hoisting sails. The best seamen were those who could do this action the fastest. In the 19th century, Americans adapted the expression "hand over fist"—describing one hand clenching a rope and the other deftly moving above it—to suggest quickness and success.

CLEAN AS A WHISTLE
Meaning: Exceptionally clean or smooth
Origin: This phrase appeared at the beginning of the 19th century, describing the whistling noise made as a sword tears through the air to decapitate a victim cleanly, in a single stroke.

TO BREAK THE ICE
Meaning: To start a conversation
Origin: "Severe winter weather is a major nuisance to operators of

boats. Until the development of power equipment, it was frequently necessary to chop ice at the river's edge with hand tools in order to make channels for plying about the river. The boatman had to break the ice before he could actually get down to business." (*Cassell Everyday Phrases*, by Neil Ewart)

PULL YOUR OWN WEIGHT
Meaning: To do one's share or to take responsibility for oneself
Origin: "The term comes from rowing, where a crew member must pull on an oar hard enough to propel his or her own weight. In use literally since the mid-19th century, it began to be used figuratively in the 1890s." (*Southpaws & Sunday Punches*, by Christine Ammer)

* * *

26 THINGS ELVIS DEMANDED TO BE KEPT AT GRACELAND AT ALL TIMES:

Fresh ground beef
Hamburger buns
Case of Pepsi
Case of orange soda
Brownies
Milk
Half-and-half
6 cans of biscuits
Chocolate ice cream
Hot dogs
Sauerkraut
Potatoes
Onions
Bacon
Fresh fruit
Peanut butter
Banana pudding
Meat loaf
Cigarettes
Dristan
Super Anahist
Contac
Sucrets
3 packs each of Spearmint, Juicy Fruit, and Doublemint gum

The Bible

Dogs are mentioned 14 times in the Bible. Cats aren't mentioned even once.

Longest name in the Bible: Mahershalalhashbaz (Isaiah 8:1).

The Bible has been translated into Klingon.

The Bible is the most shoplifted book in the United States.

The word *sermon* does not appear in the Bible.

Sixty percent of atheists and agnostics say they own at least one Bible.

First hotel to stock Gideon Bibles: the Superior Hotel in Iron Mountain, Montana, in 1908.

The word *girl* appears in the Bible once.

Most mentioned woman in the Bible: Sarah, 56 times.

Only two books in the Bible are named for women: Ruth and Esther.

Over 6 billion copies of the Bible have been sold.

According to the Bible, there were two windows on Noah's Ark.

* * *

LIFE'S LITTLE IRONIES

English novelist Arnold Bennett died in Paris in 1931. Cause of death? "Drinking a glass of typhoid-infected water to demonstrate that Parisian water was perfectly safe to drink."

Founding Fathers

JOYCE C. HALL
Hall started out selling picture postcards from a shoe box, but soon realized that greeting cards with envelopes would be more profitable. He started a new company, Hallmark Cards, a play on his name and the word for quality, and in 1916 produced his first card. But the innovation that made Hallmark so successful had little to do with the cards themselves—it was their display cases. Previously cards were purchased by asking a clerk to choose an appropriate one. Hall introduced display cases featuring rows of cards that the customer could browse through. When he died in 1982, the company he founded in a shoe box was worth $1.5 billion.

DAVID PACKARD
David Packard was an engineer with the General Electric Company. In 1938 he moved to California, where he renewed a friendship with William Hewlett. The two went into the electronics business, making oscillators that were smaller, cheaper, and better than anything else on the market. Working from a small garage in Palo Alto, the Hewlett-Packard company earned $1,000 that first year. Today the garage is a state landmark: "The Birthplace of Silicon Valley." Packard died in 1996 leaving an estate worth billions.

CHARLES FLEISCHMANN
An Austrian native who first visited the United States during the Civil War, he found our bread almost as appalling as our political situation. At the time, bread was mostly homebaked, using yeast made from potato peelings, and its taste was unpredictable. The next time he came to America, Fleischmann brought along samples of the yeast used to make Viennese bread. In 1868 he began to sell his yeast in compressed cakes of uniform size that removed the guesswork from baking. In 1937 yeast sales reached $20 million a year. After

Prohibition ended, Charles and his brother Maximillian found another use for their yeast—to make Fleischmann's distilled gin.

PAUL ORFALEA
After graduating from the University of California at Santa Barbara, Orfalea opened a small copy shop next to a taco stand in nearby Isla Vista, starting with a single copy machine. Business was brisk. He soon expanded the store, then branched out to the rest of California, and then all over the country. And all the stores bore his name, the nickname he got in college because of his curly red hair—Kinko's.

GODFREY KEEBLER
Opened a bakery in Philadelphia in 1853. His family expanded it. Today Keebler is the second-largest producer of cookies and crackers in the United States.

WILLIAM SCHOLL
As an apprentice to the local shoemaker, Billy Scholl's work led him to two conclusions: feet were abused, and nobody cared. So, in a burst of idealism, Scholl appointed himself the future foot doctor to the world. Strangely enough, it actually happened. By the time he became a doctor at 22, Scholl had invented and patented his first arch support; in fact, he held more than 300 patents for foot treatments and machines for making foot comfort aids. And his customers seemed to appreciate it—a widow once wrote him that she buried her husband with his Foot-Eazers so he would be as comfortable as he was in life. Until he died, in his 80s, Dr. Scholl devoted himself to saving the world's feet, adhering always to his credo: "Early to bed, early to rise, work like hell, and advertise."

SIR JOSEPH LISTER
Even before the mouthwash that bears his name was invented, Lister fought germs: he campaigned against filthy hospitals and against doctors who performed surgery in their street clothes. When St. Louis chemist Joseph Lawrence invented the famous mouthwash, he named it Listerine both to honor and to take advantage of Lister's well-known obsession with cleanliness.

The Time It Takes

Twenty-nine days, 12 hours, 44 minutes, and three seconds from a new moon to a new moon

Thirty-five days for a mouse to reach sexual maturity

Thirty-eight days for a slow boat to get to China (from New York)

Twelve weeks for a U.S. Marine to go through boot camp

Eighty-nine days, one hour for winter to come and go

Ninety-one days, 7 hours, 26 minutes, and 24 seconds for Earth to fall into the sun if it loses its orbit

Two hundred fifty-eight days for the gestation period of a yak

One year for Los Angeles to move two inches closer to San Francisco (due to the shifting of tectonic plates)

Two years for cheddar cheese to reach its peak flavor

Four years, eight months to receive your FBI file after making the appropriate request

Six years in a snail's life span

Twenty-five years equals the time the average American spends asleep in a lifetime

Sixty-nine years for the Soviet Union to rise and fall

One hundred years for tidal friction to slow Earth's rotation by 14 seconds

Eighteen hundred years to complete the Great Wall of China

Five hundred thousand years for plutonium-239 to become harmless

One billion years for the sun to release as much energy as a supernova releases in 24 hours

Patently Absurd

INVENTION: Musical Baby Diaper Alarm
USE: Three women from France marketed this alarm to mothers in 1985. It's a padded electronic napkin that goes inside a baby's diaper. When it gets wet, it plays "When the Saints Go Marching In."

INVENTION: Thinking Cap
USE: Improves artistic ability by mimicking the effects of autism. The cap uses magnetic pulses to inhibit the front-temporal, or "left brain," functions. This, say the two Australian scientists behind the project, creates better access to extraordinary savant abilities. They reported improved drawing skills in five of 17 volunteers in a 2002 experiment.

INVENTION: Breath Alert
USE: This pocket-sized electronic device detects and measures bad breath. You simply breathe into the sensor for three seconds, then the LCD readout indicates—on a scale of one to four—how safe (or offensive) your breath is.

INVENTION: Vibrating Toilet Seat
USE: Thomas Bayard invented the seat in 1966. He believed that "buttocks stimulation" helps prevent constipation.

INVENTION: Lavakan
USE: It's a washing machine for cats and dogs. This industrial-strength machine soaps, rinses, and dries your pet in less than 30 minutes. One of the inventors, Andres Díaz, claims that the $20,000 machines can actually reduce pet stress. "One of the dogs actually fell asleep during the wash," he said. Cats weren't quite as happy about being Lavakanned. "But it's better than having a cat attach itself to your face, which is what can happen when you try to wash one by hand."

INVENTION: See-Through Refrigerator
USE: The door is a one-way mirror so when a light is switched on inside the fridge, you can see what's inside without opening the door. You save energy . . . and pounds. Inventor Bruce Lambert says, "The mirror encourages dieting, because people can see their reflections as they approach the door."

INVENTION: Rape-L
USE: Haley manufactures skunk scent vials that wearers can clip to their undergarments to fend off sexual assaults. When attacked, the wearer simply pinches the vial and douses themselves with the scent, which is harvested from real skunks at a skunk ranch in upstate New York. The kit also contains a second vial filled with ordinary tap water "for practice," inventor John Haley explains. Suggested retail price: $19.95.

INVENTION: Beethoven Condoms
USE: The condom will play a bit of Beethoven if it breaks during use. According to news reports, "the condom is coated with a substance that changes electrical conductivity upon rupture, setting off a microchip that produces sound." Inventor Lino Missio, a 26-year-old Italian physics student, has also proposed an alternative to music: a verbal warning to the participants to stop what they're doing immediately.

* * *

DID YOU KNOW?

Hurricanes are classed by wind speed:

Category 1	74–95 mph
Category 2	96–110 mph
Category 3	111–130 mph
Category 4	131–155 mph
Category 5	156 mph and up

That Was Then

In 1912 the archbishop of Paris declared dancing the tango a sin.

In the 13th century, Europeans baptized children with beer.

When medieval Europeans burned witches, the witches' families had to pay for the firewood.

King Henry VI banned kissing in England in 1439 because he thought it spread disease.

Tablecloths originally served as big napkins. People wiped their hands and faces on them.

Ancient Roman banquet halls had "vomitoriums" so people could keep eating after they were full.

Parrot tongue and ostrich brains were considered delicacies in the Roman Empire.

Colonial governor John Winthrop introduced the table fork to America in 1620.

Knights in armor used to lift their visors when riding past the king—the original military salute.

In the Middle Ages chicken soup was considered an aphrodisiac.

In the 13th century, suits of armor weighed as much as 90 pounds.

The Pilgrims refused to eat lobsters because they thought they were really big insects.

The wok began as a Bronze-Age Mongolian helmet that doubled as a cooking pan.

World's oldest profession according to anthropologists: witch doctor.

Page of Sixes

6 Nobel Prize Categories
Peace, Chemistry, Physics,
Physiology & Medicine,
Literature, Economics

6 Wives of Henry VIII
Catherine of Aragon, Ann
Boleyn, Jane Seymour, Anne of
Cleves, Catherine Howard,
Catherine Parr

6 Rodeo Contests
Saddle bronco riding, Bareback
riding, Calf roping, Bull riding,
Steer wrestling, Team roping

**6 Parts of the
Circulatory System**
Heart, Arteries, Arterioles,
Capillaries, Venules, Veins

**6 Enemies of Mankind
(Hinduism)**
Lust, Angst, Envy, Avarice,
Spiritual ignorance, Pride

6 Categories of Dog Breeds
Working, Sporting, Hounds,
Terriers, Nonsporting, Toy

6 Grades of Meat
Prime, Choice, Good,
Standard, Commercial, Utility

6 Layers of the Earth
Crust, Upper mantle, Lower
mantle, Outer core, Transition
region, Inner core

**6 Foreign Places Named
for U.S. Presidents**
Cape Washington, Antarctica;
Monrovia, Liberia; Lincoln
Island, South China Sea;
Cleveland, Brazil; Mount
Eisenhower, Alberta, Canada;
Avenue de President
Kennedy, Paris

**6 Branches of the
U.S. Armed Forces**
Army, Navy, Air Force,
Marines, National Guard,
Coast Guard

6 Elements (Buddhism)
Earth, Water, Fire, Wind,
Space, Consciousness

**Sinister 6 (Spider-Man's
Archenemies)**
Kraven the Hunter, Dr.
Octopus, Mysterio, Vulture,
Electro, Sandman

Myth Conceptions

Myth: Your hair and nails continue to grow after you die.
Fact: They don't. Your tissue recedes from your hair and nails, making them appear longer.

Myth: You should never wake a sleepwalker.
Fact: There's no reason not to wake a sleepwalker. This superstition comes from the old belief that a sleepwalker's spirit leaves the body and might not make it back if the person is wakened.

Myth: In the Old West, pioneers circled their wagons to protect against Indian raids.
Fact: When they did circle the wagons, it was to keep livestock in.

Myth: A strong cup of coffee will help a drunk person get sober.
Fact: It's the alcohol in a person's bloodstream that makes them drunk, and no amount of coffee, no matter how strong, will change that.

Myth: SOS stands for "Save Our Ship."
Fact: It doesn't stand for anything. It was selected as a distress signal because it's easy to transmit in Morse code: 3 dots, 3 dashes, 3 dots.

Myth: Fortune cookies were invented in China.
Fact: They were invented in the United States in 1918 by Charles Jung, a Chinese restaurant owner, to amuse customers while they waited for their food. Only later were they served after the meal.

Myth: According to the Bible, angels have wings.
Fact: Nowhere in the Bible does it say that angels have wings. The idea didn't become popular until painters and sculptors began adding them.

Myth: Dogs sweat through their tongues.
Fact: Dogs cool off by breathing rapidly, not by sticking their tongues out. Their tongues don't have sweat glands—and the only large sweat glands they have are in their feet.

Myth: For every cockroach you see in your house, there are 10 more you didn't see.
Fact: According to studies conducted by the Insects Affecting Man and Animals Laboratory of the U.S. Department of Agriculture, the number is actually closer to 1,000 to 1.

Myth: The artist Vincent van Gogh cut off his entire ear.
Fact: The famous episode followed two months of hard work, hard drinking, and an argument with his best friend, Paul Gauguin. Van Gogh was despondent and cut off only a small part of his earlobe.

Myth: The largest pyramid in the world is in Egypt.
Fact: The Quetzalcoatl pyramid southeast of Mexico City is 177 feet tall, with a base covering 45 acres and a volume of 120 million cubic feet. Cheops, the largest in Egypt, though originally 481 feet tall, has a base covering only 13 acres and a volume of only 90 million cubic feet.

Myth: A limb "falls asleep" because its blood supply gets cut off.
Fact: This feeling of numbness—called neurapraxia—happens when a major nerve is pinched against a hard object or bone. This causes the harmless temporary sensation of numbness, but the blood continues to flow normally.

Interested in myths about Mars?
Turn to page 340.

Sweet Tooth

Americans consume more than 20 pounds of candy per person per year.

The kid on the Cracker Jack box is named Robert.

The seven Gummi Bears are named Gruffi, Cubbi, Tummi, Zummi, Sunni, Gusto, and Grammi.

Bellysinkers, doorknobs, and burl cakes are nicknames for doughnuts.

The double Popsicle stick was introduced during the Depression. It was designed so two people could share it.

Animal Crackers come in 18 different "species."

In 1995 Kellogg Company paid $2,400 to a man whose kitchen was damaged by a flaming Pop-Tart.

World's best-selling cookie: Oreo.

Five Jell-O flavors that flopped: celery, coffee, cola, apple, and chocolate.

Twinkie inventor Jimmy Dewar ate 40,177 Twinkies in his lifetime.

Sixty-nine percent of cake eaters eat the cake first, then the frosting.

Americans eat enough ice cream each year to fill the Grand Canyon.

Cranberry Jell-O is the only flavor that contains real fruit flavoring.

About 8 percent of students at the Dunkin' Donuts Training Center fail the six-week course.

Aspartame is 200 times sweeter than sugar. Saccharin is 500 times sweeter.

There are more places to buy candy in the United States than there are places to buy bread.

Your Average Kid

A child laughs about 400 times a day. Adults laugh about 15 times.

More children are accidentally poisoned by toxic houseplants than by household chemicals.

The average American child uses 730 crayons by the age of 10.

The price of a sleepover in the Bronx Zoo's Congo Gorilla Forest exhibit for 15 kids: $4,500.

The average American child takes his first trip to the mall at two months old.

A child just starting school knows about 6,000 words.

A four-year-old child asks about 437 questions a day.

The average kid eats 15 pounds of cereal a year.

The average child will eat 1,500 peanut butter sandwiches by high school graduation.

On average, kids ages two to five put their hands in their mouths 10 times an hour.

An American kid catches six colds a year. The average American kid in daycare catches 10 colds every year.

Forty-six percent of American kids don't get an allowance.

Sixty-five percent of kids have had at least one imaginary friend by age seven.

Kids' favorite superheroes: Spider-Man, Superman, and Captain Underpants.

Twenty-one percent of U.S. children say that if they were president, they'd "eat ice cream for every meal."

Something's Fishy

Goldfish remember better in cold water than in warm water.

One mother shark can give birth to as many as 70 baby sharks per litter.

Pregnant goldfish are known as "twits."

The great white shark is the only shark that can hold its head above water to observe activity on the surface.

Some Arctic and Antarctic fish have proteins in their blood that act as antifreeze.

Marine turtles rid their bodies of excess salt by weeping.

A shrimp's heart is in its head.

Great white sharks can hear sounds from over a mile away.

A baby oyster is called a spat.

Sponges form 99 percent of all marine species.

Maximum life span of a goldfish in captivity: 25 years.

The glue that barnacles use to stick themselves to ship hulls is twice as strong as epoxy resin.

An adult electric eel generates enough electricity to power a medium-size house.

* * *

STRANGE TOURIST ATTRACTIONS

The Hall of Mosses (Washington)

Philip Morris Cigarette Tours (Virginia)

The Soup Tureen Museum (New Jersey)

The Testicle Festival (Montana)

Safari

Hippopotamus bites are almost always fatal. Reason: they're very large bites.

The hippo weighs about 100 pounds at birth.

Elephants drink a minimum of 50 gallons of water a day.

Elephants spend 18 hours a day eating.

The ears of an African elephant can weigh up to 110 pounds each.

No matter what anyone tells you, elephants are not afraid of mice.

The elephant is the only animal with four knees.

An elephant grows six sets of teeth in its lifetime.

Lions and tigers can't purr. Cougars can.

Force exerted by the jaw of an African lion: 937 pounds. By the human jaw: 175 pounds.

Lions are the only cats that live in packs.

Lions can mate more than 50 times a day.

Elephants can't jump. Every other mammal can.

The cheetah is the only member of the cat family that cannot retract its claws.

A giraffe only sleeps about four hours a day.

Baby giraffes grow as much as one inch every two hours.

A giraffe's tongue is 17 inches long.

Baby giraffes drop six feet to the ground when they're born.

The giraffe has the highest blood pressure of any animal.

Giraffes are highly susceptible to throat infections because of their long throats—and because they can't cough.

Famous Folks

Benjamin Franklin once wrote an essay on the possibility of waterskiing.

What did Christopher Columbus look like? No one knows—his portrait was never painted.

P. T. Barnum staged the first international beauty contest.

Astronaut Neil Armstrong stepped on the moon with his left foot first.

Daniel Boone thought coonskin caps were uncivilized.

Though deaf and blind, Helen Keller learned English, French, and German.

Joan of Arc was 19 years old when she was burned at the stake.

Jimmy Hoffa's middle name was Riddle.

Mussolini's favorite cartoon character was Donald Duck.

Abraham Lincoln and William Shakespeare have no living descendants.

Charles Darwin and Albert Einstein married their first cousins.

Winston Churchill called his wife Kat. She called him Pug.

Albert Einstein couldn't read until the age of nine.

Sigmund Freud smoked 20 cigars a day.

Napoléon Bonaparte was afraid of cats.

Cleopatra was married to Ptolemy XIII and Ptolemy XIV—both her brothers.

Cleopatra tested the potency of her poisons by feeding them to her slaves.

Mahatma Gandhi is buried in California.

Myth Conceptions

Myth: The driest spot on earth is in the Saharan desert.
Fact: The driest place on earth is in Chile. It's so dry in Calama, Chile, that 400 years went by without rain; the only source of moisture was the fog in the air. (A torrential rainstorm broke the 400-year dry spell in 1972, but the record remains intact.)

Myth: Most of the world's plant life is in the dense jungles of Africa and South America.
Fact: The vast majority—85 percent, in fact—of the world's greenery is in the oceans.

Myth: All your fingernails grow at the same rate.
Fact: If you're right-handed, nails on your right hand grow faster; if you're left-handed, nails on your left will.

Myth: If you touch a baby bird, its mother will abandon it.
Fact: Whether or not a mother can detect the scent of a human depends on the animal's sense of smell. Birds have a poor sense of smell and would never know from it whether a human had touched their nests.

Myth: Air fresheners remove offending odors from the air.
Fact: Not even close. Actually they either cover smells up with a stronger scent, or make your nose numb so you can't smell the bad stuff. The only way you can get rid of odors is with expensive absorption agents like charcoal or silica gel.

Myth: Whales spout water.
Fact: Whales actually exhale air through their blowholes. This creates a mist or fog that looks like a waterspout.

The Sporting Life

The game of lacrosse is about 600 years old.

Most popular sport on earth: soccer. It is played by 100 million people in more than 50 countries.

In 2002 runner Tom Johnson ran an 80 kilometer race (about 50 miles) against a horse—and beat it by 10 seconds.

There are about 10 trillion ways to play the first 10 moves in a game of chess.

Sports celebrity to appear simultaneously on *Time*, *Newsweek*, and *Sports Illustrated*: the racehorse Secretariat, in 1973.

John McEnroe once tied his shoelaces seven times during a match at Wimbledon.

Oldest major U.S. sporting event: the Kentucky Derby, first held in 1875.

Fifteen runners started the first-ever Boston Marathon. Only 10 of them finished it.

In an average day Canada imports 822 hockey sticks from Russia.

A runner consumes about seven quarts of oxygen while running a 100-yard dash.

Horse jockeys are the only U.S. athletes legally allowed to bet on themselves.

Oldest American college sport still in existence: rowing.

In the United States, Frisbees outsell baseballs, basketballs, and footballs combined.

First announcer to say, "He shoots, he scores!" during a hockey game: Foster Hewitt, in 1933.

In pro Ping-Pong, if players use white balls, they can't wear white shirts. They can't see them.

Geography 101

Check a map: Reno, Nevada, is west of Los Angeles, California.

Westernmost state in the United States: Alaska. Easternmost: Alaska. (It crosses the international date line.)

Tallest mountain on Earth: Hawaii's Mauna Kea, 31,800 feet from the ocean floor.

Highest town in the United States: Climax, Colorado, at 11,302 feet above sea level.

Moscow is closer to Washington, D.C., than Honolulu is.

Alaska alone has as much coastline as the rest of the United States.

Coney Island isn't an island, but it used to be.

Three Mile Island is two and a half miles long.

Israel is one-fourth the size of Maine.

There were 30 more countries in the year 2005 than there were in 1990.

What's special about Cadillac Mountain, Maine, in the winter? It's the first place you can see the rising sun in the United States. In the warmer months, it's Mars Hill in Maine.

There are eight time zones in North America.

World's biggest desert: the Sahara, at 3.5 million square miles. The Gobi is number two at 500,000.

In an average minute, 20,900 gallons flow from the Amazon River into the sea.

Shortest river: the D River in Oregon. It's 120 feet long.

Page of Sevens

7 Wonders of the Ancient World
Great Pyramid of Cheops at Giza, Hanging Gardens of Babylon, Statue of Zeus at Olympia, Temple of Artemis at Ephesus, Mausoleum at Halicarnassus, Colossus of Rhodes, Pharos (Lighthouse) of Alexandria

7 Liberal Arts
Grammar, Rhetoric, Logic, Arithmetic, Geometry, Music, Astronomy

7 Deadly Sins
Pride, Envy, Wrath, Sloth, Avarice, Gluttony, Lust

7 Seas
Red, Adriatic, Black, Caspian, Mediterranean, Persian Gulf, Indian Ocean

7 Days of the Week
Sun's day, Moon's day, Tiw's day, Woden's day, Thor's day, Frig's day, Saturn's day

7 Virtues
Faith, Hope, Charity, Fortitude, Prudence, Justice, Temperance

7 Sages of Greece
Solon of Athens, Pittacus of Mytilene, Bias of Priene, Cleobulus of Lindus, Periande of Corinth, Chilon of Sparta, Thales of Miletus

7 Japanese Gods of Happiness
Laughing Buddha, Watchman, God of longevity, God of scholarship, God of nutrition, God of fishing, Goddess of music

7 Hills of Rome
Palatine, Capitoline, Quirinal, Viminal, Esquiline, Caelian, Aventine

7 Metals of Alchemy
Gold, Silver, Lead, Quicksilver, Copper, Iron, Tin

7 Muslim Heavens
Pure silver, Pure gold, Pearl, White gold, Silver, Ruby and garnet, Divine Light

7 Sisters (Pleaides)
Alcyone, Asterope, Celaeno, Electra, Maia, Merope, Taygete

7 Ancient Rivers
Nile, Tigris, Oxua, Euphrates, Indus, Yaksart, Arax

7 Taxonomic Classifications
Kingdom, Phylum, Class, Order, Family, Genus, Species

Custom Made

CLINKING GLASSES AFTER A TOAST
Nobles and knights were sometimes assassinated by enemies who'd poisoned their wine. So when they got together socially, each poured a little of his own wine into everyone else's goblet, as a precaution. That way, if one man poisoned another, he poisoned everyone— including himself. Over the years the tradition of exchanging wine has been simplified into clinking glasses as a gesture of friendship.

BUTTONS ON COAT SLEEVES
Researchers credit this to Napoléon Bonaparte. Apparently, while inspecting some troops, he spotted a soldier wiping his nose on his jacket sleeve. Disgusted, Napoléon ordered new jackets for his army—this time with buttons on the sleeves, to prevent a recurrence.

WEARING BLACK FOR MOURNING
Until King Charles VIII of France died in the late 15th century, Europeans in mourning wore white (for hope or renewal). But when Anne of Brittany, Charles's widow, went into mourning, she donned black. The result: a funeral fashion that continues today.

BUSINESS CARDS
Until the early part of the 20th century, "calling cards" were used by the upper class exclusively for social purposes. Presenting a calling card when you met or visited someone indicated that you didn't have to work for a living. But as the middle classes got into the act, the calling card became another means of making a business contact.

STRIPED BARBER POLES
Barbers were once a lot more versatile than they are today. They not only cut hair, but performed surgery as well. When the barbers finished, the towels used to soak up excess blood were hung outside to dry on a pole. As the wind dried them, they wrapped around the pole, making a design, so to speak, of red and white stripes.

APRIL FOOLS' DAY
Until 1564 it was a tradition to begin the New Year with a weeklong celebration, ending with a big party. But the calendar was different then; the new year began on March 25—which meant the annual party was held on April 1. In 1564 a new calendar was instituted, making January 1 the New Year. People who forgot and still showed up to celebrate on April 1 were called April fools.

TIPPING
Some think it began in the 17th century, when restaurants had boxes labeled T.I.P.—To Insure Promptness—on the wall beside their entrances. Patrons who wanted their food in a hurry deposited a few coins in the box before they sat down.

AN APPLE FOR THE TEACHER
Now an outmoded custom, it stems from the days when public schoolteachers were paid with whatever the community could afford. Often they were given food or goods in lieu of cash.

THE TOOTH FAIRY
In Germany, where the idea apparently originated, the tooth was not placed under a pillow. Instead, it was put in a rat hole, because it was thought that the new tooth growing in would take on the "dental quality" of the animal who found it.

COVERING A YAWN
People once thought that their souls could escape during a yawn. They covered their mouths to prevent this and, since yawns can be contagious, to try to keep people around them from "catching" the yawn. The apology after a yawn originated as an expression of regret for having exposed people to mortal danger.

* * *

THE COST OF THINGS: 1930

Christmas tree light set (eight bulbs): 88¢
Motor oil: 49¢ a gallon
Electric toaster: $1
Washing machine: $58

Random Science

If you could tap the energy released by an average-size hurricane, it would be enough to satisfy all U.S. energy needs for six months.

In any given year, about 26,000 meteorites land on the earth's surface, the vast majority dropping into the oceans. Only seven people in recorded history have been hit by one.

When glass breaks, the cracks travel faster than 3,000 mph.

Gold is so rare that all of the pure gold produced in the last 500 years would fit inside a 50-foot cube.

At least 100,000 separate chemical reactions occur in the human brain every second.

About 70 percent of the earth is covered with water, but only 1 percent of that water is drinkable.

Sound travels through steel 15 times faster than it travels through air.

To escape Earth's gravitational pull, a spacecraft has to move faster than seven miles per second—a speed that would take you from New York to Philadelphia in under 20 seconds.

Rain contains vitamin B12.

According to a University of Michigan study, men are six times more likely to be struck by lightning than women are.

If you could capture a comet's entire 10,000-mile vapor trail in a container, the condensed vapor would occupy less than one cubic inch of space.

Earth travels through space at 66,600 miles per hour—eight times faster than the speed of a bullet.

Golf

Japan has more than 13 million golfers, but only 1,200 golf courses.

Fewer people golf on Tuesday than on any other day of the week.

Eight percent of all money spent on sporting goods in the United States is used to buy golf equipment.

Before 1850, most golf balls were stuffed with feathers.

Golf was banned in England in 1457 because it was a distraction from archery.

It's about 10 times easier to shoot a hole in one while golfing than it is to score a perfect 300 game while bowling.

Amount Tiger Woods's caddie made in 2000: $1 million.

Golf probably comes from the Dutch word *kolf*, which means "club."

Golf club Alan Shepard used on the moon: six iron. (See page 355)

The world's first golf rule book was published in Scotland in 1754.

The first golf course with 18 holes was St. Andrews in Scotland, in 1764.

When it was introduced in 1848, the modern golf ball was called a "gutta-percha" ball.

A golf club remains in contact with the ball for half a thousandth of a second.

More people die playing golf than any other sport. Leading causes: heart attacks and strokes.

Earth Science 101

A 7.0 magnitude earthquake is 900 times more powerful than a 5.0 earthquake.

How much would you weigh at the exact center of the earth? Nothing.

Space dust increases the earth's weight by as much as six tons a day.

Which goes up, stalactites or stalagmites? Try this: "When the mites go up, the tights come down."

Geologically speaking, we live in the Cenozoic era, which began 65 million years ago.

Due to the rotation of the earth, an object can be thrown farther if it's thrown west.

The earth is turning to desert at a rate of 40 square miles per day.

The earth spins 1,000 mph faster at the equator than at the poles.

If the earth had no air between its atoms, it would be about the size of a baseball.

All That Glitters

Odds that a polished diamond weighs more than a carat: one in 1,000.

In a typical diamond mine, you have to dig 23 tons of ore to find a single one-carat diamond.

An ounce of gold can be beaten thin enough to cover an entire acre of ground.

The largest gold nugget ever found weighed 172 pounds, 13 ounces.

There's enough gold in the ocean to give every human nine pounds.

Diamonds are up to 90 times harder than corundum, the next-hardest mineral.

The number one use of gold in the United States: class rings.

Only 20 percent of diamonds are considered high enough quality to be classified as gems.

Diamonds will not dissolve in acid.

The thinnest man-made thread is a gold filament.

It takes about a ton of ore to provide the gold for one wedding ring.

Diamonds have been worth more than pearls for only about a century.

About 75 percent of all the gold mined each year is made into jewelry.

The diamond is the only gem composed of a single element (carbon).

A cubic foot of gold weighs more than half a ton.

Pound for pound, radium is worth more than gold.

South Africa mines almost half of the world's gold.

Bug Off!

Ants have five noses. Each one smells a different odor.

Each year insects eat a third of the world's food crop.

In a single day, a pair of termites can produce as many as 30,000 offspring.

Leaf-cutter ants can build anthills 16 feet deep and one acre square.

The horsefly can pierce a horse's hide with its mouth.

The longest earthworm ever found was 22 feet long.

Fire beetles fly into forest fires to lay their eggs.

A common housefly beats its wings about 20,000 times per minute.

Only the female mosquitoes eat blood. Males eat sap.

A queen honeybee can lay as many as 1,500 eggs a day.

A bee has 5,000 nostrils. It can smell an apple tree two miles away.

It takes three minutes for a fresh mosquito bite to begin to itch.

Animal responsible for the most human deaths worldwide: the mosquito.

Word Origins

TYCOON
Meaning: A wealthy and powerful business person
Origin: "A trumped-up Japanese title, *taikun* was a word used to magnify the role of the shogun or military commander of the country, especially when he was addressing foreigners, the point being to suggest that he was more potent and important than the emperor himself. The word meant 'emperor' or 'great prince,' borrowed from the Chinese *t'ai kiuen* ('great prince')." (*The Secret Lives of Words*, by Paul West)

THIRD DEGREE
Meaning: Intense, often brutal, questioning, especially by police
Origin: "Dating to the 1890s in America, it has no connection with criminal law. The third degree is the highest degree in Freemasonry. Any Mason must undergo very difficult tests of proficiency before he qualifies for the third degree and it is probably from these 'tests' that the exhaustive questioning of criminals came to be called the third degree." (*QPB Encyclopedia of Word and Phrase Origins*, by Robert Hendrickson)

ATCHOO!
Meaning: The sound you make when you sneeze
Origin: "Excluded from dictionaries, this imitative word corresponds oddly with the French *à tes souhaits* (pronounced 'a tay soo-eh'), their version of 'God bless.' It even sounds like it, though *à tes souhaits* follows the sneeze. Is this overlap a mere fluke, or has somebody really been listening?" (*The Secret Lives of Words*, by Paul West)

POSTHUMOUS
Meaning: Something that arises from or occurs after one's death
Origin: "Posthumous comes from the Latin *postumus*, 'last' or 'last-born,' which, strictly speaking, could be applied to the last child born

of a particular mother and father, without reference to death. The *h* crept into *postumus* by association with *humus* (earth or ground) and perhaps with some help from *humare* (to bury). The modern spelling and meaning were fixed by Posthumus Leonatus, hero of Shakespeare's *Cymbeline*, who received this name, as the audience is informed at the start of the play, because he was born after his father died." (*Devious Derivations*, by Hugh Rawson)

TATTOO
Meaning: A permanent mark on the skin made by ingraining an indelible pigment
Origin: "When Captain Cook sailed to Tahiti in 1769, he unwittingly introduced tattoos to sailors. Upon studying the island's inhabitants, Cook described how 'both sexes paint their bodys.' Cook called it 'tattow,' his rendition of the Tahitian term *tatau*. The word was derived from the Polynesian *ta*, 'to strike,' a reference to the puncturing of the skin 'with small instruments made of bone, cut into short teeth.'" (*The Chronology of Words and Phrases*, by Linda and Roger Flavell)

LUKEWARM
Meaning: Barely warm
Origin: "Luke was a Middle English word, now obsolete, meaning 'warm,' which was based on *lew*, another word for 'warm.' *Lew*, in turn, was derived from the Old English word *hleow*, meaning (guess what?) 'warm.' You have probably realized by now that lukewarm actually amounts to saying 'warm-warm,' but this sort of redundancy is common when obsolete words are carried over into modern usage." (*The Word Detective*, by Evan Morris)

SEEDY
Meaning: Somewhat disreputable; squalid
Origin: "During the seasons when rye, barley, oats, and other grains were being planted, a fellow who spent his days in the fields was likely to be covered with seeds. Once the derisive title entered common usage, it came to mean anything run-down—from shacks to individuals." (*Why You Say It*, by Webb Garrison)

Know Your -ologies

Anemology: The study of wind

Conchology: The study of shells

Dactylology: Communication using fingers (sign language)

Hippology: The study of horses

Ichthyology: The study of fish

Mycology: The study of fungi

Myrmecology: The study of ants

Neology: The study of new words

Nosology: The study of the classification of diseases

Oenology: The study of wines

Otology: The study of ears

Potamology: The study of rivers

Rhinology: The study of noses

Sinology: The study of Chinese culture

Matter Miscellany

Trash in landfills keeps its original weight, volume, and form for 40 years.

The average pencil will draw a line 35 miles long.

Even clean air may contain as many as 1,500 specks of dust per cubic inch.

A cubic yard of air weighs about two pounds.

Most avalanches travel downhill at a rate of 22 mph.

The only rock that floats in water: pumice.

Sand melts at 3,100°F.

Sound travels a mile in five seconds through the air. Under water, it travels a mile in one second.

Scientific name for the dust we kick up when in motion: the "Pigpen effect."

The average smell weighs 760 nanograms.

There are an estimated 30 billion billion molecules in a cubic centimeter of air.

It takes about 3 1/2 hours for sound waves to travel from San Francisco to New York.

Scientists don't completely understand why thrown stones skip across water.

Helium-filled balloons float because helium is seven times lighter than air.

Hot water weighs more than cold water.

Mercury is the only metal that is liquid at room temperature.

Left to its own devices, one ton of iron can turn into three tons of rust.

Lead melts at a temperature of 620°F. Tin melts at 446°F. Mix them together and they melt at 356°F.

Dry ice doesn't melt. It evaporates.

Eh Two, Canada?

Canada was the second country to legalize medical marijuana. (First: Belgium)

Canada has the second coldest national capital: Ottawa. (First: Ulaanbaatar, Mongolia)

Canada is the second largest foreign investor in Chile. (First: United States)

Canada has the second highest university enrollment rate in the world. (First: United States)

Canada has the second most tornadoes. (First: United States)

Canada is the second in pork exports. (First: Denmark)

Canada has the second highest amount of gum chewed per capita. (First: United States)

Canada has the second highest broadband Internet access in the world. (First: South Korea)

Canada was the second country to publish a national atlas. (First: Finland)

Canada has the second highest freshwater use per capita. (First: United States)

Canada has the second highest water quality. (First: Finland)

Canada is the second largest per capita emitter of greenhouse gases. (First: United States)

Canada has the second most biotech companies. (First: United States)

Canada is the second largest exporter of red meat. (First: Australia)

Canada is the second biggest market for U.S. seafood. (First: Japan)

Canada is the second largest foreign investor in Korea. (First: United States)

The Speed of Things

A penguin with a six-inch stride can run as fast as an average man.

Columbus traveled at an average speed of 2.8 miles per hour on his first voyage across the sea.

Water can flow through a plant at four miles per hour.

The speed of a roller coaster increases an average of 10 miles per hour when it's raining.

Good thing they're hauling gas: giant oil tankers get about 31 feet per gallon.

Flying fish "fly" at 40 miles per hour.

Top speed of a chicken at full gallop: 9 miles per hour. Top speed of a pigeon in flight: 90 miles per hour.

When you pop a champagne cork, it can travel as fast as 100 miles per hour.

Average speed of a golf ball in flight during the PGA Tour: 160 miles per hour.

Peregrine falcons can dive at speeds up to 240 miles an hour.

Toys

Barbie (the doll) has a last name: Roberts. Ken's last name is Carson.

World's largest manufacturer of female apparel: Mattel. (They make Barbie clothes.)

Chance of meeting someone with Barbie's human-scale measurements (36–18–33): one in 100,000. Chance of meeting someone with Ken's: one in 50.

Easy-Bake Ovens have been sold since 1964.

If you lined up all the Slinkys ever made, they could wrap around the world 126 times.

You can buy a gold-plated Slinky for $100. Sterling silver: $400.

Play-Doh was used as a wallpaper cleaner before it became a toy.

Lego has manufactured more than 189 billion pieces in 2,000 different shapes since 1949, about 30 Lego pieces for every living person on earth.

Annual sales of G.I. Joe increased by 46 percent in 2002—following the 9/11 attacks.

The import of stuffed animals and female dolls is banned in Saudi Arabia.

Nearly 21,000 people are injured every year from air rifles, paintball pistols, and BB guns.

In 1958 Crayola changed its "Prussian blue" to "midnight blue" in response to teacher recommendations that children could no longer relate to Prussian history.

World's most popular "laptop": the Etch A Sketch.

Processed Foods

First food eaten by an American in space: pureed applesauce from a tube.

There are 27 chemicals that can be added to bread without being listed on the label.

The first cereal to come in a box? Shredded Wheat.

First food product permitted by law to have artificial coloring: butter. (It's naturally white.)

One of the most popular soups in 1929: peanut butter soup.

The first canned foods appeared in 1810, but the can opener wasn't invented until 1858.

Most of the egg rolls sold in the United States are made in Houston.

Lemon Pledge has more lemons than Country Time Lemonade.

Six weeks after an aluminum can is recycled, it's back on the shelf in the form of a new can.

First Editions

World's First Dictionary: *Explaining Words, Analyzing Characters* (A.D. 100), by Xu Shen. Chinese words and definitions.

World's First Fantasy Story: *The Castaway*, published in Egypt circa 1950 B.C. The story of a man who is shipwrecked on an island ruled by a giant bearded serpent with a deep voice and an ability to predict the future.

World's First Sci-Fi Story: *True History*, by Lucian of Samosata, published in the 2nd century A.D. Adventures in outer space, in unknown seas, and on the moon. Everyone in space speaks Greek.

World's First Book of Firsts: *Origins of Ages* (100 B.C.), author unknown. Lists the founders of the ruling families of China.

World's First Novel: *Cyropaedia* (360 B.C.), by the Greek author Xenophon. An account of the life of Cyrus, founder of the Persian empire. The book offers "an idealized account of Persian society, contrasting with the unsympathetic views of most Greeks."

World's First Autobiography: *Memoirs of Aratus of Sicyon*, published after his death by poisoning in 213 B.C. Critics commend Aratus for admitting his own weaknesses in the book, but fault him for being "insultingly critical of people he disliked."

World's First Book of Ghost Stories: *Tales of Marvels* (early 3rd century), by Chinese author Tsao Pi. Stories include a haunted house and a man who convinces a ghost that he's a ghost, too.

World's First Joke Book: *Forest of Jokes*, by Harn Darn Jun, a Chinese author, around A.D. 200.

Cool Billions

If you had $1 billion and spent $1,000 a day, it would take 2,740 years to spend it.

One billion people would fill roughly 305 Chicagos.

It took until 1800 for the world's population to reach 1 billion, but only 130 years more for it to reach 2 billion—in 1930.

One billion people lined up side by side would stretch for 568,200 miles.

First magazine in history to sell a billion copies: *TV Guide*, in 1974.

More than 1 billion people on earth are between the ages of 15 and 24.

One Styrofoam cup contains 1 billion molecules of CFCs (chlorofluorocarbons)—harmful to the earth's ozone layer.

A single ragweed plant can release a billion grains of pollen.

To cook 1 billion pounds of pasta, you'd need 2 billion gallons of water—enough to fill nearly 75,000 Olympic-size swimming pools.

The ratio of billionaires to the rest of the U.S. population is 1 to 4.5 million.

Nearly 1 billion Barbie dolls (including friends and family) have been sold since 1959. Placed head to toe, the dolls would circle the earth more than three times.

The first billion-dollar corporation in the U.S. emerged in 1901—United States Steel.

One teaspoon of yogurt contains more than 1 billion live and active bacteria.

The first year in which the U.S. national debt exceeded $1 billion was 1863.

There are about 1 billion red blood cells in two to three drops of blood.

Elvis

Elvis was nearsighted. He owned $60,000 worth of prescription sunglasses when he died.

On an average day, four people call Graceland and ask to speak to Elvis.

According to *Billboard* magazine, the number one single of the 1950s was "Don't Be Cruel," by Elvis Presley.

Boris Yeltsin's favorite Elvis song: "Are You Lonesome Tonight?"

Elvis Presley got a C in his eighth-grade music class.

The lightest Elvis ever weighed as an adult was 170 pounds in 1960, following his discharge from the U.S. Army. The heaviest was at the time of his death: 260 pounds.

Elvis's favorite amusement park ride was the bumper cars.

Elvis had a pet monkey named Scatter.

The U.S. Post Office sold a record 123 million Elvis Presley commemorative stamps when they were first issued in 1993.

The Elvis Presley hit "Hound Dog" was written in about 10 minutes.

One of Elvis's favorite meals was a pound of bacon—and nothing else.

Elvis auditioned for a spot on the 1950s TV show *Arthur Godfrey's Talent Scouts* but didn't make the cut. Neither did Buddy Holly when he tried it.

Elvis is the top-earning dead celebrity in the world. His estate took in $45 million in 2004.

Graceland is the second-most-visited house in America. The first is the White House.

Seven percent of Americans believe Elvis is still alive. Curious? See page 333.

Whales & Co.

The blood vessels of a blue whale are so wide that an adult trout could swim through them.

A whale's heart beats about once every six and a half seconds.

Bottle-nosed whales can dive 3,000 feet in two minutes.

Whales can get lice.

A blue whale's heart is as big as a compact car.

Whales are the fastest-growing animals in the world.

A humpback whale can eat 5,000 fish in a single sitting.

The right whale's eyeball is about as big as an orange.

The sperm whale's brain weighs 20 pounds, the largest in the animal kingdom.

At its peak, a growing blue whale gains between 200 and 300 pounds a day.

Dolphins can hear underwater sounds from as far as 15 miles away.

Dolphins sleep with one eye open.

Baby seals are called "weaners."

Seals can dive as deep as 1,000 feet.

The northern fur seal averages 40 to 60 mates per season.

Male seals don't eat during mating season.

If a walrus eats enough food, it can grow wider than its own length.

How can you tell when a porpoise is searching for a mate? It swims upside down.

Football

The football huddle was invented at a university for the deaf . . . to keep the opposing team from seeing their hand signs.

It takes 3,000 cows to supply the NFL with enough leather for a year's supply of footballs.

John Heisman (of trophy fame) coined the word *hike* and split football games into four quarters.

Top ticket price to the first Super Bowl, in 1967: $12. Top price in 2005: $500.

Most successful high school football team in history: De La Salle Spartans of Concord, California. After more than 10 years and 151 wins, they lost to Washington's Bellevue Wolverines in September 2004.

NFL great Vince Lombardi coined the phrase "game plan."

Football has more rules than any other American sport.

In 1888 Yale football coach Walter Camp fell ill. His wife coached for the entire season.

Deion Sanders is the only man to play in the World Series and the Super Bowl.

There is a 100 percent injury rate among professional football players.

In the NFL, the host team must have 26 footballs inflated and ready.

The L.A. Rams were the first football team to have emblems on their helmets.

Nine of the 15 highest-rated television shows in history have been NFL championship games.

So few Heisman Trophy winners have made it into the Pro Football Hall of Fame—only 10 (including O. J. Simpson) —that the prize has been called "the kiss of death" for college players.

Europe

Norway consumes more Mexican food than any other European nation.

France gets 75 percent of its energy from nuclear power plants.

Belgium is about the same size as New Jersey.

Country with the lowest divorce rate on earth: Vatican City. Lowest birthrate in the world: Vatican City.

In 1952 as many as 12,000 people may have died from the four-day Great Coal-burning smog in London.

The city of Edinburgh, Scotland, is built on top of an extinct volcano.

Downtown London has sunk almost an inch since 1995. In Greenland there's a place called Thank God Harbor.

During the summer months in Reykjavik, Iceland, the sun is visible 24 hours a day.

The Battle of Waterloo wasn't fought in Waterloo. It was fought in Pancenoit, four miles away.

In Finland, saunas outnumber cars.

The Netherlands is the country with the tallest overall average adult height at 72.6 inches, followed by Denmark, Norway, Sweden, and Germany. The average adult height in the United States is 70.8 inches.

The top five non-English languages spoken at home by kids are, in rank order, Spanish, French, German, Italian, and Chinese.

There are more than 5,000 islands in the British Isles.

When Italy was founded in 1861, only 3 percent of Italians spoke Italian fluently.

Greenland, which is mostly snow and ice, was named by Erik the Red; he wanted to encourage immigration.

Everyday Origins

REFRIGERATOR MAGNETS

Mass-produced magnets designed for refrigerators didn't appear until 1964. They were invented by John Arnasto (son of the guy who invented Eskimo Pies) and his wife, Arlene, who sold a line of decorative wall hooks. Arlene thought it would be cute to have a hook for refrigerator doors, so John made one with a magnet backing. The first one had a small bell and was shaped like a tea kettle; it sold well, so the Arnastos added dozens of other versions to their line. Believe it or not, some of the rare originals are now worth more than $100.

GOLD RECORDS

In 1941 RCA Victor released Glenn Miller's "Chattanooga Choo Choo" after he performed it in the movie *Sun Valley Serenade*. It was a huge hit: 1.2 million records were sold in less than three months. So RCA came up with a great publicity gimmick to promote it: They sprayed one of the "master records" with gold paint, and on February 10, 1942, presented it to Miller during a radio broadcast in honor of his selling a million copies. Eventually the Record Industry Association of America (RIAA) copied the idea and started honoring million-selling records with an official Gold Record Award.

KITTY LITTER

In January 1948, in Cassopolis, Michigan, a woman named Kay Draper ran into trouble: The sandpile she used to fill her cat's litter box was frozen solid. She tried ashes, but wound up with paw prints all over the house. Sawdust didn't work, either. As it happened, her neighbors, the Lowes, sold a product called fuller's earth, a kiln-dried clay that was used to soak up oil and grease spills in factories. Ed Lowe, their 27-year-old son, had been looking for a new market for the stuff—he'd tried unsuccessfully to sell it to local farmers as nesting material for chickens. On the spur of the moment, he convinced Draper that this stuff would make great cat litter. He really had no idea if it would . . . but it did! He sensed the sales potential, put some fuller's earth in paper bags and labeled it Kitty Litter with a grease pen. Then he drove around, trying to sell it. (Actually, he gave it away at first to get people to try it.) Once people tried it, they invariably came back for more.

SLOT MACHINES

Other types of gambling machines date back as far as the 1890s, but the first one to really catch on was a vending machine for chewing gum introduced by the Mills Novelty Company in 1910. Their machine dispensed three flavors of gum—cherry, orange, and plum—depending on which fruits appeared on three randomly spinning wheels. If three bars reading "1910 Fruit Gum" appeared in a row, the machine gave extra gum; if a lemon appeared, it gave no gum at all (which is why *lemon* came to mean something unsatisfactory or defective.) You can't get gum in a slot machine anymore—the 1910 Fruit Gum machine was so popular that the company converted them to cash payouts—but the same fruit symbols are still used in slot machines today.

PLASTIC WRAP

Invented by accident in 1933, when Ralph Wiley, a researcher at Dow Chemical, was washing his lab equipment at the end of the day and found that a thin plastic film coating the inside of one vial wasn't coming off. The stuff was polyvinylidene chloride, and after further experimentation, Wiley found that the stuff was clingy, resisted chemicals, and was impervious to air and water. It was so tough, in fact, that he wanted to call it eonite, after an imaginary indestructible substance in the *Little Orphan Annie* comic strip. Dow decided to call it Saran Wrap instead.

WATER BEDS

The direct ancestor of the modern water bed was invented in 1853 by Dr. William Hooper of Portsmouth, England, who saw the beds as a medical device that could be used to treat bedridden patients suffering from bedsores, as well as burn victims, and arthritis and rheumatism sufferers. His water bed wasn't much more than a rubber hot water bottle big enough to sleep on. It wasn't until 1967 that San Francisco design student Charles Hall made an improved model out of vinyl and added an electric heater to keep the bed warm all the time.

What's on TV?

Thirty thousand Hawaiians signed a petition to change Maui's name to Gilligan's Island.

There was so little dialogue in the original *Mission Impossible* TV show that Peter Graves, the star, once fell asleep in the middle of a scene and no one noticed.

In a 1990 preschool poll, Mister Rogers was first choice for president of the United States.

Johnny Carson once sold vacuum cleaners door-to-door. Ed McMahon sold kitchen utensils.

Desi Arnaz's mother was one of the heirs to the Bacardi Rum fortune.

Ted Danson once appeared in a TV commercial as a package of lemon chiffon pie mix.

Ads for Super Bowl 2006 hit a record high of $2.4 million for 30 seconds.

According to *Sesame Street*, Kermit the Frog is left-handed.

Cheers has the most Emmy nominations—117—for a TV program.

Britain is the biggest market for illegally downloaded TV shows in the world, followed by Australia.

Oscar the Grouch has a pet—a worm named Slimey.

First TV show to win an Emmy for Outstanding Drama: *Pulitzer Prize Playhouse*, in 1950.

Only about a third of *Gilligan's Island* episodes are about getting off the island.

In a typical year, 14,030 answers are questioned on *Jeopardy!*

Five different dolphins "acted" in TV's *Flipper*, but only one horse played Mr. Ed.

Johnny Carson once hosted a game show called *Earn Your Vacation*.

TV actor George Reeves needed three men to help him out of his Superman suit.

Firsts

THE FIRST MOVIE THEATER
Date: June 26, 1896
Background: The first permanent movie theater was the 400-seat Vitascope Hall in New Orleans. Admission was 10¢. Patrons were allowed to look in the projection room and see the Edison Vitascope projector for another 10¢. Most of the films shown there were short scenic items, including the first English film to be released in America, Robert Paul's *Waves off Dover*. A major attraction was the film *The Kiss*, which introduced sex to the American screen.

THE FIRST WOMAN DRIVER
Date: 1891
Background: The first woman to drive a car was Madame Levassor, wife of one of the partners in the Paris motor manufacturing concern Panhard et Levassor, but better known by her former name of Madame Sarazin. After the death of her first husband, Madame Sarazin had acquired the French and Belgian rights of manufacture for the Daimler gas-powered engine. The following year she married Emile Levassor, and the patent rights passed to her new husband's firm. They began manufacturing cars under their own name in 1891, the year Madame Levassor learned to drive. The earliest evidence of her becoming a chauffeuse is a photograph showing her at the tiller of a Panhard car, dated 1892.

THE FIRST CHRISTMAS TREE WITH ELECTRIC LIGHTS
Date: December 1882
Background: The first electrically illuminated Christmas tree was installed in the New York City home of Edward H. Johnson, an associate of Thomas Edison. The first commercially produced Christmas tree lamps were manufactured in nine-socket sets by the Edison General Electric Co. in 1901. Each socket took a miniature 2-candlepower carbon-filament lamp operating on 32 volts.

THE FIRST DEPARTMENT STORE
Date: 1848
Background: Alexander Turney Stewart opened the Marble Dry Goods Palace on Broadway in New York City. Stewart had been a schoolmaster in Ireland before he emigrated in 1823 and set up his own business. At the time of its erection the Marble Dry Goods Palace was the largest shop in the world, extending the whole length of a city block. By 1876, the year of his death, Stewart's company had annual sales of $70 million, and his personal fortune was estimated at $80 million.

THE FIRST POLICE CAR
Date: 1899
Background: The first occasion in which a car was used in police work occurred when Sgt. McLeod of the Northamptonshire (England) County Police borrowed a Benz vehicle to pursue a man who was selling forged tickets for the Barnum and Bailey Circus. Top speed: 12 mph. The first car regularly employed in police work was a Stanley Steamer acquired by the Boston Police Department in 1903. It replaced four horses.

THE FIRST FILM ACTOR
Date: August 28, 1895
Background: The first motion picture to involve the use of actors was a brief costume drama titled *The Execution of Mary Queen of Scots*, which was shot by Alfred Clark in West Orange, New Jersey. The part of Mary was played by Mr. R. L. Thomas, secretary and treasurer of the Kinetoscope Company. After approaching the block and laying his head upon it, Thomas removed himself, the camera was stopped, and a dummy was substituted. The camera was then started again for the decapitation scene. This was also the first use of trick photography or special effects work in a film.

THE FIRST INCOME TAX
Date: 1451
Background: The first income tax was the Catastro introduced in Florence, Italy, under Lorenzo de' Medici. It was later replaced by the Scala, an income tax levied on a progressive basis, but this degenerated into a convenient means of political blackmail and, on the overthrow of the Medicis in 1492, was repealed.

Happy Holidays

Why is September 28 special? It's Ask A Stupid Question Day. Thanks for asking!

Nine percent of Americans buy their pets' clothing on birthdays and holidays.

Number of states that celebrate National Admit You're Happy Day: 19.

Americans spend $1.1 billion on Valentine's Day candy each year.

July 22 is National Rat-Catchers Day.

The ball that drops in Times Square every New Year's Eve is named the Star of Hope.

December 29 is National Whiner's Day.

About 15 percent of U.S. kids say they keep their Halloween candy for at least a year.

The most popular Easter egg color is blue. Next are purple and pink.

Number one holiday for telephone calls: Mother's Day.

November 19 is Have a Bad Day Day.

In Switzerland children receive holiday eggs from the Easter cuckoo.

Mother-in-Law Day was first celebrated on March 5, 1934, in Amarillo, Texas.

Seventy-six percent of Americans celebrate New Year's Eve in groups of fewer than 20.

Every Thanksgiving Americans consume 45 million turkeys— one for every five and a half people.

Americans send an estimated 900 million Valentine's Day cards each year.

More collect calls are made on Father's Day than on any other day of the year.

In the Woods

Beavers sometimes get crushed by the trees they gnaw down.

Reindeer milk has five times as much fat as cow milk.

There are 1,000 barbs in a single porcupine quill.

A typical porcupine has about 30,000 quills.

A wolf's howl can be heard as far as seven miles away.

Beavers' teeth are so sharp that Native Americans once used them as knife blades.

Some beaver dams are more than 1,000 years old.

A bison can jump as high as six feet off the ground.

If you feed a wild moose often enough, it will begin to attack people who don't feed it.

A warthog has only four warts, all of them on its head.

Full-grown grizzly bears can bite through a half-inch of steel.

A hibernating bear can go as long as six months without a bathroom break.

Bears don't hibernate in caves. They like hollow stumps or logs.

A brown bear can run faster than a horse at full gallop.

Some female turtles may wait as long as five years to lay their eggs after mating.

A female black bear can weigh 300 pounds, but her babies weigh only half a pound at birth.

If a female ferret goes into heat and can't find a mate, she'll die.

Library Classics

Emily Dickinson wrote 1,700 poems. Seven were published in her lifetime.

World's top-selling fiction author: Agatha Christie, with over 2 billion copies sold.

Charles Dickens always slept facing north. He thought it improved his writing.

Jack Kerouac's favorite pastime late in life: getting drunk and watching the *Beverly Hillbillies*.

Ernest Hemingway rewrote the final page of *A Farewell to Arms* 39 times.

The first novel ever written on a typewriter was *The Adventures of Tom Sawyer*.

Dr. Seuss's first book was rejected by 23 publishers.

Ernest Hemingway's rules for manhood: plant a tree, fight a bull, write a book, have a son.

Stephen King was 19 years old when his first story was published.

Mark Twain liked to say he only smoked once a day—"all day long."

In 1879, while on his honeymoon, Robert Louis Stevenson wrote *Travels with a Donkey*.

First American novel to sell more than a million copies: *Uncle Tom's Cabin*.

World's best-selling novel: Dan Brown's *The Da Vinci Code*—almost 40 million copies in print as of December 2005.

The Speed of Things

When the air bag in your car goes off, it expands at a rate of 150 miles per hour.

By the time you finish reading this, the earth will have traveled almost 100 miles through space.

Olympic downhill skiers reach 80 miles per hour.

Hummingbirds fly 60 miles per hour.

A greyhound can run as fast as 41 miles per hour.

Wild turkeys can run 30 mph and fly at speeds up to 55 miles per hour.

Raindrops can fall as fast as 22 miles per hour.

Elephants can run 20 miles per hour.

Top speed of an abalone on the move: five yards per minute.

Roadrunners run at a top speed of 15 miles per hour.

If aircraft carriers ran on gasoline, they'd get about six inches to the gallon.

The Post

The average stamp, when licked, has a tenth of a calorie.

Stamp collecting is the most popular hobby in the world.

Considered the world's most-used public mailbox: at the intersection of Madison and Halsted streets in Chicago. It has to be emptied six times a day.

First stamp design selected by vote of the U.S. public: the 1993 Elvis Presley 29¢ stamp.

Every day the average mail carrier delivers 2,300 pieces of mail to more than 500 different addresses along his or her route.

Zip code 12345 is assigned to General Electric in Schenectady, New York.

For every post office in the United States, India has four.

The islands of Antigua and Barbuda issued Elle Macpherson postage stamps in 1999.

The U.S. Postal Service delivers more than 600 million pieces of mail a day.

The glue on Israeli stamps is certified kosher.

If you sent it before 1963, it didn't have a zip code.

Smokey the Bear has his own zip code: 20252.

Personal letters make up only 2 percent of the mail delivered by the United States Postal Service.

Cost to mail a letter using the Pony Express: $5 per half ounce.

Cost of mailing a letter more than 400 miles in 1816 per letter sheet: 25¢.

The United States Postal Service handles about 46 percent of the world's mail.

On September 26, 1970, John Kenmuir licked 393 stamps in four minutes.

Big-Screen Actors

Comedian Stan Laurel was married eight times, but had only four wives.

Marlene Dietrich played the musical saw.

Liza Minnelli, daughter of Judy Garland, married Jack Haley Jr., son of Jack Haley, who played the Tin Man in *The Wizard of Oz*.

Before appearing in *The Exorcist*, Linda Blair was in a mustard commercial on TV.

Mae West never kissed her leading men on-screen.

Paul Newman played Billy the Kid in *The Left Handed Gun*. One problem: Billy was right-handed.

Fred Astaire's dancing shoes were size 8 1/2. His feet were insured for $650,000.

When Jerry Lewis wanted to make *The Catcher in the Rye* into a film, author J. D. Salinger said no.

Sean Connery was once selected Scotland's Mr. Universe.

Drew Barrymore's first acting role: a commercial for Gaines Burgers. (She was 11 months old.)

On average, Elizabeth Taylor remarries every four years, five months. She has been married eight times.

In her films, Shirley Temple always had 56 curls in her hair.

James Earl Jones (the voice of Darth Vader) and David Prowse (who played Vader on-screen) never met.

Ask the Experts

Q: HOW DOES QUICKSAND WORK?
A: Not by pulling you down. Quicksand is nearly always found above a spring, which creates a supersaturated condition that makes the sand frictionless and unable to support weight. In addition, quicksand is airless, which creates suction as you struggle to get free. The most effective way to escape quicksand is to position yourself on top of it and 'roll' out. (*The Book of Answers*, by Barbara Berliner)

Q: HOW DOES ONE SWALLOW A SWORD?
A: The main problem is learning how to relax the throat muscles and stop gagging. This takes weeks of practice . . . But it can be done. The sword doesn't cut the sword swallower's throat because its sides are dull. The point is usually sharp, but that's not a problem as long as the sword swallower doesn't swallow any swords long enough to poke him (or her) in the pit of the stomach. (*Know It All!*, by Ed Zotti)

Q: HOW ARE THE INTERSTATES NUMBERED IN THE UNITED STATES?
A: Believe it or not, this is one government practice that is organized and logical. All east-west interstate highways are even-numbered and increase from south to north. Thus, east-west Interstate 80 is north of I-10. North/south interstates are odd-numbered and increase from west to east. City bypasses and spurs have triple digits and are numbered odd or even depending on their directional orientation. (*Thoughts for the Throne*, by Don Voorhees)

Q: IF YOU DROPPED A PENNY FROM THE TOP OF THE EMPIRE STATE BUILDING, WOULD IT PIERCE A PERSON'S SKULL?
A: Given that the Empire State Building is 1,250 feet tall and ignoring such factors as wind resistance, a penny dropped from the top

would hit the ground in approximately 8.8 seconds, having reached a speed of roughly 280 feet per second. This is not particularly fast. A low-powered .22 or .25 caliber bullet, to which a penny is vaguely comparable in terms of mass, typically has a muzzle velocity of 800 to 1,100 FPS, with maybe 75 foot-pounds of energy. On top of this we must consider that the penny would probably tumble while falling, and that the Empire State Building . . . is surrounded by strong updrafts, which would slow descent considerably. Thus, while you might conceivably inflict a fractured skull on some hapless New Yorker, the penny would certainly not go through just like that. (*The Straight Dope*, by Cecil Adams)

Q: WHY DO FEET SWELL ON AN AIRPLANE?

A: It is a common myth that feet swell up when you ride in an airplane because of changes in atmospheric pressure due to high elevation. Feet swell up on planes, especially during long flights, for the same reason they swell up on the ground—inactivity. And it does not matter if you leave your shoes on or off; they will swell either way. If left on, they will provide external support, but will inhibit circulation a bit more and probably feel tighter during the latter part of the flight. If taken off, comfort may be increased, but the shoes are likely to be more difficult to put on once the flight is over. Podiatrists normally recommend "airplane aerobics" to help circulation—including help for swelling feet. (*The Odd Body: Mysteries of Our Weird and Wonderful Bodies Explained*, by Dr. Stephen Juan)

Q: WHY DOES HAIR TURN GRAY?

A: Gray (or white) is the base color of hair. Pigment cells located at the base of each hair follicle produce the natural dominant color of our youth. However, as a person grows older, more and more of these pigment cells die and color is lost from individual hairs. The result is that a person's hair gradually begins to show more and more gray. The whole process may take between 10 and 20 years—rarely does a person's entire collection of individual hairs (which can number in the hundreds of thousands) go gray overnight. (*How Things Work*, by Louis Bloomfield)

Battle of the Sexes

Male hospital patients fall out of bed twice as often as female patients.

One out of every 14 women in the United States is a natural blonde. Only one out of every 16 men are.

Men get more ulcers. Women get more migraine headaches.

The average woman shaves 412 square inches of skin on her body. The average man: 48.

Women blink nearly twice as much as men.

On average, females hear better than males at every age.

Forty-four percent of Americans think God is a man. One percent think God is a woman.

Thirty-five percent of the people who use personal ads for dating are already married.

When a waitress draws a happy face on a check, tips go up 18 percent. When a waiter does, tips only increase 3 percent.

American women over age 55 watch more TV than anyone else. Men between the ages of 18 and 24 watch the least.

About two thirds of all men's clothing bought in the United States is purchased by women.

On average, men are 40 percent muscle and 15 percent fat. Women are 23 percent muscle and 25 percent fat.

The average American woman thinks about politics 12 minutes a day. Average man: six minutes.

Thirteen percent of American men say they call their mothers every day. Thirty-two percent of women call their mothers daily.

Call the Doctor

In 1992, 5,840 people checked into U.S. emergency rooms with "pillow-related injuries."

Number one health complaint Americans report to their doctors: insomnia.

Choking on food is the seventh leading cause of death in America.

Ninety percent of Americans aren't aware that being overweight increases the risk of strokes.

The medical condition epistaxisis: nosebleed.

Most destructive disease in human history: malaria.

Most common physical complaint in the United States: lower back pain.

Sixty-five percent of American adolescents get acne.

Ninety-five percent of food-poisoning cases are never reported.

Surgeons who listen to music during operations perform better than those who don't.

Crocodile-tear syndrome is a nerve disorder that makes people cry when they eat.

Three surgeries most commonly performed in the United States: biopsies, cesarean sections, and hysterectomies.

Forty percent of nurses say they wouldn't want their family treated in hospitals where they work.

In 1962 Johanne Relleke of Rhodesia was stung by bees 2,443 times. He survived.

The common flu kills 20,000 people a year.

Average American

After a three-week vacation, your IQ can drop by as much as 20 percent.

One in four Americans isn't sure if the earth travels around the sun or vice versa.

Forty percent of Americans say the theory of evolution is "probably not true."

According to a 1997 poll, about two thirds of Americans believe a UFO may have crashed at Roswell.

Each year Americans use enough foam peanuts to fill ten 85-story skyscrapers.

If you're average, you'll change your residence 11 times in your life, or once about every six years.

Fifty-two percent of Americans say they'd "rather spend a week in jail" than be president.

Seventy-two percent of Americans believe in heaven. Twelve percent don't.

Average age of a new grandparent in the United States: 47.

Average annual income in the United Sates at the beginning of World War II: $1,070. In 2005: $32,500.

* * *

THE CAMEL

When a male camel spits at something, it aims for the eyes.

One-hump camels run faster than two-humped camels.

A camel can drink 25 gallons of water in half an hour.

A camel with one hump is a dromedary.
If it has two humps, it's a Bactrian camel.

TV: The Culture

During 33 seasons on the air, Mister Rogers's trolley traveled more than 100 miles on its track.

Ratio of people to televisions in the world: six to one.

In 1948, 2.3 percent of American households had a television. Today 99 percent do.

Forty-six percent of all violence on television occurs in cartoons.

Thirty-five percent of people watching TV yell at it.

The first TV weather chart was broadcast in Britain on November 11, 1936.

The last cigarette ad on TV appeared on *The Tonight Show*, December 31, 1970.

England was the first country with regular TV service, in 1936. The United States was second, in 1939.

Fifty-three percent of high school grads and 27 percent of college grads "get most of their information from TV."

Sitcom characters rarely say goodbye when they hang up the phone.

More people watch primetime television on Thursday night than on any other night.

More than half of Americans say they regularly watch TV while eating dinner.

The average American spends 1,600 hours a year watching TV, and 323 hours reading.

Everyday Origins

BALLPOINT PEN: Invented by a Hungarian who manufactured them in a factory in England, which was eventually taken over by a French company called Bic.

BAND-AID: Invented by the husband of an accident-prone woman who was constantly cutting and burning herself in the kitchen.

CELLOPHANE: Move over, waxed paper. The inventor was trying to make a stainproof tablecloth and came up with the first clear food wrap instead.

ELECTRIC BLANKET: Not based, as you might think, on the electric heating pad, but on the electrically heated flying suits that U.S. Air Force pilots wore during World War II.

JOCKEY SHORTS: A midwestern underwear manufacturer copied the design of men's bathing suits that were popular in France at the time (the 1930s).

MATCH: The first match was a stick that the inventor (who was trying to invent a new kind of explosive) had used to stir his ingredients. When he tried to remove the dried glob on the end of the stick, it ignited.

MINIATURE GOLF: Invented by an unusual man who loved his family as much as he loved playing golf. This way he could get his golfing fix and be with the wife and kiddies, too.

PAPER CUP: Because the inventor had in mind a disposable water cup that wouldn't carry germs, he called his invention health cups. Luckily, his office happened to be in the same building as the Dixie Doll Company—voilà!—Dixie Cups.

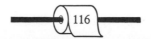

PAPER TOWEL: When a defective roll of toilet paper—too heavy and very wrinkled—arrived at the Scott company's mill, somebody had the bright idea to sell it as paper towels.

PEANUT BUTTER: Ground peanuts and peanut oil, it was the brainchild of a doctor whose patient was dying of "protein malnutrition" and, because of a stomach disorder, couldn't eat meat. Peanut butter never made it as a medicinal remedy, but it did catch on as an easy way to get kids to eat protein.

REARVIEW MIRROR: The first was introduced at the Indy 500 in 1911. Up till then there were two people in each car: the driver and the mechanic, who also acted as lookout. That year, the inventor drove his rearview-mirrored car across the finish line to finish first.

RUNNING SHOES: A miler at the University of Oregon heated some rubber in a waffle iron to get the kind of traction he wanted on the soles of his running shoes. He started a shoe business and named the shoes Nike, after the Greek goddess of victory.

SHOPPING CART: The idea didn't catch on right away since shoppers were used to carrying their own baskets around a store. The inventor (who was also the market owner) decided to hire some phonies to push the carts around and pretend they were shopping. That did the trick.

VENDING MACHINE: Would you believe that vending machines have been around since the 17th century? The first one, in England, dispensed one pipeful of tobacco for a penny.

WIRE COAT HANGER: When a worker at the Timberlake Wire and Novelty Company arrived at work and found all the coat hooks taken, he twisted some wire into what looked pretty much like the ones we use now, and proceeded to hang up his coat.

YO-YO: The word *yo-yo* means "come-come" in Tagalog. It was used as a hunting weapon in the Philippines.

Here Comes the Sun

It takes 8.3 minutes for the sun's light—traveling at 186,282 miles a second—to reach Earth. (At that speed, light can travel around Earth seven times in a second.)

The sun looks yellow-gold because we're viewing it through Earth's atmosphere. Judging from its surface temperature, the sun's color is probably closer to white.

The sun rotates once every 26.8 days.

The temperature of the sun at its core is around 73 million degrees. It takes 50 years for this energy to reach the sun's surface, where we can see it as light.

The sun contains 99.9 percent of the matter in the solar system.

The English astronomer James Jeans once figured that if you placed a piece of the sun's core the size of the head of a pin on Earth, its heat would kill a person 94 miles away.

The sun produces more energy in one second than human beings have produced in all of our history. In less than a week, the sun sends out more energy than we could make by burning all the natural gas, oil, coal, and wood on Earth.

Earth receives 2 one-billionths of the sun's power.

The amount of power that falls on each square foot of Earth's surface per minute is about 126 watts, enough to light two standard 60-watt lightbulbs.

The surface gravity on the sun is 28 times that of Earth. If you weigh 120 pounds on Earth, on the sun you would weigh 3,360 pounds.

Battle of the Sexes

Men are more likely than women to run stoplights. Women are more likely to switch lanes without signaling.

Fifty-one percent of American men say TV remote controls have "significantly" increased their quality of life. Thirty-nine percent of women agree.

Men leave their hotel rooms cleaner than women do.

Men get hiccups more often than women. No one knows why.

There are only two places in the world where men outlive women: southern Asia and Iran.

If you're an average American man, you'll spend 81 minutes in your car today. Average woman: 64.

On average, a woman's heart beats faster than a man's.

Men laugh longer, more loudly, and more often (69 times per day to 55 times for a woman) than women do.

Marriage makes a woman more likely to become depressed. A man: less likely.

Twenty-five percent of men wait until "a few weeks" before Christmas to do their holiday shopping. Fifteen percent of women start Christmas shopping in July.

Thirty-two percent of women, and 8 percent of men, say they're better at doing the laundry than their spouse is.

When snow skiing, most men fall on their faces. Most women fall on their behinds.

Presidents, 1841–1929

William Henry Harrison's inaugural address was the longest, at 8,443 words.

What was John Tyler doing when he was informed that William Henry Harrison had died, making Tyler president? He was on his knees playing marbles.

John Tyler had 15 children by two wives.

Number of times Abraham Lincoln slept in the Lincoln Bedroom: zero.

Abraham Lincoln survived two assassination attempts before being killed by John Wilkes Booth.

Ulysses S. Grant sometimes smoked as many as 20 cigars a day. He died of throat cancer.

Chester A. Arthur once sold a pair of Abraham Lincoln's pants at auction.

Grover Cleveland got more popular votes in the 1888 presidential election, which he lost, than he got in the 1884 presidential election, which he won.

President McKinley's pet parrot was named Washington Post.

Theodore Roosevelt had 24 pets in the White House, including four guinea pigs, two cats, and a bear.

Theodore Roosevelt was the most prolific writer among the presidents, authoring 40 books.

Woodrow Wilson's second wife, Edith, learned to ride a bike down the halls of the White House.

Woodrow Wilson's typewriter could be altered to print in either English or Greek.

Calvin Coolidge was sworn in as president of the United States by his father, a justice of the peace.

Average American

Americans consume 16,000 tons of aspirin every year.

Twenty-five percent of Americans believe in ghosts. Ten percent say they've seen one.

According to a poll by Progressive Insurance, 63 percent of Americans talk to their cars.

Eighty percent of Americans live in cities.

Three percent of all photographs taken in the United States are taken at Disneyland or Disney World.

One in five Americans cannot say which president is on the $1 bill.

About 4 percent of Americans are vegetarians.

Only 17 percent of Americans can identify Andrew Jackson as the guy on the $20 bill.

When asked what they think is the most stressful event of the year, 20 percent of Americans say filling out income tax forms. Twenty-five percent say visiting relatives at family gatherings.

Roughly one third of Americans live within five miles of a lake.

Foreign city most visited by Americans: Tijuana.

Some 19 percent of American taxpayers say "avoiding an audit" is their number one priority when filling out tax forms. Thirty-three percent say "taking as many deductions as possible" is.

Word Origins

JACKPOT
Meaning: A huge prize
Origin: "The term goes back to draw poker, where stakes are allowed to accumulate until a player is able to 'open the pot' by demonstrating that among the cards he has drawn, he has a pair of jacks or better." (*Dictionary of Word and Phrase Origins, Vol. II*, by William and Mary Morris)

HOOKER
Meaning: Prostitute
Origin: Although occasionally used before the Civil War, its widespread popularity can probably be traced to General Joseph Hooker, a Union soldier who was well-known for the liquor and whores in his camp. He was ultimately demoted, and Washington prostitutes were jokingly referred to as "Hooker's Division."

CALCULATE
Meaning: Add, subtract, divide, and/or multiply numbers or money
Origin: "In Rome 2,000 years ago, the merchant figured his profit and loss using what he called calculi, or 'little stones' as counters. So the Latin term calculus, 'pebble,' not only gave us calculate but . . . our word calculus . . . one of the most complicated forms of modern mathematics." (*Word Origins*, by Wilfred Funk, Litt. D.)

DOPE
Meaning: Drugs
Origin: "This word was originally a Dutch word, doop, meaning a sauce or liquid. Its first association with narcotics came when it was used to describe the viscous glop that results from heating opium. Then, by rapid extension, it came to mean any narcotic." (*Dictionary of Word and Phrase Origins, Vol. III*, by William and Mary Morris)

DOOZY
Meaning: Something wonderful, superior, or classy
Origin: "The word comes from Duesenberg, an eminently desirable motor car of the 1920s and '30s. The Duesenberg featured a chromed radiator shell, gold-plated emblem, hinged louvered hood, stainless-steel running boards, beveled crystal lenses on the instrument panel, Wilton wool carpet, and twin bugle horns. Magazine ads for the luxury car carried the slogan: 'It's a Duesie.'" (*The Secret Lives of Words*, by Paul West)

MANURE
Meaning: Animal excrement used to fertilize plants
Origin: "From the Latin manu operati, 'to work by hand.' Farming was constant manual labor, especially the fertilizing, which required mixing by hand. Genteel folks who objected to the word dung, the excrement of animals, were responsible for its euphemistic displacement with the more 'refined' manure.

"Even manure became objectionable to the squeamish; they preferred fertilizer. According to a famous story about Harry S Truman, the president was explaining that farming meant manure, manure, and more manure. At which point a lady said to the president's wife: 'You should teach Harry to say "fertilizer," not "manure."' Mrs. Truman replied, 'You don't know how long it took me to get him to say "manure."'" (*The Story Behind the Words*, by Morton S. Freeman)

ADMIRAL
Meaning: High-ranking commissioned officer in a navy or coast guard
Origin: "This is an artificial spelling of the French *amiral*. The Arabian word *amir*, commander, is commonly followed by al, as in amir-al bahr, 'commander of the sea,' from which amiral resulted." (*More About Words*, by Margaret S. Ernst)

TEMPURA
Meaning: A Japanese dish of deep-fried vegetables or seafood
Origin: "Neither a native Japanese dish, nor a Japanese name. When the Portuguese arrived in the 17th century, the Japanese noticed that at certain 'times' (Portuguese, tempora), notably Lent, they switched from meat to fish. With typical subtlety the Japanese concluded that the word meant a variety of seafood." (*Remarkable Words with Astonishing Origins*, by John Train)

Mr. Moonlight

It takes 29 days, 12 hours, 44 minutes, and 3 seconds for the moon to go through all of its phases (from one full moon to the next). This is close to the length of a month—which is why the word *month* means "moon."

The light that comes from the moon is sunlight reflected off the moon's surface. It takes 1.25 seconds for the light to travel to Earth.

The moon is 2,160 miles in diameter—about a quarter of Earth's diameter.

A 3-foot jump on earth would carry you 18 feet, 9 inches, on the moon.

There is no sound on the moon. Nor is there weather, wind clouds, or colors at sunrise and sunset.

The side of the moon we always see is called "the near side."

The side we never see from Earth is "the far side." That's probably where Gary Larson got the name of his comic strip.

Astronauts have brought over 843 pounds of moon samples back to Earth.

If you weigh 120 pounds on Earth, you would weigh 20 pounds on the moon—one-sixth of your weight on earth.

If Earth were as big as a fist, the moon would be the size of a stamp . . . placed 10 feet away.

The moon is moving away from Earth at the rate of about one-eighth inch a year.

For the Birds

In the three weeks that baby sparrows are in the nest, their parents make 5,000 trips for food.

The Arctic tern flies as far as 10,500 miles when it migrates.

Some breeds of vultures can fly at altitudes of 36,900 feet.

Male cardinals take three times as long as females to learn a new song.

A hummingbird consumes the caloric equivalent of 228 milkshakes per day.

Most hummingbirds weigh less than a penny.

The average American bald eagle weighs nine pounds—"about the size of a well fed housecat."

When a roadrunner is content, it purrs.

Most parrots are left-handed.

When mating, a hummingbird's wings beat 200 times per second.

The fastest way to wake up a penguin is to touch its feet.

Lonely parrots can go insane.

Flamingos can only eat with their heads upside down.

When a turkey is panicking, it whistles.

In some parts of Africa, ostriches are used to herd sheep.

If birds could sweat, they wouldn't be able to fly.

Old-Time Treatments

Leprosy is the oldest documented infection—first described in Egypt in 1350 B.C.

Among the "treasures" found in King Tut's tomb: several vials of pimple cream.

Doctors in ancient India closed wounds with the pincers of giant ants.

The world's first recorded tonsillectomy was performed in the year 1000 B.C.

Acne treatment, circa A.D. 350: "wipe pimples with a cloth while watching a falling star."

In medieval Japan, dentists extracted teeth with their hands.

The Hunza people of Kashmir (India and Pakistan) have a 0 percent cancer rate. Scientists link it to the apricot seeds they eat.

Oldest form of surgery in the world: trepanning (drilling holes into the skull).

In the Middle Ages, Europeans "cured" muscle pains by drinking powdered gold.

Sixteenth-century French doctors prescribed chocolate as a treatment for venereal disease.

Doctors in the 1700s prescribed ladybugs, taken internally, to cure measles.

England's Queen Victoria smoked marijuana to cure her cramps.

Between 1873 and 1880, some U.S. doctors gave patients transfusions of milk instead of blood.

During World War I, raw garlic juice was applied to wounds to prevent infection.

The ancient Chinese would swing their arms to cure a headache.

Big-Screen Actors

Tom Hanks and Elvis Presley are both related to Abraham Lincoln.

Bela Lugosi was buried in the cape he wore as Dracula.

Michael J. Fox's middle name is Andrew.

John Wayne was related to Johnny Appleseed.

After starring in two movies with Elvis, actress Dolores Hart became a nun.

The Three Stooges appeared in more movies than any other comedy team in U.S. film history.

Marlene Dietrich's beauty secret: to emphasize her high cheekbones, she had her upper molars removed.

The odds that a stage or screen actor has changed his or her name is about three out of four.

In 1947 Marilyn Monroe was crowned the first Queen of Artichokes.

Actor with the most leading roles in Hollywood films: John Wayne, at 141.

Cowboy star Tom Mix had tires made with his initials imprinted on them so that when he drove down dirt roads he would leave a trail of TMs.

Shirley Temple made $300,000 in 1938, but her allowance was only $4.25 a week.

Sylvester Stallone's payment for his first major film role, in *The Lords of Flatbush*, was 25 T-shirts.

Read All About It!

Twenty-five percent of Americans think Sherlock Holmes was a real person.

Gadsby, a 50,000-word novel by Ernest Wright, contains no words with the letter *e*.

Earliest use of the flashback in Western literature: Homer's *Odyssey*.

In how many Agatha Christie mysteries did "the butler do it"? None.

Charles Dickens's original phrase for Scrooge was "Bah! Christmas!" not "Bah! Humbug!"

One self-help book in Japan claims clenching your butt 100 times a day fights depression. Try it.

There's a Cinderella story in Finnish folklore. But the girl's name isn't Cinderella. It's Tuna.

Goldilocks was originally named Silver Hair.

The first names of Dr. Jekyll and Mr. Hyde are Henry and Edward.

Little Red Riding Hood's first name is Blanchette.

Marco Polo dictated the book about his travels while he was a prisoner of war in Genoa. When it was published, everyone thought it was fiction.

There were two streetcars in Tennessee Williams's *A Streetcar Named Desire*.

The book *Green Eggs and Ham* contains only 50 words.

Charles Dickens wrote *A Christmas Carol* in six weeks.

The Tin Woodsman's real name in the Oz books was Nick Chopper.

Real Toys of the CIA

IT LOOKS LIKE: A cigarette
BUT IT'S REALLY: A .22-caliber gun
DESCRIPTION: This brand of cigarette packs a powerful puff. Intended as an escape tool, the weapon only carries a single round, but with good aim it can inflict a lethal wound from close range. To fire the cigarette, the operator must twist the filtered end counterclockwise, then squeeze the same end between the thumb and forefinger. Warning: don't shoot the weapon in front of your face or body—it has a nasty recoil.

IT LOOKS LIKE: A pencil
BUT IT'S REALLY: A .22-caliber pistol
DESCRIPTION: Like the cigarette gun, this camouflaged .22 comes preloaded with a single shot. The weapon is fired in the same manner as the cigarette: Simply turn the pencil's eraser counterclockwise and squeeze. The only difference between the weapons is that the pencil has a greater firing distance—up to 30 feet.

IT LOOKS LIKE: Dentures
BUT IT'S REALLY: A concealment device (and much more)
DESCRIPTION: What could possibly fit inside a dental plate? A lot more than you'd think. Items such as a cutting wire or a compass can be placed in a small concealment tube and hidden under a false tooth. A rubber-coated poison pill can be carried in the same manner. The poison can either be ingested to avoid capture or poured into an enemy's food and utilized as a weapon. Radio transceivers can be placed in dental plates, with audio being transmitted through bone conduction. The CIA has even created a dental plate that alters the sound of one's voice. If all of these gadgets prove ineffective, then the dental plate itself can be removed and its sharp scalloped edge used for digging, cutting, or engaging in hand-to-hand combat.

IT LOOKS LIKE: A belt buckle
BUT IT'S REALLY: A hacksaw
DESCRIPTION: Fitted inside a hollow belt buckle is a miniature hacksaw. When the buckle is opened, a small amount of pressure is released from the saw's frame, exerting tension on the blade. This makes the saw a more efficient cutting machine, keeping the blade taut when sawing through, for example, handcuffs. The belt buckle saw will cut through anything from steel to concrete in about 15 minutes and will tear through rope and nylon. Don't wear belts? Buckles can be put on coats and luggage, too.

IT LOOKS LIKE: Eyeglasses
BUT IT'S REALLY: A dagger
DESCRIPTION: Concealed in the temple arms of these CIA glasses are two sharp blades. Disguised as the reinforcing wire found in most eyeglass frames, the daggers are designed to be used once and broken off at the hilt, inside the victim. The lenses are cutting tools, too. The lower edges are ground to razor sharpness and can be removed by heating or breaking the frames.

IT LOOKS LIKE: A felt-tip marker
BUT IT'S REALLY: A blister-causing weapon
DESCRIPTION: Don't mistake this pen for your Sharpie, and be careful: You wouldn't want it leaking in your pocket. A little over three inches long, the marker distributes an ointment that creates blisters on the skin. In order to activate the applicator, press the tip down on a surface for one minute—then simply apply a thin coating of the colorless oil over any area, such as a keyboard or door handle. The ointment will penetrate clothing and even shoes, and will cause temporary blindness if it comes in contact with the eyes. Blisters will cover the skin wherever contact is made within 24 hours and will last for about a week.

Fruits & Vegetables

CABBAGE
Originated in Asia and introduced to Europe by Alexander the Great about 325 B.C. The name comes from the Latin *caput*, meaning "head." It's high in vitamin C, but contains sulfurous compounds that, when cooked, give off odors similar to rotten eggs or ammonia.

SCALLIONS
These tiny green onions owe their name to the biblical city of Ashkelon. When the Romans conquered the city, they called the tiny onions *caepa Ascolonia* or "onions of Ashkelon." This became "scallions."

JERUSALEM ARTICHOKES
These sweet, starchy roots did not grow in Jerusalem and they are not artichokes. Native Americans used them as bread. The mix-up came when a Spanish explorer thought they were some kind of sunflower. *Girasol* ("turn to the sun") is the Spanish word for sunflower. An American heard it as "Jerusalem." No one knows why he also added "artichoke."

BROCCOLI
The word comes from the Latin *bracchium*, or "branch." It was developed about 2,500 years ago on the island of Cyprus and was a popular dish at ancient Roman banquets. (The Roman emperor Tiberius, who ruled from A.D. 14 to 37, once publicly scolded his son for eating all the broiled broccoli at a state banquet.) It was popularized in the United States by Italian immigrants.

KIWIFRUIT
Originally from China, it was imported to New Zealand in the early 1900s and renamed Chinese Gooseberry. After it arrived in the United States in 1962, a Los Angeles distributor named Frieda Caplan named it after the New Zealand national bird, the kiwi. It took 18 years before the American public started buying it.

CANTALOUPE
A type of muskmelon brought to Italy from Armenia in the 1st century A.D., and grown in the town of Cantalupo, which is where it gets its name.

George

George Washington was named after King George of England.

George Washington and Abraham Lincoln were both descended from England's King Edward I.

George Washington's name has been given to one state, seven mountains, eight streams, nine colleges, 10 lakes, 33 counties, and 121 towns across the world.

The autographs of George Washington and Abraham Lincoln are more valuable than any other presidents'.

George Washington's second inaugural address was the shortest, at just 135 words.

When he didn't wear a pocket watch, George Washington used a small sundial to tell the time.

George Washington's favorite tooth whitener: household chalk.

George Washington's feet were size 13.

When George Washington was president, there were about 350 federal employees. Today there are about 2.5 million.

* * *

REMEMBER 1980?
Ronald Reagan elected 40th U.S. president
John Lennon assassinated
Mount St. Helens erupted
#1 movie: *The Empire Strikes Back*
U.S. hockey team beat the Soviet Union at the Olympics
One percent of American homes had a PC

The Film Industry

Most expensive movie poster in history: *Metropolis* (1927), auctioned for $690,000 in 2005, edging out the previous record holder. *The Mummy* (1932), auctioned for $453,000 in 1977.

American author with the most feature films made of his work: Edgar Allan Poe.

Thirty-one percent of American adults say they won't watch a film with subtitles "no matter how good it is."

Toto the dog was paid $125 a week for his work in *The Wizard of Oz*.

James Bond, the spy, is named after James Bond, the real-life ornithologist.

Five names considered for the Seven Dwarfs: Snoopy, Dippy, Blabby, Woeful, and Flabby.

Thirty-two percent of Americans say they never go to the movies.

"What's up, Doc?" was first uttered by Bugs Bunny in the 1940 cartoon *A Wild Hare*.

Average cost of a movie ticket in 1940: 24¢.

Gone With the Wind is the only Civil War epic ever filmed without a battle scene.

In *Gone With the Wind*, Clark Gable worked 71 days and made $120,000. Vivien Leigh worked 125 days and made $25,000.

Terminator II cost $647,000 per minute of film to make.

Story most often made into a movie: Cinderella (59 times).

In 1915 someone made a silent movie version of the opera *Carmen*.

The movie *Grease* was released in Venezuela under the name *Vaselina*.

Average American

It takes the average American 2.6 days to feel relaxed on a vacation.

Per capita, more Americans volunteer their time than people of any other country.

Eighty-nine percent of Americans don't have a valid passport.

The average American will use two thirds of an acre's worth of trees in wood products this year.

Twenty-four percent of Americans say the world "was in better shape a thousand years ago."

Nearly 6 percent of all marriage proposals are made over the telephone.

There are 33 vampire fan clubs in the United States.

Eight percent of Americans twiddle their thumbs. Fifteen percent bite their fingernails.

Ten percent of Americans have at least one college degree.

Twelve percent of Americans think they've seen UFOs.

According to florists, America's favorite flower is the rose. Next: the daisy.

* * *

**OFFICIAL REQUIREMENTS OF
THE PILLSBURY DOUGHBOY:**

His skin must look like dough: "off-white, smooth, but not glossy"

Slightly luminous, but no sheen

No knees, elbows, wrists, fingers, ears, or ankles

Rear views do not include "buns"

Walks with a "swagger"

Stomach is proportional to the rest of his body

Skin and Bones

The first vertebra of your neck is called the atlas because it holds up your head.

Every seven years your body grows the equivalent of an entirely new skeleton.

The thyroid cartilage is more commonly known as the Adam's apple.

Pygmy refers to "any human group whose males are less than 4'11" in average height."

Nearly all boys grow at least as tall as their mothers.

More than half of the 206 bones in your body are in your hands and feet.

If you're a healthy, full-grown adult, your thigh bones are stronger than concrete.

Physicians in the United States treat an estimated 4 million broken bones every year.

Your big toes have only two bones. The rest of your toes have three.

Short people have fewer back problems than tall people do.

Take your weight and divide by three. That's how much your legs weigh.

The average person's skeleton accounts for about 20 percent of his or her body weight.

After spending 84 days in *Skylab*, astronauts were two inches taller.

Most Americans say that if they had to resort to cannibalism, "they'd eat the legs first."

Eggshells are proportionately as strong as bone.

It's impossible to lick your elbow. Try it.

Antarctica

If Antarctica were to melt, the sea level would rise over 200 feet.

Aristotle first posed the idea that there was a continent at the South Pole.

Antarctica is the only continent without reptiles.

Antarctica doesn't have a permanent population. In summer about 4,000 people live there; in winter, around 1,000.

In Antarctica, sunsets can be green.

Antarctica is the only continent that has never seen a war.

The temperature in Antarctica once dropped 65 degrees in 12 minutes.

Coldest place on earth: Vostok, Antarctica. Average annual temperature: −72°F.

Smallest and shallowest ocean on earth: Arctic Ocean.

The first sighting of Antarctica was in 1820; the first verified landing was in 1821 by a Russian expedition.

Only 2 percent of Antarctica is ice free.

It's been as cold as −128.5°F, the lowest temperature ever recorded in the world.

Emilio Marcos Palma was the first person born in Antarctica on January 7, 1978. He's the only person in history known to be the firstborn on a continent.

The Antarctic Treaty, signed in 1959, prohibits anything of a military nature in Antarctica.

Dogs are banned from Antarctica to protect the seal population.

Antarctica is actually a desert, with about the same precipitation (less than two inches a year), as the Sahara.

Bloodstream

A pumping human heart can squirt blood as far as 30 feet.

You can lose up to a third of your blood and still survive.

The jugular vein is an artery, not a vein.

The human body has about 60,000 miles of blood vessels.

In the time it takes to turn a page, you'll lose 3 million blood cells and make 3 million more.

Red blood cells live four months. In that time they make 75,000 trips to the lungs and back.

The most nutritious "food" in the world is blood.

The Rh factor in blood occurs much more frequently (40–45 percent) in Europeans and people of largely European ancestry.

Blood is thicker than water: blood has a specific gravity of 1.06, water's is 1.00.

Identical twins always have the same blood type.

The average number of industrial compounds and pollutants found in an American's blood and urine: 91.

* * *

SHOWBIZ BLOOD

The blood in movies is inserted into a "squib," a blood pack taped to a small explosive charge that's triggered remotely at the appropriate time. The charge blows the blood pack contents through a hole in the costume.

Strange Bird Feats

The **Hummingbird** is the only bird that can fly backward. It achieves this feat by beating its wings up and down at great speed. (Some species have a wing speed of 80 beats per second.)

The home of the **Great Indian Hornbill** is a prison. When the female is ready to lay her eggs, she hides in a hole in a tree. The male then seals up the hole, leaving just a narrow slit through which he passes food. The female stays in there until the chicks are a few months old, then she breaks out and helps the male with feeding duties.

The eyes of the **Woodcock** are set so far back in its head that it has a 360-degree field of vision, enabling it to see all round and even over the top of its head.

The **Quetzal**, of Central America, has such a long tail (up to three feet) that it can't take off from a branch in the normal way without ripping its tail to shreds. Instead, it launches itself backward into space like a parachutist leaving an aircraft.

The **Wandering Albatross** has the largest wingspan of any bird and can glide for six days without beating its wings. It can also sleep in midair.

The **Male Bowerbird** of Australia attracts a female by building an elaborate love bower. After building a little hut out of twigs, he decorates it with flowers and colorful objects such as feathers, fruit, shells, and pebbles, even glass and paper if the nest is near civilization. One particular species (the atlas bowerbird) actually paints the walls by dipping bark or leaves into the blue or dark green saliva he secretes. The entire bower-building procedure can take months, and the bird will often change the decorations until he is happy with them. When finally satisfied, he performs a love dance outside the bower, sometimes offering the female a pretty item from his collection.

Immutable Laws

Zappa's Law: There are two things on Earth that are universal: hydrogen and stupidity.

Baruch's Observation: If all you have is a hammer, everything looks like a nail.

Lowe's Law: Success always occurs in private, and failure in full public view.

Todd's Law: All things being equal, you lose.

Thompson's Theorem: When the going gets weird, the weird turn pro.

The Unspeakable Law: As soon as you mention something . . . if it's good, it goes away. If it's bad, it happens.

Green's Law of Debate: Anything is possible if you don't know what you're talking about.

Hecht's Law: There is no time like the present to procrastinate.

The Queue Principle: The longer you wait in line, the greater the likelihood that you are standing in the wrong line.

Issawi's Law of Progress: A shortcut is the longest distance between two points.

Ginsberg's Theorem: 1. You can't win; 2. You can't break even; 3. You can't even quit the game.

The Salary Axiom: The pay raise is just large enough to increase your taxes and just small enough to have no effect on your take-home pay.

Wellington's Law of Command: The cream rises to the top. So does the scum.

Todd's Two Political Principles: 1. No matter what they're telling you, they're not telling you the whole truth. 2. No matter what they're talking about, they're talking about money.

Kirby's Comment on Committees: A committee is the only life form with 12 stomachs and no brain.

Phobias

The average American develops his or her first phobia at age 13.

Most common phobia in the world: odynophobia—the fear of pain.

Experts say that the most common phobia in the United States is arachnophobia: fear of spiders.

Arachibutyrophobia: the fear of having peanut butter stuck to the roof of your mouth.

Fear of lawsuits: liticaphobia

Fear of clowns: coulrophobia

What's a suriphobe? Someone who's afraid of mice.

An anemophobic person is someone who's afraid of high winds.

Fear of making decisions: decidophobia

Fear of slime: myxophobia

How would you know a cherophobe if you met one? He or she would be afraid of having fun.

Fear of constipation: coprastasophobia

If you have keraunothnetophobia, you're afraid of satellites falling to earth.

Fear of France: Francophobia

A fear of ventriloquist dummies: automatorsophobia

Fear of the moon: selenophobia

A cremnophobe is someone who is afraid of falling down the stairs.

Telesphobia is the name given to "the fear of being last."

A fear of becoming bold: phalacrophobia

An ergasiophobe is someone who's afraid of work.

It's Just Business

Biggest civilian employer in America: the U.S. Postal Service.

Wal-Mart is the world's largest private employer. It had over 1.6 million employees in 2005.

Ninety percent of U.S. businesses are family owned.

The original Macy's made a total of $11.06 on its first day of business in 1858.

The Ford Motor Company earned an average two-dollar profit on every Model T it manufactured.

Three names considered before picking "Nike" for their shoe company: Falcon, Bengal, and Dimension 6.

IBM holds the most U.S. patents.

Harley-Davidson tried to trademark its engine sound and the word *hog*. Both attempts failed.

In the 1940s the Bich pen was changed to Bic. The company thought Americans would call it Bitch.

Each employee at Ben & Jerry's headquarters gets three pints of free ice cream a day.

Every time a box of Wheaties with Tiger Woods on the front was sold, he got a dime. The farmer who grew the wheat got a nickel.

Miller Brewing donated $150,000 to its Thurgood Marshall Scholarship Fund in 1993, and spent $300,000 promoting the donation.

* * *

BIG WORD, LITTLE OBJECT

The scientific name for any object that's shaped like a football: a prolate spheroid.

It's a Living

When Confucius was 16, he worked as a grain inspector.

Before he became an explorer, Amerigo Vespucci (for whom America is named) was a pickle merchant.

Benjamin Franklin gave guitar lessons.

Benjamin Franklin was America's first newspaper cartoonist.

Will Rogers once served as honorary mayor of Beverly Hills.

Margaret Hamilton, who played the Wicked Witch of the West, was once a kindergarten teacher.

Bob Hope and Billy Joel were once boxers.

Frank Sinatra once boxed under the name Marty O'Brien.

Rod Stewart once worked as a gravedigger.

Johnny Carson, Michael Douglas, and Clint Eastwood were all once gas station attendants.

Sean Connery once had a job polishing coffins.

Dustin Hoffman used to type entries for the Yellow Pages.

Danny DeVito once studied to be a hairdresser.

Drew Carey once worked in Las Vegas—as a waiter at Denny's.

Fresh off the Farm

The average U.S. farm has 467 acres of land. The average Japanese farm has three acres.

Ninety percent of the world's food crops come from only 12 species of plants.

Ninety-nine percent of the pumpkins sold in the United States end up as jack-o'-lanterns.

A typical banana travels 4,000 miles before being eaten.

U.S. hens lay enough eggs in a year to circle the equator 100 times.

It takes 4,000 grains of sugar to fill a teaspoon.

A watermelon is 92 percent water. An apple is 84 percent water.

If a cow eats onions, its milk will taste like onions.

It takes ten pounds of milk to make one pound of cheese.

The United States produces 2–4 billion pounds of chicken and turkey feathers every year.

Ears of corn always have an even number of rows of kernels.

It takes about 21 pounds of milk to make one pound of butter.

It takes 720 peanuts to make a pound of peanut butter.

Honey is easy to digest because it has already been digested by a bee.

Honey never goes bad.

One in every five potatoes grown in the United States ends up as french fries.

It takes 16,550 kernels of durum wheat to make a pound of pasta.

The Friendly Skies

How do airports scare birds off their runways? One British airport plays Tina Turner albums.

Denver's International Airport is larger than the entire city of Boston.

Each year U.S. airlines use more than 20 million airsickness bags.

About 21,000 commercial airline flights are scheduled daily in the United States. Only about 5,000 planes are available to fly them.

If you take a plant with you on a long airplane flight, it will suffer from jet lag.

The automated baggage handler at the Chicago O'Hare Airport can sort 480 bags per minute.

The airport in Calcutta, India, is called Dum Dum.

As many as 10,000 pieces of luggage are lost or "mishandled" by U.S. airlines every day.

* * *

THE COST OF THINGS: 1936

First-class stamp: 3¢
Quart of milk: 12¢
Six-pack of Coca-Cola (bottles): 25¢
Full dinner at New York's Roxy Grill: 75¢
Three-minute call from New York to San Francisco: $4.30
Average starting salary for a college graduate: $20–$25 a week
13-day cruise from New York to Bermuda: $123
FDR's presidential salary: $75,000 a year

Ask the Experts

Q: IS A DOG YEAR REALLY THE EQUIVALENT OF SEVEN HUMAN YEARS?
A: No—it is actually five to six years. The average life expectancy of a dog is 12 to 14 years. However, most dogs mature sexually within six to nine months, so in a sense there is no strict correspondence to human years. (*The Book of Answers*, by Barbara Berliner)

Q: WHY ARE THERE HOLES IN SWISS CHEESE?
A: Because of air bubbles. During one of the stages of preparation, while it is still "plastic," the cheese is kneaded and stirred. Inevitably, air bubbles are formed in the cheese as it is twisted and moved about, but the viscous nature of the cheese prevents the air bubbles from rising to the surface and getting out. As the cheese hardens, these air pockets remain, and we see them as the familiar "holes" when we slice the wheel of cheese. (*A Book of Curiosities*, compiled by Roberta Kramer)

Q: DO FISH SLEEP?
A: Hard to tell if they sleep in the same sense we do. They never look like they're sleeping, because they don't have eyelids. "But they do seem to have regular rest periods . . . Some fish just stay more or less motionless in the water, while others rest directly on the bottom, even turning over on their side. Some species . . . dig or burrow into bottom sediment to make a sort of 'bed.' Some fish even . . . prefer privacy when they rest; their schools disperse at night to rest and then reassemble in the morning." (*Science Trivia*, by Charles Cazeau)

Q: SHOULD YOU TOSS THE COTTON AFTER OPENING A BOTTLE OF PILLS?
A: Yep. "The cotton keeps the pills from breaking in transit, but once you open the bottle, it can attract moisture and thus damage the pills or become contaminated." (*Davies Gazette*, a newsletter from Davies Medical Center in San Francisco)

Q: WHAT ARE THE "BABY CARROTS" SOLD AT SUPER-MARKETS?

A: Take a closer look. Right there on the bag, it says clearly "baby-cut." These aren't now and never were baby carrots. In the early 1990s a carrot packer in Bakersfield, California, thought of a clever way to use his misshapen culls. Mechanically he cut them into short pieces, then ground and polished them until they looked like sweet, tender young carrots. Baby-cut packers today don't rely on culls . . . They use a hybrid carrot called Caropak that grow long and slender; it doesn't taper much and has little or no core. In the processing shed, the carrots are cleaned, cut into pieces, sorted by size, peeled in abrasive drums, then polished. Bagged with a little water and kept cold, they stay crisp and bright orange. (*San Francisco Chronicle*)

Q: HOW MUCH GOLD DOES THE UNITED STATES STORE IN FORT KNOX?

A: The U.S. Bullion Depository at Fort Knox contains approximately 315 million troy ounces of gold. At the official government price of $42.222 per troy ounce, the gold in the vault is worth $13 billion. At a market price of $300 an ounce, the gold would be worth $94.5 billion. (*Do Fish Drink Water?*, by Bill McLain)

Q: HOW MUCH IS ONE HORSEPOWER?

A: Although it was originally intended to be measured as the average rate at which a horse does work, one horsepower has now been standardized to equal exactly 550 foot-pounds of work per second, or 746 watts of power. Speaking of watts, they're named after James Watt, the Scottish engineer who invented an improved steam engine and then created the term *horsepower*. He needed some way to convince potential customers that his engine could outperform the horse. By devising a system of measurement based on the power of a horse, customers could easily compare the work potential of his engine versus that of the beast. (*Everything You Pretend to Know and Are Afraid Someone Will Ask*, by Lynette Padwa)

The Film Industry

The shark model in *Jaws* was called Bruce—Steven Spielberg named it after his lawyer.

In Japan the James Bond film *Dr. No* was originally translated as *We Don't Want a Doctor.*

Close Encounters of the Third Kind is a remake of Spielberg's 1964 amateur film *Firelight.*

Film with the most destructive car chase ever: *The Junkman* (1982). One hundred and fifty cars were destroyed.

In June 1989, two original carbon scripts of *Citizen Kane* sold for $231,000.

Most costumes used for a film was 32,000: *Quo Vadis* (1951).

Record for most costume changes by an actor in one film: 65, by Elizabeth Taylor in *Cleopatra* (1963).

The word *love* appears in more film titles than any other word. Second: *Paris.*

When actors are filmed in a car through the windshield, there's usually no rearview mirror.

Number of Dalmatians used in the filming of the movie *101 Dalmatians*: 233.

Five hundred pairs of false sideburns were used in the making of *Gone With the Wind.*

No insurance company will underwrite Jackie Chan's productions.

Shakespeare's *Hamlet* has been adapted into a film 49 times. *Romeo and Juliet*, 27 times.

Americans spent $3.9 billion in movie rentals in the first half of 2005.

There are 10,800 feet of film in a two-hour movie.

Popcorn eaters are three times more likely to cry in the movies than non–popcorn eaters.

The Plant World

Of the 80,000 known species of plants, only 50 are cultivated regularly.

A typical redwood tree's roots are only five to six feet deep—and spread out over an acre.

Mesquite bushes growing in Death Valley can have roots reaching 100 feet down for water.

Plants, like people, run fevers when they're sick.

There are more varieties of orchid than of any other flower (30,000 at last count).

The kernel inside a peach pit is poisonous.

Seventy percent of the world's oxygen supply is produced by marine plants.

The saguaro cactus does not grow its first arm until it's at least 75 years old.

Largest living thing on earth: an underground mushroom in Oregon, 3.5 miles across.

The tomato comes in more than 4,000 varieties.

Auto Industry

The first state to require license plates on cars: New York, in 1901.

First car to offer seatbelts: the 1950 Nash Rambler.

Best-selling passenger car ever: Toyota Corolla. At least 30 million have been sold since it was introduced in 1969.

About 200 million tires are discarded every year in the United States.

Raised-bump reflectors on U.S. roads are called Botts' Dots. (Elbert Botts invented them.)

The world's most popular car color is red.

The little statue on the grill of every Rolls Royce has a name: "Spirit of Ecstasy."

The slowest time for car dealers is just before Christmas.

* * *

FOUR USES FOR A BANANA PEEL

1. To get rid of a wart, tape a one-inch square of the inside of a banana peel over the wart. Change the dressing every day or so until the wart is gone—probably within a month or two.

2. Use the same treatment to get rid of a splinter. Tape a piece of peel over the splinter. By morning the splinter should be at the surface.

3. To draw the color from a bruise, hold a banana peel over it for 10 to 30 minutes.

4. To relieve a headache, tape or hold the inner side of a banana peel to the forehead and the nape of the neck. The peels increase the electrical conductivity between the two spots.

Around the Globe

World's muddiest river: the Yellow River, in China.

The only country in the Middle East without a desert: Lebanon.

The city of Tsuenchen, China, was designed to resemble a carp when viewed from above.

The official name of India is Bharat.

Leading cause of death in Papua, New Guinea: falling out of a tree.

Ninety-five percent of the population of Egypt live within 12 miles of the Nile River.

The largest country in Africa is the Sudan.

The Sahara desert is larger than the entire United States.

At their closest point, the Russian and U.S. borders are less than two miles apart.

Widest waterfall in the world: Victoria Falls in Africa, at almost a mile wide.

Only 20 percent of the Sahara is covered with sand; the rest is rocky.

In the 19th century, India imported ice harvested from ponds in the United States.

Half the world's population live in temperate zones, which make up 7 percent of the earth's land area.

About one quarter of all nations drive on the left side of the road. Most are former British colonies.

On the Road

The United States has almost 4 million miles of roads and streets.

Each mile of a four-lane freeway takes up more than 17 acres of land.

Fifteen percent of drivers get 76 percent of all traffic tickets.

If you could drive to the sun at 60 mph, it would take 176 years, not including pit stops.

The worst day for automobile accidents is Saturday.

Longest Main Street in the United States: the one in Island Park, Idaho. It's more than 33 miles long.

Canada has the world's longest street: Yonge Street stretches 1,178 miles.

Forty percent of car-theft victims left their keys in the ignition.

According to statistics, yellow cars and bright blue cars are the safest to drive.

Seventy-six percent of U.S. commuters drive to work alone.

If you're an average American, you'll spend about six months of your life waiting at red lights and five years stuck in traffic.

Odds of winning if you challenge a traffic ticket in court: about one in three.

Accident rates rise 10 percent in the first week of daylight saving time.

Oxymorons

Military Intelligence
Light Heavyweight
Jumbo Shrimp
Drag Race
Friendly Fire
Criminal Justice
Genuine Imitation
Mandatory Option
Limited Nuclear War
Standard Deviation
Protective Custody
Industrial Park
Freezer Burn
Eternal Life
Pretty Ugly
Loyal Opposition
Natural Additives
Educational Television
Nonworking Mother
Full-Price Discount
Limited Immunity
Active Reserves
Student Teacher

Superheroes

"Superhero" has been jointly trademarked by DC Comics and Marvel comics.

The most valuable comic book in the world: Action Comics #1, which features the origin and first appearance of Superman.

In the original comic, Superman couldn't fly.

Kryptonite made its first appearance on the Superman radio show, not in the comic book.

Muhammad Ali once appeared in a DC Comics edition. He knocked out Superman to save him from aliens.

Superman had a pet monkey named Beppo.

Superman is 6 feet 2 inches, but Clark Kent is only 5 feet 11 inches. (He slouches.)

Official DC statistics state that Batman stands 6 feet 2 inches and weighs 220 pounds.

Wonder Woman's bulletproof bracelets were made of a metal called feminum.

Wonder Woman's creator, William Moulton Marston, invented the polygraph.

Marvel comics put a hyphen in Spider-Man's name so he wouldn't be confused with Superman.

On Halloween 2004, an estimated 2.15 million U.S. children dressed up as Spider-Man, making it the year's most popular costume.

Johnny Canuck was a Canadian cartoon in 1869 and was reinvented as a superhero in 1942.

Captain Marvel's appearance was modeled after actor Fred MacMurray.

Makes Sense

We taste only four things: sweet, sour, salt, and bitter. It's the smells that really give things flavor.

Talking with your mouth full expels taste molecules and diminishes the taste of food.

Women have a keener sense of smell than men.

Like fingerprints, each of us has an odor that is unique. One result: much of the thrill of kissing comes from smelling the unique odors of another's face.

By simply smelling a piece of clothing, most people can tell if it was worn by a woman or man.

Smells stimulate learning. Studies show that students given olfactory stimulation along with a word list retain much more information and remember it longer.

Many smells are heavier than air and can be smelled only at ground level.

We smell best if we take several short sniffs, rather than one long one.

* * *

PHRASES COINED BY SHAKESPEARE

apple of [one's] eye
bag and baggage
bated breath
be-all and the end-all
brave new world
budge an inch

caught red-handed
cold comfort
full of sound and fury
good riddance
in a pickle
play fast and loose

Eh, Canada?

There's a 75 percent chance that a public road in Canada will be unpaved.

The United States absorbs more than 85 percent of all Canadian exports.

In its history, six flags have been flown over Canada.

Nearly one fourth of all the freshwater in the world is in Canada.

The Trans-Canada Highway is the longest national highway in the world.

The baseball glove was invented in Canada in 1883.

Other inventions by Canadians: the electric range, the electron microscope, standard time, and the zipper.

Four Canadians have been featured on U.S. postage stamps.

At the Haskell Free Library and Opera House, the audience is seated in America, and the opera is performed in Canada.

Canadian journalist Sandy Gardiner coined the term *Beatlemania*.

Some 50,000 Canadians fought in the American Civil War, including about 200 for the South.

There are some 2 million lakes in Canada, covering about 7.6 percent of the country's landmass.

There are no skunks in Newfoundland.

In Canada if a debt is higher than 25¢, it is illegal to pay it with pennies.

Stretched in a continuous line, Canada's coastline would circle the earth more than six times.

The Business World

The Bayer Aspirin Company trademarked the brand name Heroin in 1898.

Bowing to pressure from antismoking groups, Hasbro took away Mr. Potato Head's pipe in 1987.

At one time, tulip bulbs were traded on the Amsterdam Stock Exchange.

End to end, the number of Crayola crayons made in a year (3 billion) would circle the globe six times.

Denny's restaurants used to be known as Danny's restaurants.

Tony the Tiger turned 50 in 2005. The Jolly Green Giant turned 77.

Prior to 1953 the slogan of L&M cigarettes was "just what the doctor ordered."

Ramses condoms are named after Ramses II, an Egyptian pharaoh who fathered more than 160 children.

Original name for the Bank of America: the Bank of Italy.

The millionth trademark issued by the U.S. Patent Office: Sweet'N Low.

Weird Plants

Welwitschia mirabilis, from the deserts of Namibia, can live for over 2,000 years, yet its central trunk never grows more than three feet in height. Instead, the energy is transmitted into its two huge leaves that never fall and continue growing throughout the plant's life. The leaves can be as long as 20 feet.

The **banyan tree** (*Ficus benghalensis*) of India has more than one trunk. When the tree reaches a certain size, it sends down ropelike roots, which, when they reach the soil, take root and thicken to form additional trunks. The tree can spread outward almost indefinitely. A 200-year-old specimen in the Calcutta Botanic Gardens had more than 1,700 trunks. During Alexander the Great's Indian campaign, 20,000 soldiers are said to have sheltered under a single banyan tree.

As a defense mechanism, the merest touch causes the **sensitive plant** (*Mimosa pudica*) to collapse in a tenth of a second. The wilting pose deters grazing animals from eating it. A few minutes later, when the danger passes, the plant reverts to its upright position.

Puya Raimondii of Bolivia can take up to 150 years to bloom. But once it flowers, it promptly dies. Although it is an herbaceous plant, it is built like a tree, with a stem strong enough to support a human adult.

The **grapple tree** (*Harpagophytum procumbens*) of South Africa produces a fruit called the Devil's Claw. The fruit is covered in fierce hooks, which latch on to passing animals. In trying to shake the fruit off, the animal disperses the seeds but at the same time, the hooks sink deeper into the creature's flesh. If the animal touches the fruit with its mouth, the fruit will attach itself to the animal's jaw, inflicting great pain and preventing it from eating. Antelopes are the usual victims, but it has been known to kill a lion.

Twisters

A tornado swept a toddler out of his bed and set him down safely 50 feet away without removing his blankets.

After a tornado a woman walked into her front yard to find a sturdy, 40-foot tree uprooted—even though the lawn furniture remained exactly where she had left it.

A tornado picked up a tie rack with 10 ties attached and carried it for 40 miles without removing one tie.

While a couple slept, a tornado lifted their cottage then dropped it into a nearby lake. They remembered only a loud bang before they woke up in deep water.

Tornadoes have plucked all the feathers off chickens.

A tornado scooped up five horses that were hitched to a rail, then set the whole arrangement down, intact, horses uninjured, a quarter-mile away.

In 1987, in China, 12 children walking home from school were sucked up by a tornado and safely deposited 12 miles away in sand dunes.

After a tornado killed migrating ducks at a migratory bird refuge, it rained dead ducks 40 miles away.

TV: The Culture

Most common place to lose the remote control: under furniture.

Average length of time a child watches an episode of *Sesame Street*: eight minutes.

If you're an average American, you spend four to six hours every day watching TV.

Approximately 14 percent of U.S. homes have a TV in the kitchen.

The average color TV lasts for eight years.

In 1959 former First Lady Eleanor Roosevelt made a TV commercial for Good Luck margarine.

For years the globe on the *NBC Nightly News* spun in the wrong direction.

Mr. Ed's real name was Bamboo Harvester.

Twenty percent of men say their TV has taught them more about life than their parents have.

First animated characters on TV commercials: the Ajax pixies. They sold cleanser.

An average American seven-year-old watches 20,000 commercials a year—about 55 every day.

The world's first animated TV ad was created by Dr. Seuss in 1949, for the Ford Motor Co.

Words most frequently used in U.S. advertisements: *new and improved.*

The first time live models advertised (Playtex) bras on TV was in 1987.

Third graders with TV sets in their bedrooms score lower on standardized tests. With computers, they score higher.

Founding Fathers

RICHARD REYNOLDS

The nephew of cigarette mogul R. J. Reynolds. He spent 10 years working for his uncle's tobacco company, then in 1912 struck out on his own. After several setbacks, he went back to his uncle and borrowed enough money to start the U.S. Foil Company—which made foil cigarette packaging for R.J. Reynolds Co. In the mid-1930s Richard learned of a new type of foil made from aluminum. Sensing the product's potential, he built a plant to manufacture it. He began selling it as Reynolds Wrap.

WARREN AVIS

In the 1930s he was a Ford salesman. Then during World War II he joined the air force and became a combat flying officer. He found that, often, the hardest part of flying was figuring out how to get from the airport to his final destination. In 1946 he started a car rental company at Detroit's Willow Run Airport. He talked Ford into selling him cars at a discount by convincing them that having renters "test-drive" new Fords would help the automaker sell its cars. By the time he sold Avis Rent-A-Car in 1954, the chain had expanded to 154 locations around the country.

ARTHUR PITNEY AND WALTER BOWES

In 1901 Pitney created a machine that could stick postage stamps on letters. In 1920 he joined forces with Bowes. Because of World War I, there was a letter-writing boom, and the post office needed a machine to keep up. In 1920 Congress passed a bill allowing the Pitney-Bowes machine to handle the mail.

GLEN W. BELL

After he got out of the marines in 1946, Bell sold his refrigerator for $500 and used the money to start Bell's Drive-In in San Bernardino, California. San Bernardino is also the birthplace of McDonalds, and

when Bell realized how well the McDonald brothers were doing, he decided it would be easier to switch to Mexican food than it would be to compete against them directly. His first restaurants were called Taco Tia. But after a while he renamed them Taco Bell, after himself.

DR. KLAUS MAERTENS
In the 1940s he made orthopedic support shoes for older women. He expanded his line to include shoes for people suffering from skiing injuries, and simple, functional work boots that could stand up to almost anything. In 1959 Maertens licensed his designs to a small British shoe company, R. Griggs, which began selling English versions of the shoes under the anglicized trade name Dr. Marten's.

JASPER NEWTON DANIEL
He was born in Tennessee in 1850, the youngest of 13 children, and ran away when he was only six years old. Little Jasper ended up living with a neighbor named Dan Call and earned his keep by helping him make moonshine whiskey. In 1863 Call sold his still to Jasper, who was then only 13. Known as Jack, Jasper Daniel had a knack for making—and selling—whiskey, and distributed it to both sides during the Civil War. He used his war profits to build a real distillery. A slight man at 5 feet 2 inches and 120 pounds, Daniel relied on his personality as much as the quality of his whiskey to make sales. He always wore a mustache and goatee, a planter's hat, and a knee-length frock coat. He never appeared in public without his "costume." When postwar liquor laws changed, Daniel was the first man to register a distillery in the United States, which he called Jack Daniel Distillery No. 1.

CHARLES HENRY DOW AND EDWARD D. JONES
Journalists at the turn of the century, Dow and Jones created the first index of U.S. stock prices—the Dow Jones average. It later appeared in the newspaper they founded, the *Wall Street Journal*.

GABRIEL DANIEL FAHRENHEIT
German scientist of the late 17th and early 18th centuries. Invented a new thermometer that used mercury instead of alcohol. Its new scale—which marks water's freezing point at 32° and its boiling point at 212°—was named Fahrenheit after him and became popular in English-speaking countries.

Our Solar System

Only 48 percent of the sun's energy actually reaches Earth.

Uranus has 21 moons.

Approximately 26,000 meteorites crash to Earth each year.

There are more than 7,000 asteroids in the solar system. Only one (Vesta) is visible to the naked eye.

Number of stars in the Seven Sisters (the Pleiades): about 250.

It takes Pluto 25 years to receive as much solar energy as Earth receives in one minute.

Mercury is 800°F at its equator, but has ice at its north and south poles.

An astronaut orbiting Earth can see as many as 16 sunrises and sunsets every 24 hours.

The footprints on the moon will last forever—or until a meteor hits them.

On average, every square meter of the surface of Earth receives 240 watts of sunlight.

The three most common elements in the universe: hydrogen, helium, and oxygen.

Wind speeds on Neptune can reach 1,500 mph.

Scientists think there's gold on Mars, Venus, and Mercury.

Neptune's summer is 40 years long.

The sun spews out more than a million tons of matter every second.

Earth is closest to the sun on January 3.

Presidential Firsts

George Washington was the first and only president elected by a unanimous electoral vote.

The first president to shake hands in greeting was Thomas Jefferson. Earlier presidents bowed.

James Madison was the first president to wear long pants instead of knee breeches.

John Quincy Adams was the first president with a pet reptile. He kept a pet alligator in the East Room of the White House. He enjoyed "the spectacle of guests fleeing from the room in terror."

Andrew Jackson was the first president to ride a train.

Jackson was also the first president to be handed a baby to kiss during his campaign. He refused to kiss the infant and handed it over to his secretary of war.

Martin Van Buren was the first president actually born in the United States.

The first U.S.-born president to be born outside the original 13 states: Abraham Lincoln (Kentucky).

The first president to have a "First Cat" at the White House: Abraham Lincoln.

Abraham Lincoln was the first president to wear a beard in office.

James Garfield was the first president to use a phone in the White House. His first words to inventor Alexander Graham Bell, who was on the other end, were "Please speak a little more slowly."

The first president to act in a movie was Teddy Roosevelt. He starred as himself in a 1908 comedy.

Richard Nixon was the first president to host a rock concert at the White House. He invited the Guess Who and the Turtles to play for his daughters.

Looney Laws

In Brooklyn, New York, it's illegal to let a dog sleep in your bathtub.

In Atlanta, it's illegal to tie a giraffe to a streetlight or telephone pole. Dogs are OK.

Whale harassment is a federal offense punishable by up to $10,000 in fines.

A monkey was once tried and convicted for smoking a cigarette in Indiana.

In St. Louis, Missouri, it's illegal to drink beer from a bucket when you're sitting at the curb.

Snoring is legal in Massachusetts only when all bedroom windows are closed and locked.

Kentucky citizens are required by state law to bathe at least once a year.

It's illegal to ship live mice through the U.S. mail.

In Downey, California, more than two police officers are prohibited from gathering at the same doughnut shop at the same time.

In Cleveland, Ohio, it's illegal to catch mice without a hunting license.

In Kentucky, it's illegal to marry your wife's grandmother.

In Yukon, Oklahoma, it's illegal for patients to pull their dentist's teeth.

In Sarasota, Florida, it's illegal to wear a swimsuit while singing in a public place.

In Oklahoma, you can be fined for making funny faces at dogs.

In some states, it's illegal to dance to the "Star Spangled Banner."

It's against the law to drink beer in Cedar City, Utah, if your shoelaces are untied.

More Oxymorons

Half Dead
Inside Out
Even Odds
Baby Grand
Fresh Frozen
Upside Down
Original Copy
Random Order
Irrational Logic
Business Ethics
Jumbo Shrimp
Tax Return
Good Grief
Open Secret
Baked Alaska
Plastic Glasses
Friendly Takeover
Unofficial Record
United Nations
Science Fiction
Peacekeeping Missiles
Somewhat Addictive
Truth in Advertising

Stormy Weather

Most raindrops are round or doughnut shaped, not "raindrop" shaped.

Clouds don't float—they fall very, very slowly.

Lightning is more likely to strike the same place twice than it is a new place once.

Wettest place on earth: Tutunendo, Colombia. Average rainfall: 38.6 feet per year.

The average lightning bolt is only an inch in diameter.

Thunder is caused when air rushes into the vacuum created by a bolt of lightning.

An estimated 16 million tons of rain falls to earth every second.

Less than a gallon of water is in a cubic mile of fog.

Half of all forest fires are started by lightning.

Lightning bolts are only about two inches wide.

The odds are good that the Empire State Building will be struck by lightning twice this month.

Foggiest place on the West Coast: Cape Disappointment, Washington (107 days per year).

In ancient Rome, any house hit by lightning was considered consecrated.

Take 1 million cloud droplets and squish them together to form a single raindrop.

About 75,000 umbrellas are lost every year on buses and subways in London.

Danger Ahead

Nearly 1,000 people every year die as a direct result of volcanic activity.

A British newspaper reported that 60,000 people a year are treated for injuries caused by opening canned goods.

About 8,000 Americans are injured by musical instruments each year.

The annual odds of dying by falling from your bed: two in a million.

Every year about 8,000 people die from food poisoning in the United States.

On average, 100 people choke to death on ballpoint pens every year.

Twenty-eight percent of household injuries in the summer are caused by yard work.

Odds of getting hit by a meteor this year: one in five billion.

* * *

PRESIDENTIAL STATISTICS

On an average day, the president of the United States receives 20,000 letters.

No only child has ever been elected president of the United States.

Five U.S. presidents have had the first name James, more than any other name.

Eleven presidents have been military generals.

Sixty-three percent of U.S. presidents have been members of a fraternity of some kind.

Baby Talk

More babies are conceived in December than in any other month.

Babies are born without kneecaps.

More boys are born during the day. More girls are born at night.

One out of every 270 pregnancies results in identical twins.

A newborn's skin is wrinkled because it's too big for its body.

On average, babies born in May are seven ounces heavier than those born in other months.

The longest recorded interval between the birth of twins was 136 days.

A newborn baby's heart beats twice as fast as an adult's.

The average newborn cries 113 minutes a day.

A newborn baby's body contains 26 billion cells. An adult has about 100 trillion cells.

For every 100 girls born, there are 105 boys born.

A newborn's brain will triple in weight during its first year.

The navel divides the body of a newborn baby into two equal parts.

If a child ate as much, comparatively, as a growing bird, he or she would eat three lambs and one calf each day.

Three things pregnant women dream of most during their first trimester: frogs, worms, and potted plants.

The average baby spends 27.5 months in diapers.

More babies are born in the month of September than in any other month.

Toy Origins

SCRABBLE

Created in 1931 by an out-of-work architect named Alfred Botts. He hoped he could support his family by inventing a successful word game, but before the game was refined, he had his job back. That was just as well; when he finally showed his handmade Criss-Cross to toy companies, they insisted it had no potential—it was too intellectual.

In 1948 Botts and a friend went into business manufacturing the game—now called Scrabble—in an old schoolhouse. It was an unsophisticated cottage industry that enabled the friend to barely eke out a living. But in the summer of 1952, for no apparent reason, Scrabble suddenly became a fad. In two years the partners went from selling fewer than 10,000 games a year to selling more than 4 million. To meet the growing demand, the rights were sold to Selchow-Righter, and 30 years later, Scrabble ranks as the second-best-selling game in history.

RUBIK'S CUBE

Devised by Hungarian mathematician Erno Rubik in 1974 as an aid for teaching math concepts to his students. Rubik realized the puzzle's possibilities as a toy and ended up selling 2 million of the cubes in Hungary alone—a total of one cube for every five Hungarians. In 1980 the Ideal Toy Corporation bought the rights, and the puzzle became a worldwide craze. Rubik reportedly became "the first self-made millionaire in a Communist country."

LINCOLN LOGS

In 1916 Frank Lloyd Wright went to Tokyo to supervise construction of the Imperial Palace Hotel, a magnificent building assembled with an inner frame of wood so it would withstand earthquakes better. Wright brought his son John with him, and as John watched workers move the huge timbers required for the structure, he came up with an idea for a wooden construction toy. When he returned to America, John created Lincoln Logs.

SILLY PUTTY
In 1945 an engineer at a General Electric laboratory in New Haven, Connecticut, was assigned the task of trying to create synthetic rubber. One day he combined boric acid with silicone oil. The result: a bizarre substance with a variety of fascinating properties (it bounced, stretched, and could be broken with a hammer), but no practical use. It became a New Haven conversation piece.

Several years later a marketing man named Peter Hodgson saw a group of adults playing with the stuff at a cocktail party. Hodgson was putting together a mail-order catalog for a toy store at the time, and decided to include this "nutty putty" in it.

The response was amazing. Even without a photo, the putty outsold everything in the catalog except crayons. Hodgson knew he had a winner—so he bought $147 worth of putty from G.E. and packaged it in little plastic eggs (it was Easter time). In the first five years, over 32 million containers of the stuff were sold worldwide.

SLINKY
Richard James, a marine engineer, was trying to invent a spring that could be used to offset the effects of a boat's movement on sensitive navigational instruments. One day he knocked a sample spring off a high shelf—but instead of simply falling, it uncoiled like a snake and "crawled" down to the floor. James realized he had a toy product, gave it a name, and formed the James Toy Company to manufacture it.

* * *

THE COST OF THINGS: 1946
One pound of round steak: 41¢
Average hourly wage at the Ford Motor Company: $1.38
Dinner and show featuring comedian Sid Caesar: $2.75 per person
Average wage for a registered nurse: $200 per month
One year's tuition at Yale University: $600

Inside Toothpaste

Water. Toothpaste is 30 percent to 45 percent water. Which means you're paying about $2 a pound for that water.

Chalk. The same variety that schoolteachers use. What is chalk? It's the crushed remains of ancient ocean creatures. The exoskeletons retained their sharpness during the eons when they were buried, and they are one of the few things tough, yet gentle enough, to clean the hardest substance in the body, tooth enamel.

Titanium dioxide. This stuff goes into white wall paint to make it bright. On your teeth, it paints over any yellowing for at least a few hours, until it dissolves and is swallowed.

Glycerin glycol. To keep the mixture from drying out, glycerin glycol is whipped in. You may know it as an ingredient in antifreeze.

Seaweed. A concoction made from the seaweed known scientifically as *Chrondrus crispus*. This oozes and stretches in all directions and holds the paste together.

Paraffin. This petroleum derivative keeps the mixture smooth.

Detergent. What good would toothpaste be without the foam and suds? The answer is: it would be perfectly fine . . . but the public demands foam and suds.

Peppermint oil, menthol, and saccharin. These counteract the horrible taste of detergent.

Formaldehyde. The same variety that's used in anatomy labs. It kills the bacteria that creep into the tube from your brush and the bathroom counter.

Does this list of ingredients for toothpaste turn you off? Take heart. Studies have shown that brushing with water can be almost as effective.

America Eats

Americans will eat 90 acres worth of pizza today.

The potato chips Americans eat each year weigh six times as much as the *Titanic*.

According to the USDA, the average American ate 1,950 pounds of food in 2003.

The average family eats 6,000 pounds of food in a year.

Americans buy 40 million Ritz crackers every day.

If you're an average American, you'll eat 5,666 fried eggs in your lifetime.

The average American eats the equivalent of 28 pigs in his or her lifetime.

The average American eats 21.4 pounds of snack foods each year.

The average American consumes 87 hot dogs a year.

Twenty-nine percent of Americans say that most of the meals they eat are made from leftovers.

Nine boxes of Jell-O are sold every second.

As late as 1950, pork was the most popular meat in America.

The average American family spends more than $2,000 a year dining out.

Americans, on average, eat 100 pounds of beef a year—about 50 percent of it as hamburger.

The single most ordered item in American restaurants: french fries.

Americans consume an average 736 million pounds of peanut butter each year.

Americans throw away an estimated 27 percent of their food every year.

Left & Right

If you're left-handed, you're definitely outnumbered. Lefties make up only 5 to 15 percent of the population.

If you're a female southpaw, you're even more unusual—there are roughly 50 percent more left-handed males than females.

The artwork found in ancient Egyptian tombs portrays most Egyptians as right-handed. But their enemies are portrayed as left-handers, a sign they saw left-handedness as an undesirable trait.

Ancient Greeks never crossed their left leg over their right, and believed a person's sex was determined by their position in the womb—the female, or "lesser sex," sat on the left side of the womb.

Roman customs dictated that they enter friends' homes "with the right foot forward" . . . and turn their heads to the right to sneeze. Their language showed the same bias: the Latin word for left is *sinister* (which also means evil or ominous), and the word for right is *dexter* (which came to mean skillful or adroit). Even the word *ambidextrous* means "right-handed with both hands."

Lefties are more likely to be on the extreme ends of the intelligence scale than the general population: a higher proportion of mentally retarded people and people with IQs over 140 are lefties.

Why are lefties called southpaws? In the late 1890s, most baseball parks were laid out with the pitcher facing west and the batter facing east (so the sun wouldn't be in his eyes). That meant left-handed pitchers threw with the arm that faced south. So Chicago sportswriter Charles Seymour began calling them southpaws.

What did traditional Christians believe was going to happen on Judgment Day? According to custom, God blesses the saved with his right hand—and casts sinners out of heaven with his left.

Our Solar System

Only city whose main street can be seen from space: Las Vegas, Nevada.

The weight of the sun's light on Earth's surface: two pounds per square mile.

Top speed of astronauts traveling to the moon: 24,679 mph.

The longest a lunar eclipse can last: seven minutes, 58 seconds.

Galileo called Saturn "the planet with ears."

A light-year (the distance light travels in a year) is about 6 trillion miles.

There are 169 known moons in our solar system (so far).

Do you know how long it takes Earth to go around the sun? Forty-six percent of Americans don't.

Twenty-four people have traveled to the moon, but only 12 have landed on the surface and walked around.

The closest black hole, known as V4641 Sgr, is 1,600 light-years from Earth.

Jupiter is large enough to fit all the planets of the solar system inside it.

A year on Jupiter is 12 times longer than a year on Earth.

Forty-one percent of the moon is not visible from Earth at any time.

The average meteor is no larger than a grain of sand.

Some material brought back from the moon is 4.72 billion years old.

Beverage Origins

GATORADE

According to *60s!*, by John and Gordon Javna: "In 1965, Dr. Robert Cade was studying the effects of heat exhaustion on football players at the University of Florida (whose team name is the Gators). He analyzed the body liquids lost in sweating and within three minutes came up with the formula for Gatorade. Two years later, Cade sold the formula to Stokely-Van Camp. Soon, annual sales were well over $50 million and Gatorade could be found on the training tables of over 300 college sports teams, 1,000 high school squads, and all but two pro football teams."

7-UP

According to *Parade* magazine: "In October 1929, just before the stock market crash, St. Louis businessman Charles L. Grigg began marketing a beverage called Bib-Label Lithiated Lemon-Lime Soda. His slogan: 'Takes the "Ouch" out of grouch.' The drink was a huge success during the Depression, perhaps because it contained lithium, a powerful drug now prescribed for manic-depressives. The drink's unwieldy name was later changed to 7-UP. The '7' stood for its 7-ounce bottle, the 'UP' for 'bottoms up,' or for the bubbles rising from its heavy carbonation, which was later reduced. The lithium was listed on the label until the mid-'40s."

DR. PEPPER

In Virginia in the 1880s, a pharmacist's assistant named Wade Morrison fell in love with his boss's daughter. The pharmacist decided Morrison was too old for his daughter and encouraged him to move on. He did, settling down in Waco, Texas, where he bought his own drugstore. When one of his employees developed a new soft drink syrup, Morrison named it after the man who got him started in the pharmacy business—his old flame's father, Dr. Kenneth Pepper.

For Word Nerds

Lethologica is the inability to remember a word.

Hawaii's state fish is the humuhumunukunukuapua'a.

Loosely translated, the word *carnival* means "flesh, farewell."

Aglet is the plastic or metal tip of a shoelace.

Pogonology is the study of beards.

A poem written to celebrate a wedding is called an epithalamium.

A melcryptovestimentaphiliac is someone who compulsively steals ladies' underwear.

A selenologist studies the moon.

A "beer can fancier" is called a canologist.

The only contemporary words that end in -*gry* are angry and hungry.

Monday is the only day of the week that has a one-word anagram: dynamo.

A misodoctakleidist is someone who hates practicing the piano.

It's easy to spot someone with hexadactylism: he or she has six fingers on one hand or six toes on one foot.

Snapping your fingers is called a fillip.

If you have a compulsive urge to dance, you're a dinomaniac.

The ball on top of a flagpole is called a truck.

The longest English word you can type with only the left hand: stewardesses.

Basketball

Charles Barkley entered the league with the nickname Round Mound of Rebound.

Until 1937 the referee tossed a jump ball after every basket in basketball.

Michael Jordan always wore the shorts of his North Carolina basketball uniform under his Bulls uniform, beginning the trend for baggier shorts in the NBA.

Earvin "Magic" Johnson was, at 6 feet 9 inches, the tallest point guard in NBA history.

Tulsa guard Marcus Hill has a collection of over 300 pairs of shoes.

Hakeem Olajuwon was the first player to be named NBA MVP, NBA Defensive Player of the Year, and NBA Finals MVP in the same season.

The NBA instituted the three-pointer before the 1979–1980 season.

Wilt Chamberlain holds nearly 100 NBA records.

The first professional basketball league was formed in 1898; players earned $2.50 for home games, $1.25 for games on the road.

Shaquille O'Neal was sworn in as a Miami Beach reserve police officer on December 8, 2005.

Four players in NBA history have compiled 20,000 points, 10,000 rebounds, and 4,000 assists: Kareem Abdul-Jabbar, Wilt Chamberlain, Karl Malone, and Charles Barkley.

Kareem Abdul-Jabbar holds the record for the most play-off game appearances: 237.

Basketball superstition: the last person to shoot a basket during the warm-up will have a good game.

As a 5 foot 11 inch sophomore, Michael Jordan was cut from his high school varsity basketball team.

Word Origins

PHONY

Meaning: A fraudulent person or thing

Origin: "Newspaperman H. L. Mencken suggested that a maker of fake jewelry named Forney is the origin of this word, but few experts agree with him. The majority opinion is that phony is an alteration of fawney, British slang for a worthless ring. The word probably comes from the fawney rig, a con game in which a worthless ring is planted, and when someone 'finds' it he is persuaded by a 'bystander' that he should pay the bystander for his share in the find." (*Word and Phrase Origins*, by Robert Hendrickson)

EROTIC

Meaning: Relating to sexual desire or excitement

Origin: "Erós was the god of love, and the fairest of the gods in the Greek pantheon. But he was vain and spoiled and for sport shot his love-poisoned arrows into the hearts of men and gods. At his festival, the erotia, married couples of the day were supposed to patch up their differences and end all quarrels. From the Greek name Eros comes the word erotic, meaning 'full of sexual desire,' or 'morbidly amorous.'" (*Word Origins*, by Wilfred Funk)

COCKTAIL

Meaning: An alcoholic drink consisting of spirits mixed with other ingredients

Origin: "One idea is that it came from cockfighting. A cock's courage was fired up by slipping him a mixture of stale beer, gin, herbs, and flour, which was called cock-ale. More likely, the term was coined by Antoine Peychaud, a New Orleans restaurateur. During the 1800s, Antoine made drinks mixed from a number of different liquors. He served the wicked brew in little egg cups called coquetier in French. Wanting to give his drinks a special name, he simply Americanized the French word by changing it to cocktail." (*Straight From the Horse's Mouth*, by Teri Degler)

PARASITE
Meaning: An organism that lives in or on another organism at the other's expense
Origin: "In ancient Greek it meant a professional dinner guest. It came from the Greek para ('beside') and sitos ('grain, food'). Put together, parasitos first meant 'fellow guest' and acquired, even then, its present-day meaning." (*Dictionary of Word and Phrase Origins, Vol. III*, by William and Mary Morris)

POOPED
Meaning: Exhausted
Origin: "Englishmen headed for the New World found that violent waves did the most damage when they crashed against the stern (rear end), or poop of a vessel. Any ship that came out of a long bout with nature was said to be badly 'pooped.' Sailors who described the splintered stern of a ship often confessed that they felt as pooped as their vessel looked. Landsmen borrowed the sea-going expression and put it to use." (*Why You Say It*, by Webb Garrison)

BUTTERFLY
Meaning: An insect
Origin: "The most generally accepted theory of how this insect got its name is a once-held notion that if you leave butter or milk uncovered in a kitchen, butterflies will land on it . . . and eat it. Another possibility is that the word is a reference to the color of the insects' excrement." (*Dictionary of Word Origins*, by John Ayto)

GENUINE
Meaning: Real, not fake
Origin: "Originally meant 'placed on the knees.' In Ancient Rome, a father legally claimed his new child by sitting in front of his family and placing his child on his knee." (*Etymologically Speaking*, by Steven Morgan Friedman)

ADDICT
Meaning: A person with an uncontrollable (usually bad) habit
Origin: "Slaves given to Roman soldiers as a reward for performance in battle were known as addicts. Eventually, the term came to refer to a person who was a slave to anything." (*Etymologically Speaking*, by Steven Morgan Friedman)

What People Believe

According to Middle Eastern tradition, the original forbidden fruit was a banana.

According to some spiritualists, the human aura cannot be photographed through polyester.

Buddhist monks at Japan's Yakushido Temple perform a purification ritual by "setting fire to their own pants."

There are more churches per capita in Las Vegas than in any other U.S. city.

In Greek mythology, Nike is the goddess of victory.

The ancient Sumerians had a goddess of beer.

Four most common names for popes: John, Gregory, Benedict, and Clement, in that order.

As pope, John Paul II performed at least three exorcisms.

In 1997, 87 percent of people surveyed said they were "likely" to go to heaven, more than the number (79 percent) who said Mother Teresa was likely to go to heaven.

Among other things, the ancient Egyptians worshipped cabbages.

Fastest-growing religion in Ireland: Buddhism.

* * *

THE COST OF THE THINGS: 1950s

Roll of film: 38¢
Toilet paper (20 rolls): $2.39
Combination 19-inch television/FM radio/phonograph: $495
Corvette (1953): $3,498
Jackie Robinson's salary (1951): $39,750 per year

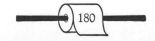

Fashion Sense

The ancient Romans dyed their hair with bird droppings.

About three quarters of American adults wear some kind of fragrance.

The average fashion model weighs 23 percent less than the average American woman.

When she died in 1603, Queen Elizabeth I owned 3,000 dresses. When Empress Elizabeth of Russia died in 1762, she owned 15,000 dresses.

Queen Elizabeth I owned 2,000 pairs of gloves.

Percentage of Americans who say a unibrow is a turnoff: 35.

Bozo the Clown wore size 83AAA shoes.

The average person owns 25 T-shirts.

Don't believe the Scots. The kilt originated in France.

Blue neckties sell best. Red ties are second.

Julius Caesar wore a laurel wreath crown to hide the fact that he was balding.

In 1907 egret plumes were worth twice their weight in gold.

The first person to wear silk stockings: England's Queen Elizabeth I. They were a gift.

In 1797 James Hetherington invented the top hat and wore it in public. He was arrested for disturbing the peace.

* * *

REDUNDANCIES

knots per hour
temporary reprieve
cluster together

disappear from view
total extinction
violent explosion

Fat & Fat Free

Average caloric requirement for existing (breathing, eating, sleeping): 1,000–1,500 per day.

Thirty-five percent of American dieters blame candy for their failure to lose weight. Twenty-one percent blame cheese.

Melting an ice cube in your mouth burns about 2.3 calories.

You'd have to walk five miles to burn off the calories of a hot fudge sundae.

You burn more calories sleeping than you do watching TV.

Your body gives off enough heat in 30 minutes to bring half a gallon of water to a boil.

To lose one pound of fat, you need to walk at least 35 miles (briskly).

A karaoke singing of "We Are the World" burns 20.7 calories.

About 36 percent of people who make a New Year's resolution to diet and exercise break it by January 31.

Play a round of golf, then drink two cocktails. You've just gained more calories than you burned.

* * *

REMEMBER 1981?
President Reagan and Pope John Paul II shot; both recovered
Charles and Diana married
Sandra Day O'Connor became first woman
appointed to Supreme Court
52 U.S. hostages released from Iran
AIDS identified for the first time
MTV debuted

Film Firsts & Mosts

First movie shown in the White House: *Birth of a Nation*, in 1916. Woodrow Wilson was president.

Nanook of the North (1922) was the first documentary film ever made.

The first movie stars to leave their hand- and footprints at Grauman's: Mary Pickford and Douglas Fairbanks, April 30, 1927.

The Jazz Singer (1927) was only about 25 percent talkie, and ad-libbed at that.

The first movie to premiere at Grauman's Chinese Theatre: Cecil B. DeMille's *King of Kings* (1927).

The first scripted "all-talking" feature-length picture was the gangster film *Lights of New York* (1928).

The first movie shown in a drive-in theater: *Wife Beware*, in 1933.

According to a 2005 Harris Poll, America's favorite movie stars are, in order: Tom Hanks, Mel Gibson, Julia Roberts, Johnny Depp, Harrison Ford, Denzel Washington, and John Wayne (d. 1979).

Drew Barrymore was five years old when she made her first appearance in a feature film (*Altered States*, 1980).

First movie star to appear on a postage stamp: Gene Kelly.

Highest-grossing sports movie in history: *Rocky IV*, followed by *Jerry Maguire*.

The longest film ever released was Andy Warhol's ****, aka *The 24 Hour Movie*. When it flopped, Warhol released a 90-minute version that didn't do very well either.

Highest price ever paid for a movie prop: $275,000, for 007's Aston Martin from *Goldfinger*.

Let It Snow!

The tiniest snowflake ever recorded: 1/500 of an inch in diameter. Largest snowflakes: 15 inches in diameter and eight inches thick. They fell in Montana in 1887.

In the United States, more snow falls in February than in any other month.

When groundhogs predict the start of spring, they're wrong 72 percent of the time.

Coldest towns on earth: Verkyoyanks and Oymyakon, Siberia, with temperatures as low as –95°F.

Hawaii is the only state that has never recorded a temperature below 0°F.

Very thin, weak ice is known as "cat ice" because it can't even support the weight of a cat.

On January 20, 1973, it was –16°F in Deadwood, South Dakota, but 52°F in Lead— only one and a half miles away.

When the ground temperature is below freezing, it can't hail.

Largest 24-hour snowfall on record in the United States: Valdez, Alaska, in January 1990—47.5 inches.

Twenty-three percent of the world's landmass is buried under snow at least part of the year.

About one third of the earth's surface never gets snow.

The largest hailstone ever recorded was 17.5 inches in diameter—bigger than a basketball.

On average, Salt Lake City gets more snow than Fairbanks, Alaska.

Presidential Firsts

PRESIDENT: John Quincy Adams
NOTABLE FIRST: First president interviewed in the nude.
BACKGROUND: President Adams loved to skinny-dip. In hot weather he'd sneak out for a swim in the Potomac. One morning Anne Royall—a reporter who had been trying to interview him for months—sneaked up while he was swimming, sat on his clothes, and refused to leave until he granted her an interview. He did.

PRESIDENTS: Thomas Jefferson and James Madison
NOTABLE FIRSTS: The only presidents to be arrested together.
BACKGROUND: One afternoon in the spring of 1791, future presidents Jefferson and Madison were riding in a carriage through the Virginia countryside when a rural sheriff pulled them over and arrested them on the spot. Their crime: riding in a carriage on Sunday.

PRESIDENT: Benjamin Harrison
NOTABLE FIRST: First president with a fear of electricity.
BACKGROUND: President Harrison knew two things about electricity: The White House had just been wired for it, and it could kill people (the electric chair was becoming a common form of execution). That was all he needed to know—he didn't want anything more to do with it. Throughout his entire term, he and his wife refused to turn the lights on and off themselves. They either had the servants do it or left the lights off or on all night.

PRESIDENT: Theodore Roosevelt
NOTABLE FIRST: First and last (that we know of) president to wear another president's body part during his inauguration.
BACKGROUND: The night before he was sworn into office in 1901, Roosevelt was given an unusual gift—a ring containing strands of hair that had been cut from President Abraham Lincoln's head the night he was assassinated. Roosevelt wore the ring to his inauguration the next day.

PRESIDENT: William Howard Taft
NOTABLE FIRST: First president to throw out the first pitch of the baseball season.
BACKGROUND: Weighing in at over 330 pounds, Taft handlers feared his girth might make him seem weak when he ran for office again. So, in 1910, one of them suggested to the president that he begin playing a sport to prove that he still had his youthful vigor. When Taft vetoed the idea, his aide suggested that he at least make a ceremonial appearance at a sporting event—say, to throw out the first ball of the baseball season. Taft agreed, and on April 14, 1910, he waddled out to the pitcher's mound at Griffith Stadium in Washington, D.C., and pitched a ball to home plate. (It went wild.) Continuing the tradition started by Taft, subsequent presidents' pitches were just as wild. By 1929, rather than actually pitch the ball, most presidents just threw it onto the field from their seat in the stands.

PRESIDENT: Warren G. Harding
NOTABLE FIRST: First president to bet (and lose) White House china in poker games.
BACKGROUND: Harding was an enthusiastic poker player; unfortunately, he wasn't very good at it and was often short of cash. End result: When he was low on cash during poker games with his buddies, he used individual pieces of fine White House china for poker chips. It is not known how many pieces of the china were lost in this way.

* * *

WORD PLAY

We have to **polish** the **Polish** furniture.
How can he **lead** if he can't get the **lead** out?
A skilled farmer sure can **produce** a lot of **produce**.
The dump was so full it had to **refuse refuse**.
The soldier decided to **desert** his **dessert** in the **desert**.
No time like the **present** to **present** the **present**.
A small-mouthed **bass** was painted on the big **bass** drum.
The white **dove dove** down into **Dover**.

Once Upon a Time

In France it was once considered bad luck to cut your fingernails on Friday.

Ancient Romans paid their taxes with honey.

The Aztecs restricted the smelling of certain flowers to the upper classes.

Pogo sticks were first used by sacrificial dancers in Borneo.

The world has been at peace only 8 percent of the time over the last 3,500 years.

Germans once believed a pregnant woman could avoid premature delivery by carrying one of her husband's socks.

Peanut butter sandwiches weren't popular until the 1920s.

United States

At last count, Minnesota had 99 lakes named Mud Lake.

Oregon has the most ghost towns of any state.

There are no natural lakes in the state of Ohio. They are all man-made.

The Great Salt Lake in Utah is six times saltier than seawater.

Michigan borders no ocean but has more lighthouses than any other state.

Most crowded state: New Jersey, with an average of 1,000 people per square mile.

If you're anywhere in the state of Florida, you're within 60 miles of a beach.

According to one study, 24 percent of Iowans have some sort of lawn ornament in their yard.

Tennessee got its name in 1796. Before then it was known as Franklin.

Prohibition didn't end in Mississippi until 1966.

The state capital of Texas has been moved 15 times.

George Washington nicknamed New York the Empire State.

Alaska has the highest percentage of baby boomers. Utah has the lowest.

Arizona has official state neckwear: the bolo tie.

The only state with no straight-line boundary is Hawaii.

More roses are grown in Texas than in any country on earth.

Until 1867 Alaska was known as Russian America.

Maine is the only state with a one-syllable name.

Slogan stamped onto New Hampshire license plates by state prison inmates: "Live free or die."

Lost in Translation

Amen is the same in more languages than any other word. *Taxi* is second.

A group of non-English speakers chose "diarrhea" as one of the prettiest-sounding English words.

The language of Taki, spoken in parts of Guinea, consists of only 340 words.

Say it three times fast: *Geschwindigkeitsbegrenzung* is German for "speed limit."

How many languages in the world? About 5,000.

The French typing equivalent of "the quick brown fox jumped over the lazy dog" is "Take this old whiskey to the blonde judge who's smoking a cigar."

In England a cat is sometimes called a moggy. Noses are conks.

Number of languages spoken in India: about 845.

The German language has about 185,000 words. French has fewer than 100,000.

The English language has the most words with nearly 1 million.

Native Americans spoke more than 133 different languages.

Nine most-used words in the English language: and, be, it, of, the, will, I, have, you.

The French word for walkie-talkie is *talkie-walkie*.

There are more than 500 words for macaroni in Italian.

More than 700 different languages are spoken in Papua New Guinea.

Most popular "American" expression on earth: OK.

The World Eats

On any given day, half the people in the world will eat rice.

Iceland consumes more Coca-Cola per capita than any other nation.

The French eat an average of 200 million frogs each year.

Peruvians eat about 65 million guinea pigs each year.

In Japan you can buy cocoa flavored with 2 percent chili-pepper sauce.

You can buy horseradish ice cream in Tokyo.

In Denmark, Danish pastries are called Vienna bread.

Best-selling candy bar in Russia: Snickers.

The average Briton drinks four cups of tea per day.

Damper is an unleavened bread made by the Australian bush people.

Germans eat more potatoes per capita than any other people, averaging 370 pounds per year.

The most popular Campbell's soup in Hong Kong is water-cress and duck gizzard.

Domino's Pizza sells a reindeer sausage pizza, but only in Iceland.

Tibetans drink a tea made of salted rancid yak butter.

* * *

REDUNDANCIES

baby calf
circle around
slippery slime
hollow tube
illegal poaching

old adage
NFL football team
merge together
sandwiched between
reflect back

The Wild West

Billy the Kid's first crime? Stealing clothes from a Chinese laundry.

In the Old West, more cowboys died crossing swollen rivers than during gunfights.

Billy the Kid was buried in a shirt five sizes too big.

Buckeroo is the anglicized form of *vaquero*, the Spanish word for cowboy.

Two black aces and eights are called the "dead man's hand." It's what Wild Bill Hickok was holding when he was shot dead in the Number Ten Saloon in Deadwood, Dakota Territory.

Wild Bill Hickok had a brother. His nickname was Tame Bill.

Jesse James issued his own press releases.

Legendary Johnny Ringo didn't die with his boots on—his killer made him take them off before shooting him.

1860 ad for Pony Express riders: Wanted: Young, skinny, wiry fellows not over 18. Must be expert riders willing to risk death daily. Orphans preferred.

There were no ponies in the Pony Express.

The gunfight at the O.K. Corral lasted 30 seconds and left three bad guys dead and three good guys wounded.

John Henry "Doc" Holliday was a doctor of dentistry.

The notorious Black Bart (Charles E. Bolton) robbed 27 Wells Fargo stagecoaches in his day; on his release from San Quentin prison, he disappeared and was never heard from again.

Jesse James's father was a Baptist minister.

Cowboys called jail the hoosegow after the Spanish word *juzgado*, meaning "court of justice."

Food for Thought

You can think 625 thoughts on the caloric energy of one Cheerio.

Eat one lump of sugar and you've eaten the equivalent of three feet of sugar cane.

According to food researchers, thyme helps prevent tooth decay.

The calories in a bagel with cream cheese can run an electric toothbrush for 52 hours, 20 minutes.

The darker green a vegetable is, the more vitamin C it contains.

A bowl of Wheaties contains twice as much sodium as a bowl of potato chips.

One big difference between canned and fresh vegetables is salt. There's up to 40 times more in cans.

The USDA recommends five servings of fruits and veggies a day. The average adult eats 4.4. Kids eat 3.4.

The only food that provides calories with no nutrition is sugar.

The peanut is one of the most concentrated sources of nourishment.

The most popular fruit in the United States: apples, followed by oranges and bananas.

Broccoli was first introduced to the United States in the 1920s. Today 27 percent of Americans say broccoli is their favorite vegetable.

Pound for pound, oysters have 20 times as much cholesterol as eggs.

Spinach consumption in the United States rose 33 percent after the Popeye comic strip became a hit in 1931.

You burn 26 calories with a one-minute kiss.

The Metric System

HISTORY. In the years following the French Revolution of 1789, the French Republic tried to make a clean break from the past by inventing a new form of government, new names for the seasons, a new calendar with new names for all of the days and months, and other such innovations. Over the next 30 years most of these reforms fell by the wayside, but one of them didn't—the metric system.

THE METER. Originally intended to be exactly one 10-millionth the length of the distance between the North Pole and the equator. The only problem: Measuring instruments weren't precise enough to measure such a vast distance accurately, so the length that was chosen for the meter turned out to be the wrong one. By the time scientists discovered this, however, the meter's length—39.37 inches—was so widely accepted that they decided not to change it.

LITERS, KILOGRAMS, GRAMS. Once the scientists designing the metric system settled on the length of the meter, they used it to create measurements for mass and volume. They designed a cube with each side exactly one-tenth of a meter (a decimeter) long and filled it with water. The space that the water filled was designated as a liter, and the amount the water weighed was called a kilogram, which was then subdivided into 1,000 units called grams.

* * *

Note: One reason the metric system caught on with scientists was that in the traditional measurement system, there were no standard units smaller than an inch or larger than a mile, which made it tough to measure extremely large and extremely small distances. With the metric system, it was much easier to invent new measurements when they became necessary.

Your Hair

How many hairs on your head? If you're blond, about 150,000. Brunet, 100,000. Redhead, 60,000.

There are 550 hairs in the average eyebrow.

About 10 percent of men and 30 percent of women shave solely with an electric razor.

There are about 15,500 hairs in an average beard.

Women start shaving at a slightly younger age than men do.

Half of Caucasian men go bald. Eighteen percent of African American men do.

American Indians rarely go bald.

Hair is unique to mammals.

Fifty percent of Americans have gray hair by the time they're 50 years old.

Number of hair follicles on an average adult: 5 million.

City dwellers have longer, thicker, denser nose hairs than country folks do.

The older you get, the slower your hair grows.

Cutting hair does not influence its growth.

Hair covers the whole human body, except for the soles of the feet, the palms, mucous membranes, and lips.

The average life span of a human hair: three to seven years.

Your hair is as strong as aluminum.

Women shave an area nine times as large as men do.

Medical studies show that intelligent people have more copper and zinc in their hair.

Word Geography

SUEDE
From: Sweden
Explanation: *Gants de Suede* is French for "gloves of Sweden." It was in Sweden that the first leather was buffed to a fine softness, and the French bought the *gants de Suede*. Suede now refers to the buffing processes—not to any particular kind of leather.

TURKEY
From: Turkey
Explanation: *Turk* means "strength" in Turkish. The turkey bird is a large European fowl named after the country of its origin. American colonists mistakenly thought a big bird they found in the New World was the same animal . . . so they called it a turkey.

CHEAP
From: Cheapside, a market in London
Explanation: The Old English word was *ceap* (pronounced "keep"), which meant "to sell or barter." Because Cheapside was a major market where people went to barter for low prices, the word gradually took on a new pronunciation . . . and meaning.

MAYONNAISE
From: Port Mahon, Spain (according to legend)
Explanation: The *-aise* suffix is French for "native to" or "originating in." Mahonnaise was supposedly created to celebrate a 1756 French battle victory over the British on the Spanish isle of Port Mahon.

DENIM
From: Nimes, France
Explanation: The tough cloth used in jeans was also made in Nimes. It was called *serge di Nimes*—later shortened to *di nimes*, which became *denim*.

COFFEE
From: Kaffa, Ethiopia
Explanation: According to legend, coffee beans were first discovered in the town of Kaffa. By the 13th century, the Kaffa beans had traveled, becoming *qahwah* in Arabia, *café* in Europe, and finally *coffee* in the New World.

COLOGNE
From: Cologne, Germany
Explanation: Scented water that was produced there beginning in 1709 was named for the city.

SLAVE
From: Slavonia, Yugoslavia
Explanation: After large parts of Slavonia were subjugated by Europeans in the Middle Ages, a Slav become synonymous with someone who lived in servitude. Eventually *Slav* became *slave*.

LIMERICK
From: Limerick, Ireland
Explanation: The town was popularly associated with humorous verses that had five lines, the first two rhyming with the last, the middle two rhyming with each other. The poems became an English fad in the mid-19th century, and people naturally identified them with the town's name.

HAMBURGER
From: Hamburg, Germany
Explanation: People in the immigration-port city of Hamburg—called Hamburgers—liked to eat raw meat with salt, pepper, and onion-juice seasoning, a treat brought to them via Russia that we call steak tartare today. A broiled version using chopped meat eventually became popular in America.

TURQUOISE
From: Turkey/Europe
Explanation: Another Turkish origin. Turquoise comes from a number of places, but was probably first imported to Europe from Turkey. So it was called turquoise, which means "Turkish stone."

Crazy World Records

Farthest distance a pumpkin has been hurled without the use of explosives: 3,718 feet.

T. D. Rockwell had his name and address tattooed on his body in 27 different languages, including Morse code, shorthand, and semaphore.

Record for most haircuts given in an hour: 23, by Scot Sandy Dobbie.

A New York man carried a milk bottle on his head continuously for 24 miles.

In 1923 French sports reporter Pierre Labric rode his bicycle down the 347 stairs of the Eiffel Tower. It took him three minutes and 17 seconds. His bike was wrecked.

The World's Largest Office Chair is in Anniston, Alabama. It's 33 feet tall.

The world's longest zipper, with over 12,600 teeth, was presented to President Ronald Reagan in 1985. It's now in the Smithsonian.

A museum in Old Lyme, Connecticut, dedicated to nuts also has the world's largest nutcracker.

Longest underwater kiss on record: 2 minutes and 18 seconds.

Elaine Davidson, of Edinburgh, Scotland, has a record-breaking total of 720 body piercings, including 192 on her face and head.

Al Gliniecki of Gulf Breeze, Florida, tied 39 cherry stems into knots in three minutes using his tongue.

Incredible Animals

The world's longest earth-worms—found only in a small corner of Australia—can grow to as long as 12 feet and as thick as a soda can.

Ancient Romans trained elephants to perform on a tightrope.

Squids have the largest eyes in nature—up to 16 inches across.

Australia's mallee bird can tell temperature with its tongue, accurate to within two degrees.

Not only does the three-toed sloth sleep 20 hours a day, it also spends most of its life upside down.

By using air currents to keep it aloft, an albatross may fly up to 87,000 miles on a single feeding trip without ever touching the ground. That's more than three times around the earth.

The chamois—a goatlike mountain antelope—can balance on a point of rock the size of a quarter.

Robins become drunk after eating holly berries and often fall off power lines.

Octopus eyes resemble human eyes—the U.S. Air Force once taught an octopus to "read" by distinguishing letterlike shapes.

A woodpecker's beak moves at a speed of 100 mph.

Polar bears are so perfectly insulated from the cold that they spend most of their time trying to cool down.

Whales can communicate with each other from over 3,000 miles away (but the message takes over an hour to get there).

The Office

The average office chair with wheels will travel eight miles this year.

One percent of U.S. businesses allow their employees to take naps during working hours.

Twenty-four percent of commuters say that when stuck in traffic, they think "deep thoughts."

Four out of every ten people are satisfied with their jobs.

If you work nights, you're nearly twice as likely to have an accident than if you work days.

Once you file something, there's a 98 percent chance you'll never look at it again.

The average American worker receives 201 phone, paper, and e-mail messages per day.

The average American worker has held eight different jobs by the age of 40.

Thirty-two percent of managers say "looking too young" can make a salesperson's job more difficult.

The average American CEO's pay has increased more than 600 percent since 1990.

Need time off? Move to Italy. On average, Italians get 42 vacation days per year.

The average office worker spends 50 minutes a day looking for lost files and other items.

For every 1,470 résumés an employer receives, one person is hired.

Twenty-six percent of American men say their workplace filing system consists of "putting things in piles."

People who work at night tend to weigh more than people who work during the day.

Choppers

Three things a helicopter can do that a plane can't:

1. Fly backward
2. Rotate as it moves through the air
3. Hover motionless

It takes both hands and both feet to fly a helicopter, which, many say, makes it much more complex than flying a plane.

The helicopter pilot has to think in three dimensions. In addition to cyclic control (forward, backward, left, and right), and collective control (up and down, and engine speed), there is rotational control (spinning in either direction on the axis).

In 1956 Bell Aircraft Corporation introduced the *UH-1*. The Huey became the best-known symbol of the U.S. military during the Vietnam War.

The first U.S. president to fly in a helicopter: Dwight D. Eisenhower, in 1957.

In 1969 the Russian Mi-12 became the largest helicopter ever flown. It could lift a payload of 105,000 kilograms (231,485 pounds).

In 1982 a Bell 206 completed the first solo crossing of the Atlantic by a helicopter.

In 1483 Leonardo da Vinci made drawings of a fanciful craft he called a helical air screw, but it never got off the drawing board. His concept of "compressing" the air was similar to that used by today's helicopters. However, when a prototype was built recently at the Science Museum of London, it didn't work.

Household Hints

Tomatoes have more flavor at room temperature than they do when chilled.

Ketchup cleans copper. Apply, wait a minute, and rinse. Voilà!

Is your soup too salty? Slice up two potatoes and boil them in it for a short time.

Chew gum while peeling onions. It may keep you from crying.

Egg whites will turn pink when left overnight in a copper bowl.

If you don't remove an avocado's pit, it won't turn black, even when you peel it.

Add honey to peanut butter to keep it from sticking to the roof of your mouth.

How long does it take a frozen sandwich to thaw at room temperature? About three hours.

If you refrigerate your rubber bands, they'll last longer.

Pour leftover cola into your toilet. It'll give it a nice shine.

If you have to give your dog a pill, put it far back on its tongue, then blow in its nose.

Baby wipes are the perfect fix for carpet stains.

If you can find where ants are coming in, a barrier of sprinkled cinnamon or ground pepper will stop them.

Lipstick on your collar will disappear with petroleum jelly.

Mix baby powder with your kitty litter to keep it smelling fresh.

Yes, your down comforter can be washed in the washing machine—cold water, gentle cycle. Toss a few tennis balls into the dryer to fluff it up again.

Disappearing ink: try rubbing alcohol on ink stains before washing.

United States

Only state with official vegetables: New Mexico, which honors both the chili and the frijole.

Hawaii is the only state in the United States with a royal palace: Iolani Palace.

There are 122 Hawaiian islands.

In 39 of the 50 states in the United States, the travel industry is the largest single employer.

New Jersey is number one in the nation for hazardous waste sites, with more than 1,000.

Technically speaking, there are only 46 states in the United States. Kentucky, Massachusetts, Pennsylvania, and Virginia are commonwealths.

The Thousand Islands of New York and Ontario actually number about 1,500.

There's a producing oil well beneath the Oklahoma State capitol building.

Official state dance of Utah: square dance.

In what state can you find the Alabama swamps? New York. Wyoming Valley? Pennsylvania.

States with the lowest percentage of senior citizens: Alaska, Utah, Colorado, Texas, and Georgia.

States with the highest percentage of senior citizens: Florida, Pennsylvania, West Virginia, North Dakota, Iowa.

The most crowded street corner in the United States: 59th and Lexington in New York City.

State with the highest percentage of people who walk to work: Alaska.

Ask the Experts

Q: WILL RUBBER TIRES PROTECT A CAR FROM BEING STRUCK BY LIGHTNING?
A: No. Lightning is strong enough to travel through or around the rubber. According to the Boston Museum of Science, your tires would have to be solid rubber a mile thick to actually insulate you from a lightning bolt. Does that mean, then, that you should avoid your car in a thunderstorm? No, the good news is that your car is the safest place to be if you're outside during a storm—the lightning will most likely travel around the metal shell of your car and not do any damage to it or you. That is, if you have a metal car and don't park under a tree or touch the metal. The bad news is that if you have a convertible or plastic car, or if you touch the metal skin of your automobile when lightning strikes, you may be in for a profoundly shocking experience. (*Just Curious, Jeeves*, by Jack Mingo and Erin Barrett)

Q: DO THE POLICE REALLY OUTLINE A MURDER VICTIM'S POSITION WITH CHALK?
A: At one time, maybe, but according to investigators we surveyed, it's really not done anymore. Why? While chalk or tape might make for dramatic TV, they also contaminate the crime scene, and contamination is a major headache for crime scene investigators. (*The Straight Dope*, by Cecil Adams)

Q: DO ANIMALS CRY?
A: Only one other land animal cries: the elephant. Marine animals that cry include seals, sea otters, and saltwater crocodiles (the so-called crocodile tears). All of these animals cry only to get rid of salt. However, one scientist, Dr. G. W. Steller, a zoologist at Harvard University, thinks that sea otters are capable of crying emotional tears. According to Dr. Steller, "I have sometimes deprived females of their young on purpose, sparing the lives of their mothers, and they would weep over their affliction just like human beings." (*The Odd Body*, by Dr. Stephen Juan)

Q: WHY DO WORMS GO ONTO THE SIDEWALK WHEN IT RAINS?

A: Most people assume that earthworms come to the surface during heavy rains to avoid drowning in their tunnels. In fact, worms can live totally submerged in water, so drowning isn't the problem. But the rainwater that filters down through the ground contains very little oxygen, so the real reason earthworms come to the surface is to breathe. Once above ground, earthworms are very sensitive to light, and even a brief exposure to the sun's rays can paralyze them. Unable to crawl back into their burrows, they eventually dry out and die on the sidewalk. (*101 Questions & Answers About Backyard Wildlife*, by Ann Squire)

Q: WHAT CAUSES TRAFFIC JAMS, AND WHY DO THEY SUDDENLY CLEAR UP?

A: It's the shock-wave effect. Highway drivers operate best at speeds of 35 mph and higher. When highway traffic volume nears its capacity, some stragglers begin driving under 35 mph and a traffic jam is born. Slower speeds, theoretically, should increase control and maneuverability, but drivers grow fearful as their pace declines. The shock-wave effect occurs because drivers look for the reason they had to slow down in the first place: They overreact to any stimuli, particularly the brake lights of cars ahead of them. A few drivers at 25 mph can set off a shock-wave effect for miles behind them and create bumper-to-bumper traffic without any ostensible reason. Why do these traffic jams suddenly disappear? Usually, it's because there is enough breathing room ahead to prompt even slowpoke victims of the shock-wave effect to risk peeling away at 35 mph or more. (*Imponderables*, by David Feldman)

Q: WHY DO CLOCKS RUN CLOCKWISE?

A: No one knows for sure, but here's one answer: "Before the advent of clocks, we used sundials. In the Northern Hemisphere, the shadows rotated in the direction we now call 'clockwise.' The clock hands were built to mimic the natural movements of the sun. If clocks had been invented in the Southern Hemisphere, [perhaps] 'clockwise' would be in the opposite direction." (*Why Do Clocks Run Clockwise, and Other Imponderables*, by David Feldman)

Know Your -ologies

Semiology: The study of signs and signaling

Cetology: The study of whales and dolphins

Vexillology: The study of flags

Deontology: The study of moral responsibilities

Axiology: The study of principles, ethics, and values

Phantomology: The study of supernatural beings

Histology: The study of tissues

Trichology: The study of hair

Malacology: The study of mollusks

Dendrochronology: The study of trees' ages by counting their rings

Morphology: The study of the structure of organisms

Oology: The study of eggs

Eschatology: The study of final events as spoken of in the Bible

Ashes to Ashes

Among other things, ancient Egyptian embalmers preserved mummies with cinnamon.

King Tut had garlic bulbs buried in his tomb with him.

Ancient Egyptian tombs are decorated with pictures of watermelons.

Neanderthals are believed to have buried their dead.

The Japanese express grief and mourning after the death of a loved one by wearing white, not black.

It is legal for a dead person to vote if he or she died after mailing in an absentee ballot.

When a person is dying, hearing is the last sense to go. Sight is the first.

The most common word spoken by a dying person is "Mother" or "Mommy."

According to a German doctor who weighed patients at the moment of death, the human soul weighs three-fourths of an ounce.

In 2003, 29 percent of Americans were cremated after they died.

In the Congo professional corpse painters charge admission to see their work.

Tombstones were originally put over graves so the dead couldn't escape.

Gail Borden (inventor of condensed milk) is buried beneath a headstone shaped like a milk can.

* * *

WORD PLAY

The **wind** was way too strong to **wind** the sail.
After a **number** of injections, my jaw finally got **number**.
You **sow**! You'll reap what you **sow**!

Time & Space

Every four seconds, somebody in the world opens a can of Spam.

Put 23 people in a room and there's a 50 percent chance two will share a birthday.

Thursday is the least busy day for barbershops.

Friday the 13th comes at least once every year, but never more than three times a year.

There are 20 days in the Aztec week.

About 90 percent of time capsules are never recovered.

Every thousand years, spring gets two-thirds of a day shorter.

A moment lasts 90 seconds.

If you're too young to be a baby boomer and too old to be a Generation Xer, you're a Cusper.

It would take two and a half minutes to fall from the top of Mt. Everest.

It's estimated that you'll spend a year of your life looking for misplaced objects.

If it happened before A.D. 476, it's ancient. After A.D. 476, it's medieval.

The Incas measured time by how long it took a potato to cook.

* * *

REMEMBER 1983?

U.S. invaded Grenada
Reagan proposed the Star Wars program
Truck bomb in Lebanon killed 241 U.S. soldiers
Thriller became bestselling album of all time
M*A*S*H ended after 251 episodes
Terms of Endearment won 5 Oscars

Myth America

SAVAGES
Myth: Scalping was a brutal tactic invented by the Indians to terrorize the settlers.
Truth: Scalping was actually an old European tradition dating back hundreds of years. Dutch and English colonists were paid a "scalp bounty" by their leaders as a means of keeping the Indians scared and out of the way. Finally the Indians caught on and adopted the practice themselves. The settlers apparently forgot its origins and another falsehood about Native American cruelty was born.

THANKSGIVING
Myth: The Pilgrims ate a Thanksgiving feast of turkey and pumpkin pie after their first year in the New World, and we've been doing it ever since.
Truth: Thanksgiving didn't become a national holiday until Abraham Lincoln declared it in 1863, and the Pilgrims ate neither the bird we call turkey, nor pumpkin pie.

MANHATTAN ISLAND
Myth: In 1626 Peter Minuit bought Manhattan Island from the Canarsee tribe for $24 worth of beads and other trinkets.
Truth: Minuit did give 60 guilders (roughly $24) worth of beads, knives, axes, clothes, and rum to Chief Seyseys of the Canarsee tribe "to let us live amongst them" on Manhattan Island. But the Canarsee actually got the best of the deal because they didn't own the island in the first place. They lived on the other side of the East River in Brooklyn, and only visited the southern tip of Manhattan to fish and hunt. The Weckquaesgeeks tribe, which lived on the upper three fourths of the island, had a much stronger claim to it and were furious when they learned they'd been left out of the deal. They fought with the Dutch settlers for years until the Dutch finally paid them, too.

BUNKER HILL

Myth: The Battle of Bunker Hill, where the Americans first faced the redcoats, was the colonists' initial triumph in the Revolutionary War.

Truth: Not only did the British wallop the Americans in the encounter, the whole thing wasn't even fought on Bunker Hill. The American troops had actually been ordered to defend Bunker Hill, but there was an enormous foul-up and somehow they wound up trying to protect nearby Breed's Hill, which was more vulnerable to attack. They paid for it. When the fighting was over, the Americans had been chased away by the British troops. Casualties were heavy for both sides: about 450 Americans were killed, and a staggering 1,000 (out of 2,100) redcoats died.

THE PILGRIMS

Myth: The Pilgrims landed at Plymouth Rock.

Truth: This tale originated in 1741, more than 100 years after the Pilgrims arrived. It has been attributed to a then-95-year-old man named Thomas Fraunce, who claimed his father had told him the story when he was a boy. However, his father didn't land with the Pilgrims—he reached America three years after they did. The Pilgrims first landed in Provincetown, Massachusetts.

YANKEE DOODLE

Myth: "Yankee Doodle" was originally a patriotic song.

Truth: It was composed in England as an anti-American tune. The phrase "stuck a feather in his cap and called it macaroni" referred to a foppish English group called the Macaroni Club, whose members wore ludicrous "continental" fashions they mistakenly believed to be elegant. The British laughed at "Yankee Doodle dandies," bumpkins who didn't know how silly they really were.

SO HIGH, SOLO

Myth: Charles Lindbergh was the first person to fly nonstop across the Atlantic Ocean.

Truth: He was the 67th person to fly nonstop across the Atlantic. The first nonstop flight was made by William Alcock and Arthur Brown in 1919, eight years before Lindbergh's flight. Lindbergh was famous because he did it alone.

The Auto Industry

The automobile was invented in 1886. The used car lot (of 17 cars) was "invented" in 1897.

In 1924 a new Ford cost $265.

The first Rolls-Royce sold for $600, in 1906. Today they sell for more than $200,000.

Whale oil was used in automobile transmission fluids as late as 1973.

The average car has 15,000 parts.

No matter how cold it gets, gasoline won't freeze. When the temperature gets below −180°F, it just turns gummy.

Toughest car ever: a 1957 Mercedes-Benz 180D racked up 1,184,880 miles in 21 years.

When used to make ethyl alcohol, an acre of potatoes will produce enough fuel to fill 25 cars.

It takes six months to build a Rolls-Royce and 13 hours to build a Toyota.

Goodyear once made a tire entirely out of corn.

The average 1995 luxury car had more than one mile of wiring.

The tubeless auto tire was invented by a man named Frank Herzegh. He made one dollar for it.

The first reported car theft in America took place in St. Louis, Missouri, in 1905.

It takes about two and a half gallons of oil to make a car tire.

The right rear tire on your car will wear out before the other three will.

No butts about it: Nissan has invented an artificial butt to test car seats.

More Americans have died in automobile accidents than have died in all U.S. wars.

Magazine Stand

The first American magazine (1741) was called *The American Magazine*.

Time magazine's Man of the Year for 1988: "Endangered Earth."

Who *has* appeared on the most covers of *People* magazine? Princess Diana—54 times.

Sixty-eight percent of gossip columnists say the best place to interview a celebrity is in their kitchen. Thirteen percent say their bedroom. Four percent say the yard.

Queen Elizabeth II was *Time* magazine's "Man of the Year" for 1952.

A typical *Playboy* centerfold weighs 15 percent less than a typical woman of the same age and height.

Mia Farrow appeared on the first cover of *People* magazine.

Fifty percent of all magazines printed in the United States are never sold.

First subject ever photographed by *National Geographic*: the city of Lhasa, Tibet, in 1905.

Time magazine's Person of the Century was Albert Einstein.

Mad was a comic book before it was converted into a magazine in 1956.

Playboy founder Hugh Hefner owns the crypt next to Marilyn Monroe at the Westwood Village Memorial Park Cemetery. Monroe was his first centerfold.

First person to appear on the cover of *Rolling Stone* magazine: John Lennon.

The Plant World

A variety of mimosa is called the sensitive plant because it wilts when touched.

The flowers of Africa's baobab tree open only in the moonlight. They are pollinated by bats.

A species of fern has the most chromosomes of all living things: 630 pairs.

The Venus flytrap only grows wild in one place: a 100-mile stretch of Carolina swampland.

Oldest vegetable known to humans: the pea.

Artichokes are flowers.

Peaches used to be known as Persian apples.

Peanuts are one of the ingredients used to make dynamite.

The stuff that gives freshly mowed grass its smell: hexanol.

An average apple contains about six teaspoons of sugar.

Mushrooms share a common ancestry with insects, not plants.

Chair Leaders?

In search of a "World's Largest" title, Bassett Furniture built a 20-foot 3-inch Mission chair. They sent it on tour to Bassett stores across the United States, calling it the World's Largest Chair, until Anniston, Alabama, publicly refuted their claim. Now they call it the World's Largest Chair on Tour.

A furniture company in Wingdale, New York, used more than a ton and a half of wood to build its 25-foot-tall Fireside Chair.

A custom furniture maker in Lipan, Texas, erected a 26-foot rocking chair in 2001.

Anniston, Alabama, has a 33-foot office chair in the vacant lot next to Miller Office Supply. A spiral staircase leads to the seat of the chair, which was constructed from 10 tons of steel.

The winner in the battle of the giant chairs is Promosedia in the province of Udine, Italy. Equivalent in size to a 7-story building, this chair was constructed in 1995 to advertise the chair-building region, known as the Chair Triangle. The 65-foot chair is indisputably the largest in the world. (So far.)

* * *

BATHROOM MISCELLANY

In medieval Europe, wedding ceremonies often took place in baths. Participants stood in a large tub as food was passed around on small boats.

Some 19th-century chamber pots were decorated with portraits of popular enemies on the inside. One popular target: Napoléon.

Women Are From Venus

Forty-six percent of women "wish they could do something about their thighs."

Two out of three times, it's the woman who starts a flirtation.

Fifteen percent of American women say they send flowers to themselves on Valentine's Day.

Fifty-seven percent of women would rather go on a shopping spree than have sex.

About 10 percent of American women keep their last name when they marry.

Life expectancy for women in the United States: 80.1 years. In 1900 it was 48.7 years.

The average female mannequin is 8 feet tall. The average woman is 5 feet 4 inches tall.

The average American female will have 3.3 pregnancies in her lifetime.

A woman can detect the odor of musk, which is associated with male bodies, better than any other smell.

Eighty percent of migraine sufferers are women.

In 1950 only 7 percent of American women dyed their hair. Today 75 percent do.

As of 2003, more than 11 million American women earned more than their husbands.

In 1960, 3 percent of American lawyers were women. In 2005 the number was up to 30 percent.

Seventy-five percent of divorced women will remarry.

America Eats

America's four favorite leftovers: pasta (including lasagna), pizza, chicken, and meatloaf.

America's least favorite veggie: brussels sprouts.

More than 50 percent of Americans say they take 15 minutes or less for lunch every day.

Top three most hated foods in the United States: tofu, liver, and yogurt.

About a third of all ethnic restaurants in the United States are Chinese.

About 1 million people drink cola for breakfast.

If you feed a rhesus monkey a "typical American diet" it will die within two years.

The average American eats 82 pounds of chicken a year.

A New Yorker could eat out every night of his or her life and never eat at the same restaurant twice.

Potato chips are the biggest-selling snack food in the United States and Canada. In fact, of 100 people eating snack food, 70 of them are eating potato chips.

Americans eat 12 billion bananas a year.

A typical supermarket displays more than 25,000 items.

Only 55 percent of dinners served in the United States include even one homemade dish.

Creature Features

Ninety-five percent of the creatures on earth are smaller than a chicken egg.

Animal in your house closest to the average-size animal in the entire animal kingdom: the housefly.

Only about 3 percent of mammals practice monogamy.

Mammals have been on the earth 200 million years. Homo sapiens: 150,000 years.

If it's a mammal, it has a tongue (or at least had one at one point).

If it has hair, feathers, or skin, it also has dandruff (dander).

Ninety percent of the wildlife species on the island of Madagascar are found nowhere else.

The E. coli bacteria has the fewest chromosomes: one pair.

Six of the most-hated creatures in the United States: cockroaches, mosquitoes, rats, wasps, rattlesnakes, and bats.

Seven thousand new insect species are discovered every year.

Last animal in the dictionary: the zyzzyva, a tropical American weevil.

* * *

WAR HEROES

What made the Dickin Medal for Valor unique during and after World War II? It was awarded to animals. From 1945 to 1949, 32 carrier pigeons, 18 dogs, three horses, and one cat were recipients of the medal.

Animal Myths

MYTH: Bats are blind.
FACT: Bats aren't blind. But they have evolved as nocturnal hunters, and can see better in half-light than in daylight.

MYTH: Monkeys remove fleas in each other's fur during grooming.
FACT: Monkeys don't have fleas. They're removing dead skin—which they eat.

MYTH: Male sea horses can become pregnant and give birth.
FACT: Actually, the female sea horse expels eggs into the male's brood pouch, where they are fertilized. And while the male does carry the gestating embryos until they are born 10 days later, he doesn't feed them through a placenta or similar organ (as had previously been thought). Instead, the embryos feed off nourishment in the egg itself—food provided by the female. Basically, the male acts as an incubator.

MYTH: Porcupines can shoot their quills when provoked.
FACT: A frightened porcupine tends to run from danger. If a hunter catches it, though, a porcupine will tighten its skin to make the quills stand up . . . ready to lodge in anything that touches them.

MYTH: Whales spout water.
FACT: Whales actually exhale air through their blowholes. This creates a mist or fog that looks like a waterspout.

MYTH: Moths eat clothes.
FACT: Moths lay their eggs, which eventually develop into larva, on your clothes. It's the larvae that eat tiny parts of your clothes; adult moths do not eat cloth.

MYTH: Bumblebee flight violates the laws of aerodynamics.
FACT: Nothing that flies violates the laws of aerodynamics.

Murphy's Law

In 1949 the U.S. Air Force decided to conduct a series of tests on the effect of rapid deceleration on pilots so they could get a better understanding of how much force people's bodies can tolerate in a plane crash. Volunteers were to wear a special harness fitted with 16 sensors that measured the acceleration, or g-forces, on different parts of their body. The harness was the invention of an air force captain named Edward A. Murphy—but it was assembled by someone else. The tests went off as expected, but no one will ever know the results because all 16 of the sensors failed. Each one gave a zero reading.

When Murphy examined the harness, he discovered that the sensors had been wired backward. There are varying accounts of what he said next, but at a press conference a few days later, he was quoted as having said, "If there are two or more ways to do something and one of those results in a catastrophe, then someone will do it that way."

Within months the expression became known throughout the aerospace industry as Murphy's Law and from there it spread to the rest of the world. But as it spread it also evolved into the popular, more pessimistic form, "If anything can go wrong, it will go wrong."

THE SCIENCE BEHIND IT
Since 1949 any number of permutations of Murphy's Law have arisen, dealing with subjects as diverse as missing socks and buttered bread falling to the floor. Some of these laws are grounded in very solid science:

MURPHY'S LAW OF BUTTERED BREAD: A dropped piece of bread will always land butter side down.
Scientific analysis: The behavior of a piece of bread dropped from table height is fairly predictable: As it falls to the ground it is more likely than not to rotate on its axis, and the distance to the ground is not sufficient for the bread to rotate the full 360 degrees needed for it to land face up. So more often than not, it will land face down.

MURPHY'S LAW OF LINES: The line next to you will move more quickly than the one you're in. (This also applies with a line of traffic.)

Scientific analysis: On average, all the lanes of traffic, or lines at a Wal-Mart, move at roughly the same rate. This means that if there's a checkout line on either side of you, there's a two in three chance that one of them will move faster than the one you're in.

MURPHY'S LAW OF SOCKS: If you lose a sock, it's always from a complete pair.

Scientific analysis: Start with a drawer containing 10 complete pairs of socks, for a total of 20 socks. Now lose one sock, creating one incomplete pair. The drawer now contains 19 socks, 18 of which belong to a complete pair. Now lose a second sock. If all of the remaining socks have the same odds of being lost, there's only one chance out of 18 that this lost sock is the mate of the first one that was lost. That means there's a 94.4 percent chance that it's from one of the complete pairs.

MURPHY'S LAW OF MAPS: The place you're looking for on the map will be located at the most inconvenient place on the map, such as an edge, a corner, or near a fold.

Scientific analysis: If you measure out an inch or so from each edge of the map and from each fold, and then calculate the total area of these portions of the map, they'll account for more than half the total area of the map. So if you pick a point at random, there's a better than 50 percent chance that it will be in an inconvenient-to-read part of the map.

* * *

FACTS TO BUG YOU

The praying mantis is the only insect that can turn its head like a human.

The hairs on the butt of a cockroach are so sensitive that they can detect air currents made by the onrushing tongue of a toad.

Mating soapberry bugs remain locked in embrace for up to 11 days, which exceeds the life span of many other insects.

On the Road

Forty-one percent of people ages 18 to 24 wear seat belts. Only 18 percent of people over age 65 do.

If your car is more than 42 feet long, you can't drive it on U.S. public roads.

First American car race: Chicago, in 1895. Average speed: 7.5 mph.

Divide the U.S. population by two—that's how many cars there are in America.

Chance that a driver will swerve out of their lane of traffic while talking on a cell phone: 7 percent.

In 1920 Detroit became the first city in the United States to put in a stoplight.

Busiest stretch of highway in the United States: New York's George Washington Bridge.

The average car in Japan is driven 4,400 miles a year. In the United States, it's 9,500 miles a year.

Sport-utility vehicle drivers are twice as likely to talk on a cell phone as are drivers of other kinds of cars.

According to one study, 85 percent of parents use child car–safety seats incorrectly.

Chance that a public road in the United States is unpaved: 1 percent.

There are more fatal traffic accidents in July than in any other month.

More road rage incidents occur on Friday between 4 and 6 p.m. than at any other time.

Aches & Pains

If it's a drug, it has a side effect.

Aspirin has never been approved by the FDA. It has never been rejected, either.

Fifth most popular plastic surgery performed on U.S. males: breast reduction.

You can't get athlete's foot if you don't wear shoes.

Chocolate is good for you: It has more antioxidant properties than green tea. The darker the better—and the warmer the better, as in a nice cup of hot chocolate.

The swine flu vaccine of 1976 caused more sickness and death than the flu itself did.

What do pediatricians do when their kids get colds? Sixty-three percent say they "let them run their course."

A few drops of tincture of mullein, easy to find at a vitamin or health food store, will stop a dry cough every time.

Crushed cockroaches, when applied to a stinging wound, are said to ease the pain.

There's no medical treatment for tinnitus, ringing in the ears. On the bright side, it sometimes goes away all by itself.

Peppermint tea is the perfect remedy for everything from stomach upsets to ulcers.

Chewing on parsley or cardamom seeds will get rid of bad breath.

Experts say that a belly laugh can help relieve constipation.

It takes about 30 minutes for aspirin to find a headache.

Animal Names

GORILLA
First used in a Greek translation of 5th century B.C. Carthaginian
explorer Hanno's account of a voyage to West Africa. He reported
encountering a tribe of wild hairy people, whose females were,
according to a local interpreter, called gorillas. In 1847 the American
missionary and scientist Thomas Savage adopted the word as the
species name of the great ape and by the 1850s it had passed into
general use. (*Dictionary of Word Origins*, by John Ayto)

FERRET
Ferret comes from Latin *furritus*, for "little thief," which probably
alludes to the fact that ferrets, which are related to pole cats, like to
steal hens' eggs. Its name also developed into a verb, to ferret out,
meaning "to dig out or bring something to light." (*Cool Cats, Top
Dogs, and Other Beastly Expressions*, by Christine Ammer)

SKUNK
Because the little striped mammal could squirt his foul yellow spray
up to 12 feet, American Indians called him *segankw* or *segonku*, the
Algonquin dialect word meaning simply "he who squirts." Early pioneers corrupted the hard-to-pronounce Algonquin word to skunk,
and that way it has remained ever since. (*Animal Crackers*, by Robert
Hendrickson)

HOUND
Before the Norman conquest of England, French hunters bred a
keen-nosed dog that they called the St. Hubert. One of their rulers,
William, took a pack to England and hunted deer—following the
dogs on foot. Saxons had never before seen a dog fierce enough to
seize its prey, so they named William's animals *hunts*, meaning
"seizure." Altered over time to *hound*, it was long applied to all hunting dogs. Then the meaning narrowed to stand for breeds that follow
their quarry by scent. (*Why You Say It*, by Webb Garrison)

LEOPARD
It was once wrongly believed that the leopard was a cross between a "leo" (a lion) and a "pard" (a white panther)—hence the name "leopard." (*Why Do We Say It?*, by Nigel Rees)

PYTHON
According to Greek legend, the god Apollo's earliest adventure was the single-handed slaying of Python, a flame-breathing dragon who blocked his way to Pytho (now Delphi), the site he had chosen for an oracle. From the name of this monster derives the name of the large snake of Asia, Africa, and Australia, the python. (*Thou Improper, Thou Uncommon Noun*, by Willard R. Espy)

CARDINAL
One would think that such an attractive creature would have given its name to many things, but in fact it is the other way around. The bird's name comes from the red-robed official of the Roman Catholic Church, who in turn was named for being so important—that is, from the adjective *cardinal*, from the Latin *cardo*, meaning "hinge" or "pivot." Anything cardinal was so important that events depended (hinged or pivoted) on it. (*It's Raining Cats and Dogs*, by Christine Ammer)

MOOSE
Captain John Smith, one of the original leaders at Jamestown, wrote accounts of the colony and life in Virginia, in which he defined the creature as Moos, a beast bigger than a stagge. Moos was from Natick (Indian) dialect and probably derived from *moosu*, 'he trims, he shaves,' a reference to the way the animal rips the bark and lower branches from trees while feeding. (*The Chronology of Words and Phrases*, by Linda and Roger Flavell)

FLAMINGO
This long-legged pink wading bird is named for the people of Flanders, the Flemings, as they were called. Flemings were widely known for their lively personalities, their flushed complexions, and their love of bright clothing. Spaniard explorers in the New World thought it was a great joke naming the bird flamingo, which means "a Fleming" in Spanish. (*Facts On File Encyclopedia of Word and Phrase Origins*, by Robert Hendrickson)

Thomas Edison

He wasn't blind, but Edison preferred reading in Braille.

Edison proposed to his second wife by Morse code.

In one four-year period, Edison obtained an average of one patent every five days.

In the 1860s Edison developed a device to electrocute cockroaches.

In 1888 Edison invented the talking doll.

Thomas Edison invented the light socket and the light switch.

The first sound recording ever made was "Mary Had a Little Lamb," by Edison in 1877.

First sport on film: boxing (Edison filmed it in 1894).

The first thing Edison filmed with his movie camera was a person sneezing: "Record of a Sneeze" (1894).

* * *

SUPERSTITIOUS?

If cooking bacon curls up in the pan, a new lover is about to arrive.

If the bubbles on the surface of a cup of coffee float toward the drinker, prosperous times lie ahead; if they retreat, hard times are promised.

When a slice of buttered bread falls butter-side-up, it means a visitor is coming.

Finding a chicken egg with no yolk is unlucky.

If meat shrinks in the pot, your downfall is assured. If it swells, you'll experience prosperity.

Your Body

If your stomach didn't produce a new layer of mucus every two weeks, it would digest itself.

Every day an adult body produces 300 billion new cells.

When your face blushes, the lining of your stomach turns red, too.

Nearly everyone's right lung is bigger than their left lung.

A single isolated heart cell will "beat" for as long as it has a fresh supply of blood.

Side by side, 2,000 cells of the human body would cover about one square inch.

Your kidneys, weighing about five ounces each, process about 425 gallons of blood a day.

Your liver—the largest organ in your body—processes about a quart of blood a minute.

The acid in your stomach is strong enough to dissolve razor blades.

You'll take about 23,000 breaths today.

You exhale air at an average speed of four miles per hour.

Your stomach has 35 million digestive glands.

Two percent of Americans have an extra nipple somewhere on their body.

Pain travels through your body at a rate of 350 feet per second.

The largest cell in the human body is a female egg. The smallest is a male sperm.

A full bladder is about the size of a softball.

Tendons, which anchor muscle tissue to bones, have half the tensile strength of steel.

You use about 200 muscles each time you take a step.

Your body uses 300 muscles to balance itself when you're standing still.

Skin & Bones

You can sweat as much as three gallons of water a day in a hot climate.

The thickest skin on your body is on your foot. It's three times thicker than the skin on your palms.

Ichthyosis is the condition that gives human skin the appearance of fish scales.

The average person's skin weighs twice as much as their brain.

The average person sheds 40 pounds of dead skin in their lifetime.

Technical term for goose bumps: horripilation.

Muscle cells live as long as you do. Skin cells live less than 24 hours.

In the old days, freckles were called moth-patches and were considered an affliction.

Draw a one-inch by one-inch square on your forehead. That square is home to 8 million bacteria.

Take your weight, multiply it by 0.6. That's roughly how many pounds of water are in your body.

If you're typical, your body contains about four ounces of salt.

* * *

GROSSEST FACT IN THIS BOOK:

You inhale about 700,000 of your own skin flakes daily.

The Friendly Skies

Two years before he made his first flight, Wilbur Wright told friends, "man won't fly for 50 years."

The Wright brothers made four flights on December 17, 1903. The first was the shortest.

Charles Lindbergh carried a Felix the Cat doll with him on his famous flight.

Henry Ford was Charles Lindbergh's first passenger in the *Spirit of St. Louis*.

Charles Lindbergh's first words after his historic flight: "Are there any mechanics here?"

First pilot ever to fly a loop-the-loop: Lincoln Beachy, November 18, 1913, in San Diego.

On February 18, 1930, a cow flew in an airplane for the first time.

First animal to be ejected from a supersonic jet: a bear, in 1962. It parachuted safely to earth.

Castor oil is used as a lubricant in jet planes.

The higher a plane flies, the less fuel it uses.

Every year, more than 500,000 passengers are bumped from U.S. airlines due to over-booking.

Air Canada was the first North American airline to ban smoking.

Fourteen of the world's 20 busiest airports are located in the United States.

In an average hour, there are 61,000 Americans airborne over the United States.

Myth America

TAKING A STAND

Myth: Custer's Last Stand at Little Bighorn was a heroic effort by a great soldier.

Truth: General George Armstrong Custer had unwarranted contempt for the American Indians' fighting ability. His division was supposed to be a small part of a major attack led by General Alfred Terry, who was planning to meet Custer in two days with his troops. Custer was instructed to wait for Terry. Instead, he led his 266 men into battle. They were all slaughtered.

REPUTATION ON THE LINE

Myth: Henry Ford invented the auto assembly line.

Truth: No, chalk this one up to Ransom E. Olds, creator of the Oldsmobile. Olds introduced the moving assembly line in the early 1900s and boosted car production by 500 percent. The previous year the Olds Motor Vehicle Company had turned out 425 cars. The year after, they made more than 2,500 of them. Ford improved Olds's system by introducing the conveyor belt, which moved both the cars and needed parts along the production line. The belt cut Ford's production time from a day to about two hours. A significant contribution, but not the original.

WITCH HUNT

Myth: Witches were burned at the stake during the Salem witch trials of 1692.

Truth: No witches were ever burned in Salem. A hundred fifty men and women were arrested under suspicion of witchcraft. In all, 19 people and two dogs were put to death as "witches and warlocks," all of them hanged except for one person, who was pressed to death by stones. Ten others were convicted, but not put to death. A few months later the governor of Massachusetts dissolved the witch court. The judges didn't mind; they were running out of people to accuse.

RECLUSE
Myth: While writing *Walden*, Henry David Thoreau lived in isolation in the woods of Massachusetts.
Truth: Thoreau's two-year retreat to Walden Pond was like a little boy pretending that his backyard tree house is in the middle of the jungle. In truth, Thoreau built his famous cabin a scant two miles from his family's home and spent very little time in isolation. "It was not a lonely spot," wrote Walter Harding in *The Days of Henry Thoreau*. "Hardly a day went by that Thoreau did not visit the village or was visited at the pond." Thoreau was even known to return home on the weekends to raid the family cookie jar.

INCOGNITO
Myth: To escape Union capture, Confederate president Jefferson Davis fled Richmond disguised in his wife's dress.
Truth: Rather than admit defeat by surrendering to the Union army, Davis fled to Texas with the hope of reorganizing his troops. However, on May 10, 1865, he was apprehended in Georgia. Clad in a gray suit as he hastily greeted the Union troops, he accidentally grabbed his wife's cloak to protect him from the cold. Secretary of War Edwin M. Stanton presented the false story of Davis disguising himself in a dress to the *New York Herald*, which published it on May 16, 1865.

ROBIN HOOD
Myth: "Jesse James was a man who killed many a man. / He robbed the Glendale train. / He stole from the rich and he gave to the poor. / He'd a hand and a heart and a brain."
Truth: Jesse Woodson James, who was born in Missouri in 1847, did indeed rob from the rich. Most of the money that he stole, however, he kept for himself. A child of slave-owning aristocrats, Jesse James made a name for himself as one of the Confederate marauders known as Quantrell's Raiders during the Civil War. His move to robbing banks after the war was inspired by a deep hatred of the Northern industry that was becoming widespread in the pastoral South. It is true that he killed many a man—most of them innocent bystanders.

Europe

Netherlands used to be known as the United States.

Europe is the only continent without a desert.

The Berlin Wall was 26.5 miles long.

Oldest unchanged flag in history: Denmark's. It has remained the same since the 13th century.

Reykjavík, Iceland, one of the coldest cities in the world, is heated almost entirely by hot springs.

The British Isles have no mountains higher than 5,000 feet.

World's largest harbor: Rotterdam Harbor in the Netherlands.

Florence, Italy, was the first city in Europe to have all of its streets paved.

Europe is the most densely populated continent in the world.

The world's largest cemetery: the Friedhof Ohlsdorf in Hamburg, Germany. It covers 990 acres.

Many restaurants in France allow dogs and even offer special menus for them.

Denmark has the highest income tax in the world, as high as 52.6 percent.

Finland has more islands than any other country: 179,584.

Largest empire in all of human history: the British empire of the 19th century.

Venice, Italy, is built in a lagoon on top of 118 islands.

Biggest French-speaking city: Paris. Second: Montreal.

England is two-thirds the size of the New England states.

Netherlands is the only country with a national dog: the Keeshond.

Parks & Recreation

The federal government owns about 29 percent of the land in the United States.

If any of the heads on Mt. Rushmore had a body, it would be nearly 500 feet tall.

Big Bend National Park (Texas) is home to 350 species of birds—more than any other national park.

There are 898 steps in the Washington Monument.

More than half of all the geysers in the world are in Yellowstone National Park.

The U.S. Capitol has 365 steps—one for each day of the year—from the basement to the top of the dome.

Number of marine wildlife sanctuaries in the United States where fishing is illegal: zero.

Officially designated wilderness in the United States: 4.7 percent.

Walt Disney World generates about 56 tons of trash every day.

At last count, 1,013 buildings in the United States have a sign that reads "George Washington slept here."

Disney World is twice the size of Manhattan.

Cost of a single-day ticket to Disneyland in 1955: $10. In 2005: $56.

* * *

REDUNDANCIES

old fossil
new beginning
fellow countrymen
appreciated in value
3 a.m. in the morning

old geezer
illegal scam
successful escape
strangled to death
awkward predicament

Super Bowl

Each year Americans consume 8 million pounds of guacamole on Super Bowl Sunday.

New York jewelers Tiffany & Co. are responsible for making the Super Bowl trophy.

Electronics companies sell five times as many big-screen TVs during Super Bowl week.

The Super Bowl is broadcast to over 182 countries in the world.

Roger Staubach holds the record for most career Super Bowl fumbles, with five.

The average Super Bowl get together includes 18 people.

Advertisers pay an average of just over $2 million per 30-second commercial during a Super Bowl game.

The Dallas Cowboys have played in a record eight Super Bowls and have won five of them.

The largest margin of victory in a Super Bowl is 45 points. In Super Bowl XIV, the San Francisco 49ers defeated the Denver Broncos 55–10.

Joe Montana is the only player to be named Super Bowl MVP three times. He won all three awards while playing quarter-back for the San Francisco 49ers.

Steve Cristie kicked the longest field goal in Super Bowl history, in 1994: 54 yards.

More than 86 million Americans watched the Super Bowl in 2005.

What's in the Drain?

Believe it or not, Roto Rooter claims they've found the following items in clogged pipes:

HOME AND GARDEN: Broom handles, doorknobs, garden hoses, bungee cords, and a hummingbird feeder.

HEALTH AND BEAUTY AIDS: Glass eyes, gold teeth, dentures, contact lenses, toothbrushes, hearing aides, and toupees.

CLOTHING AND LINENS: Women's lingerie, long johns, towels, robes, a complete bedspread, and, of course, a multitude of missing socks.

ELECTRONICS: TV remotes, pagers, an alarm clock, a Timex that took a licking and kept on ticking, and a Rolex that took a licking and died.

SPORTING GOODS AND TOYS: An eight ball, golf balls (30 in one drain), a shrimp net, a tear-gas projectile, and a Teenage Mutant Ninja Turtle doll.

PETS: Birds, bats, beavers, cats, ducks, fish, frogs, possums, skunks, a piranha, a two-and-a-half-pound trout, and lots of snakes—including a 6-foot rattlesnake.

VALUABLES: $400 in coins, $58 in change in a Laundromat pipe, canceled checks, a $4,000 diamond, and $50,000.

GROCERIES: A Cornish game hen and a six-pack of Budweiser.

Storms

In 10 minutes, a hurricane releases more energy than all the world's nuclear weapons combined.

More ships have been sunk by hurricanes than by warfare.

Dust storms in Arizona caused 119 car crashes in 2003.

The state with the most lightning and thunderstorms: Florida, the "Sunshine State."

Ninety percent of all the tornadoes in the world occur in the United States.

At this moment, nearly 2,000 thunderstorms are taking place around the world.

About 65 percent of all hurricanes tracked since 1900 have occurred in August and September.

More thunderstorms—3,000 a day—hit the tropics than any other place on earth.

The Australians used to name hurricanes after unpopular politicians.

In Australia the term for a hurricane is *Willy Willy*.

At any given moment, about half of the earth is covered by clouds.

Tornadoes move with wind speedsof from 100 to 300 mph.

An estimated 25 million cloud to ground lightning bolts kill an annual average of 73 people in the U.S.

An average spot on earth receives 33.86 inches of rain and precipitation annually.

Scientists learn about the moisture in clouds by studying the dew on spiderwebs.

Odds that a thunderstorm will strike Daytona, Florida, in the next four days: 100 percent.

Bug Off!

Cockroaches stowed away on the *Apollo XII* flight.

A flea can jump 30,000 times without taking a break.

The first job of a newborn queen bee is to kill the other newborn queens so she can rule alone.

Queen bees only sting other queen bees.

There are 290,000 beetle species on earth, the most of any animal.

If a grasshopper is hungry enough, it will eat the paint off your house.

Most snails are born with their shells.

The average caterpillar has 2,000 muscles in its body. The average human, less than 700.

A female flea can drink 15 times her weight in blood
a day.

Queen termites can lay 86,000 eggs a day.

Constipation kills more fruit flies than any other ailment.

REM

It wasn't until 1954 that scientists recognized that REM (rapid eye movement) during sleep was caused by dreaming. Here's more:

Once you're in REM the muscles of your middle ear begin vibrating (scientists don't know why). Pulse and breathing speed up. (But we breathe less oxygen and use fewer calories than in other stages of sleep.) Eyes dart all over the place, "seeing" what we're dreaming.

We can dream without REM, but scientists have established that these dreams are simple and uneventful. REM dreaming, on the other hand, is the more exciting, dramatic kind. We do REM dreaming about two hours a night. In a lifetime, this adds up to five or six years of REM dreaming.

You may think that because your body seems to go off-line, your mind does, too. Not so. Your brain spends the night integrating the information and experiences you've gained during the day, and most of this happens during REM sleep. Laboratory tests showed that if mice learned complex tasks and then were deprived of their REM time, they forgot what they learned. In tests on University of Ottawa students, researchers noticed that the faster students learned things, the more REM time they required. Slower learners needed less REM time.

Life stresses and changes also increase the need for REM. Using a group of divorcing women in their early 30s as subjects, psychoanalyst Rosalind Cartwright conducted a study that demonstrated they needed more REM time to assimilate their big changes.

Most people don't reach REM until about an hour and a half after going to sleep; people with depression, however, get to REM in about half that time. They also experience it more intensely.

REM occupies approximately 22 percent of sleeping time.

Call the Doctor

The longest case of constipation ever recorded lasted 102 days.

The longest recorded sneezing fit was 978 consecutive days.

According to Guinness, the longest recorded bout of hiccups lasted for 65 years.

People with brain disorders suffer from far fewer headaches than the general public.

As far as anyone can tell, only humans get headaches.

Big blisters are called vesicles; small ones are called bullae.

Ten body parts have three-letter names: eye, hip, arm, leg, ear, toe, jaw, rib, lip, gum.

Only 33 percent of patients admitted to emergency rooms for heart attacks have actually had one.

The first open-heart surgery was performed in 1893.

The most common disease in the world: tooth decay.

* * *

SUPERSTITIOUS?

Stuffing a cat's tail up your nose will cure a nosebleed.

It's bad luck to see three butterflies on one leaf at the same time.

Carrying a badger's tooth brings good luck, especially at gambling.

To make a sleeping woman talk, put a frog's tongue on her heart.

Pictures of an elephant bring good luck, but only if they face a door.

A Spider's Web

Although it's only about 0.00012 inch in diameter, a spider's silk is stronger than steel of equal diameter. It is more elastic than nylon, more difficult to break than rubber, and is bacteria and fungi resistant. These qualities explain why at one time web was used to pack wounds—to help mend them and stop bleeding.

Spiders have up to six types of spinning glands, each producing a different type of silk. For instance, the cylindrical gland produces silk used for egg sacs (males often lack this) and the aciniform gland produces silk used for wrapping prey. Some spiders have glands that produce very fine silk. They comb and tease the fine strands until it's like Velcro—tiny loops and hooks that entrap insect feet.

Silk is extruded through special pores called spinneretes which consist of different sized "spigots." Silk starts out as a liquid. As the liquid silk contacts the air, it hardens. The spider may need different silk for different purposes. By changing how fast the liquid is extruded or by using a different silk gland, it can control the strength and quality of the silk.

Why doesn't a spider get stuck on its own web? The spider weaves in nonsticky silk strands and only walks on those. Also, spiders have a special oil on their legs that keeps them from sticking.

The spider is a hunter and its web is a snare, designed to hold its prey. So the design of its web and the place where the spider builds it depend on the kind of insects it is trying to catch.

Male spiders of some species use vibrations to communicate to the female. They strum the female's web and must send just the right vibration to convince the female that they are mates . . . and not dinner.

Education

The students at the first Montessori school were the underprivileged preschoolers of Rome's slums.

Schoolhouses were traditionally painted red because it was the cheapest color available.

The first chalkboard was used in a school in 1714.

Dartmouth was the last Ivy League college to go coed. It held out until 1972.

In 2004, for the first time in its history, Harvard admitted more women than men to its freshman class.

Every year Harvard University denies admission to an estimated 80 percent of the high school valedictorians who apply.

Thirty-five percent of American students don't like to go to school.

Sixty-one percent of American students find school boring.

Of all the students in the world, Americans spend more school time in physical education: 12 percent. France and New Zealand are next, with 11 percent.

The average American spends 15.2 years of his or her life at school. Norwegians spend the longest of any country: 16.9 years.

The most common school colors in the United States are white and blue.

A quarter of America's college students hold full-time jobs.

Three out of four college students expect to become millionaires.

On average, college grads earn $1.4 million in their lifetime. Grad school grads: $3 million.

March of Science

In July 1981 Japanese factory worker Kenji Urada became "the first known fatality caused by a robot."

Australia has a robot that shears sheep. Japan has one that makes sushi.

As of 2005 there were more cell phones in the United Kingdom than people.

There are more telephones than people in Washington, D.C.

The first e-mail was sent over the Internet in 1972.

Grace Hopper coined the term *computer bug* when a moth shorted out her computer.

The world's highest public telephone booth is on the Siachen Glacier in India.

In 1997 about one third of American homes had computers. In 2005 it was two thirds.

A $100,000 computer 20 years ago computed about as much as a $10 chip can today.

Finland is the only nation in the world that has more cell phones than regular phones.

Worldwide an estimated 85 percent of all phone calls are conducted in the English language.

The distress signal before SOS: CQD— "Come quick danger."

In Saudi Arabia there are solar-powered pay phones in the desert.

In 1995, personal computers outsold televisions in the United States, and the number of e-mail messages exceeded stamped letters.

On an average weekday, people in New York City make 36 million phone calls.

About half the world's telephones are in the United States.

The Bard

More than 40 states have Shakespeare theater companies and/or annual festivals honoring the Bard.

Second most-published playwright in history, after Shakespeare: Neil Simon.

During his lifetime, Shakespeare's last name was spelled 83 different ways.

William Shakespeare earned about $40 a year from his writing.

Shakespeare's son's name was Hamnet, just one letter away from *Hamlet*.

Shakespeare's love sonnet "Shall I compare thee to a summer's day . . ." was written to a young man.

Hamlet has been made into more films than any other Shakespeare play: 49.

There are no real known images of Shakespeare.

Not one of the characters in Shakespeare's plays smokes.

Longest word used by Shakespeare: honorificabilitudinitatibus. It means "with honor." James Joyce also used it in *Ulysses*.

London's Globe Theatre burned to the ground in 1613 during a performance of *King Henry VIII*, the last play Shakespeare wrote.

William Shakespeare and Miguel de Cervantes died on the same day in 1616.

At the Library

The total number of original books that have been published: 65 billion.

Number of books in print in 1948: 78,000. In 2005: more than 1.8 million.

The Library of Congress has 530 miles of bookshelves.

One out of every four books sold in the United States is a mystery or suspense novel.

The average American adult can read between 150 and 200 words a minute.

Americans bought $23.7 billion worth of books in 2004.

The average American household has 15 cookbooks.

In the last five years 70 percent of adult Americans have not been in a bookstore.

The average dictionary contains entries for 278,000 words.

First nationwide best-selling book in the United States: the memoirs of Ulysses S. Grant.

Top-selling comic book of all time: *X-Men #1*: 8.1 million copies.

One third of high school graduates never read another book.

Twenty percent of all publications sold in Japan are comic books.

The CliffsNotes edition of *The Scarlet Letter* outsells Nathaniel Hawthorne's book three to one.

Seventy percent of books published do not earn back their advance.

Women buy 55 percent of the fiction sold.

The first American cookbook, *The Compleat Housewife*, was published in 1746.

Men Are From Mars

Men gamblers bet more money when they bring their wives.

Men without hair on their chest are more likely to get cirrhosis of the liver than men with hair.

Forty-eight percent of men believe balding has a negative effect on business and social relationships.

Eighty-five percent of obscene phone calls are made by males.

Most common plastic surgery performed on American men: liposuction.

If a man's tie is too tight, his vision gets worse.

If the average male never shaved, his beard would be 13 feet long the day he dies.

The average American man has $27 in his wallet right now.

Forty-three percent of single American men say they didn't go on a date in 2001.

The average single man is one inch shorter than the average married man.

If you're an average American male, you'll spend 2,965 hours shaving in your lifetime.

Most married men sleep on the right side of the bed. Divorced men often switch to the left.

When you adjust for the weight difference, men are stronger than horses.

In 1898 all cheerleaders were male. Today 3 percent are.

Nineteen percent of men say they wouldn't mind being stupid, "as long as they had a perfect body."

Triskaidekaphobia

Fear of the number 13 originated in Norse mythology. Aegir summoned 12 gods to a banquet in Valhalla. Guest number 13 showed up uninvited: Loki, god of evil.

Another possible connection comes from Christianity. Jesus and the 12 apostles dined together at the Last Supper, Judas, Christ's betrayer, being the 13th.

Predating the Christians, the Turks hated the number 13 so much that it was almost expunged from their vocabulary.

The Romans associated the number 13 with death and misfortune. There were 12 months in a year and 12 hours in a day (according to the Roman clock), so 13 was seen as a violation of the natural cycle.

For ancient Egyptians, 13 represented the final rung of the ladder by which the soul reached eternity.

Even before that, at religious feasts in ancient Babylon, 13 people were selected to represent the gods. At the end of the ceremony, the 13th "god" was put to death.

Thirteen is the number of members in a witch's coven.

According to *The Encyclopedia of Superstitions,* if 13 people gather in a room, one will die within a year. In 1798, *Gentleman's Magazine* explained the superstition by saying: "It seems to be founded on calculations adhered to by insurance offices."

The 13th card in the tarot deck is the skeleton—Death.

On the other hand, consider the ill-fated *Apollo 13* lunar mission, which left the launchpad at 13:13 hours on April 13 . . . and then exploded, almost killing the entire crew.

Ice Cream Treats

ICE CREAM SODAS
In 1874 soda-fountain operator Robert M. Green sold a drink he made out of sweet cream, syrup, and carbonated soda water. One day he ran out of cream . . . so he used vanilla ice cream instead.

ESKIMO PIES
Christian Nelson owned a candy and ice cream store in Onawa, Iowa. One day in 1920 a kid came into the store and ordered a candy bar . . . and then changed his mind and asked for an ice-cream sandwich . . . and then changed his mind again and asked for a marshmallow nut bar. Nelson wondered why there wasn't any one candy-and-ice-cream bar to satisfy all of the kid's cravings—and then decided to make one himself: a vanilla bar coated with a chocolate shell. Once he figured out how to make the chocolate stick to the ice cream, he had to think of a name for his product. At a dinner party someone suggested *Eskimo*, because it sounded cold. But other people thought it sounded too exotic—so Nelson added the word *pie*.

SUNDAES
In the 1890s many religious leaders objected to people drinking ice cream sodas on Sunday. It was too frivolous. When "blue laws" were passed prohibiting the sale of the sodas, ice-cream parlor owners created the "Sunday," which was only sold on the Sabbath; it contained all of the ingredients of a soda except the soda water. A few years later the dish was being sold all week, so the name was changed to sundae.

BASKIN-ROBBINS 31 FLAVORS
After World War II, Irvine Robbins and Burton Baskin built a chain of ice cream stores in Southern California. One day in 1953, Robbins says, "we told our advertising agency about our great variety of flavors and we said, almost in jest, that we had a flavor for every day of the month—thirty-one. They hit the table and said that was it, the thirty-one. So we changed the name of the company to Baskin Robbins 31. Like Heinz 57."

Shark Attack!

Sharks can detect the heart-beats of other fish.

Mako sharks have been known to jump into the fishing boats that are pursuing them.

Approximately 10 times more men than women are attacked by sharks.

While in a feeding frenzy, some sharks bite their own bodies as they twist and turn.

A 730-pound mako shark caught off Bimini in the Bahamas contained in its stom-ach a 120-pound swordfish, with the sword still intact.

Sharks have a sixth sense. They can navigate by sensing changes in the earth's magnetic field.

Greenland sharks have been observed eating reindeer that have fallen through ice.

Three men who spent five days adrift in the Atlantic in 1980 had a shark to thank for their rescue. They fell asleep, but when the attacking shark nudged their raft, they woke up in time to flag down a pass-ing freighter.

Some sharks can detect one part of blood in 100 million parts of water.

Bull sharks have been known to pursue their victims onto land.

The jaws of an eight-foot shark exert a force of 20 tons per square inch.

The average shark can swallow anything half its size in one gulp.

The original idea for steak knives derived from shark teeth.

Sharks will continue to attack even when disemboweled.

It's Slinky

When the Slinky first hit the shelves of Macy's department store in New York City in 1949, the toy was so popular they had to be removed from the store's shelves because the crowds of people were creating a fire hazard.

Slinkys have been used as makeshift radio antennae for soldiers during the Vietnam War, and as therapeutic tools for stroke victims.

All of the following Slinky toys have really been made: gold-plated Slinkys, felt-covered Slinky Pets with animal faces and tails, even a Slinky board game called the Amazing Slinky Game.

In 1999 Slinky appeared on a U.S. postage stamp.

It takes 80 feet of wire to make a Slinky.

Richard James, inventor of the Slinky, did not name the new toy. His wife, Betty, found the word in the dictionary—it took her two days of searching before she found the right word to describe the toy.

Slinky was taken aboard a NASA space shuttle to test the power of a Slinky in zero gravity.

* * *

PRECIOUS DETAILS

The ridges on the edges of coins are called "reeds." They were added to metal currency to deter counterfeiting and to prevent people from shaving the precious metals off the rims. Despite the fact that coins are no longer made of pure metals, the reeds remain.

Dime: 118 reeds

Quarter: 119 reeds

Half dollar: 150 reeds

Susan B. Anthony dollar: 133 reeds

Tax Dollars at Work

In 1789 the total U.S. federal government debt was $190,000.

The IRS estimates that $20 to $40 billion are lost to tax fraud every year.

In 1952 Albert Einstein called income taxes "the most difficult thing to understand."

There are 284 bathrooms in the Pentagon.

There are 412 doors in the White House.

Sixty-five percent of all paper bought by the federal government is used by the Defense Department.

Taxpayers spent $57,000 on gold-embossed playing cards for *Air Force One* in 1992.

When astronauts returned from the moon, they had to file a customs report declaring the moon rocks they brought back.

According to one government study, pigs can become alcoholics.

The U.S. government spent $277,000 on "pickle research" in 1993.

The United States spends $40 billion a year collecting "intelligence" from around the world.

The White House was known as the White House even before it was painted white.

The Pentagon spends $8,612 every second.

The Pentagon spent $50 million on Viagra for American troops and retirees in 1999.

George W. Bush's 2001 tax cut added 14,368 pages to the U.S. Tax Code.

NASA spent $200,000 on a "sanitary napkin disposal unit" for female astronauts in 1992.

Sleep

The higher your IQ, the more you dream.

If you're an average sleeper, you'll roll over 12 times in bed tonight.

In 1900 the average American slept 9 hours, 20 minutes. Now it's 7 hours, 20 minutes.

One in 10 children sleepwalks.

It takes the average person seven minutes to fall asleep each night.

According to doctors, babies dream in the womb.

Do you have insomnia? Some experts suggest wearing mittens and socks to bed.

There are more than 300 patents on antisnoring devices.

If you drop off to sleep as soon as you go to bed, it's a sign that you're sleep deprived.

Quitting smoking can reduce the amount of sleep you need each night by as much as an hour.

More than 50 percent of Americans fall asleep on their sides.

Only about 5 percent of people dream in color.

It's impossible to snore in the weightlessness of space.

The average adult has four dreams a night and one nightmare a year.

If you go without sleep for 10 days straight, you could die.

Mr. President

John Quincy Adams and Dwight D. Eisenhower have been the only bald presidents, thus far.

Thomas Jefferson invented a coding device called the "wheel cipher." It's still used by the U.S. Navy.

Thomas Jefferson and John Adams both died on July 4, 1826.

Herbert Hoover never accepted his presidential salary. He turned it over to charity instead.

Woodrow Wilson was the last president to type all of his own letters.

Calvin Coolidge was born on the Fourth of July.

Franklin Delano Roosevelt was elected president four times but never carried his home county—Duchess County, New York.

Franklin Delano Roosevelt's favorite food: fried cornmeal mush. Eisenhower's: prune whip.

Dwight Eisenhower helped popularize Izod alligator shirts.

John F. Kennedy and his staff played touch football on the White House lawn.

Lyndon Johnson used to give electric toothbrushes with presidential seals as gifts.

Texas-born Lyndon Johnson inspired a boom in cowboy hats.

Hearing aid sales rose 40 percent when Ronald Reagan got his.

George H. W. Bush was the youngest navy pilot of World War II. He enlisted on his 18th birthday, June 12, 1942.

Bill Clinton once called a proposed new tax a "wage-based premium."

Geology 101

If a volcano has erupted within the last 10,000 years, it's considered active.

Shifts in the earth's crust have moved the pyramids of Egypt three miles south in 4,500 years.

Only 6 percent of land on earth is suitable for growing crops.

If scientists didn't know a fault was there until an earthquake hit, it's called a "blind" fault.

The earth is 100 million years older than the moon.

The Rock of Gibraltar is mostly gray limestone.

The earth weighs an estimated 100,000 tons more than it did a year ago.

The continent of Australia is drifting northward at a rate of 2.25 inches per year.

Iceland has so much geothermal power that it plans to end fossil fuel use by 2030.

Fingers & Toes

The pores in your feet release about a quarter cup of sweat a day.

There are 250,000 sweat glands in a pair of human feet, more than any other part of the body.

Injured fingernails grow faster than uninjured ones.

If you never trimmed your fingernails, on your 80th birthday they'd be about 13 feet long.

Fingers don't have muscles.

Your fingernails are made from the same substance as a bird's beak.

Humans are the only primates that don't have pigment in the palms of their hands.

Fingernails grow 1/25 of an inch per week.

If you're like most people, your fingernails grow four times as fast as your toenails.

Ingrown toenails are hereditary.

There's an estimated 1 trillion bacteria on each of your feet.

Hand surgeons say that if you had to lose a finger, the index finger is the best one to lose.

In hand-to-hand combat, left-handed people are more likely to survive.

Horizontal ridges on your fingernails are indicators of high stress.

McDonald's

When the first McDonald's opened in Des Plaines, Illinois, in 1955, the hamburgers cost 15¢ each. The first day's take was $366.12.

If you'd spent $2,250 on 100 shares of McDonald's stock when it went public in 1965, your shares would have been worth over $1.8 million as of December 31, 2003.

If you want to manage a McDonald's, you'll train at a Hamburger University either in Oak Brook, Illinois, or in one of the 10 international Hamburger U.'s.

On an average day, McDonald's feeds 43 million people.

McDonald's sells "McSpaghetti" in the Philippines and "McLak" salmon burgers in Norway.

The average American will eat at McDonald's 1,811 times in his or her life.

Only 4 percent of Americans can say they didn't eat at McDonald's last year.

McDonald's makes 40 percent of its profits from Happy Meals.

McDonald's is the largest single purchaser of American beef, buying nearly 1 billion pounds per year.

There are an average of 178 sesame seeds on a McDonald's Big Mac bun.

World's highest fast-food restaurant: McDonald's in La Paz, Bolivia, at 11,000 feet above sea level.

December 10, 2005: McDonald's opened its first drive-thru in China.

The Plant World

Poison oak is not an oak and poison ivy is not an ivy. Both are members of the cashew family.

The thickest tree on earth: El Tule, a cypress in Mexico. It has a girth of 138 feet.

The squirting cucumber can shoot its seeds up to 40 feet.

Half of the genes in a banana are the same as in a human.

Lemons contain more sugar than strawberries do.

The sap from the Venezuelan cow tree looks, feels, and tastes like cow's milk.

If you plant bamboo today, it may not sprout flowers and produce seeds for 100 years.

A tree planted near a streetlight will keep its leaves longer into the fall than other trees.

The trunk of the African baobab tree can grow as large as 100 feet in circumference.

A single mushroom can produce as many as 40 million spores in an hour.

A 4,770-year-old bristlecone pine named Methuselah is the oldest living thing on earth.

In the densest jungle, only 1 percent of sunlight ever reaches the forest floor.

The Eyes Have It

If you're an average blinker, your eyes will be blinked closed for about 30 minutes today.

As you read this sentence, your eyes are moving back and forth 100 times per second.

Your eyes don't freeze in the cold because of the salt in your tears.

One in 500 people have one blue eye and one brown eye.

A human eyeball weighs about an ounce.

A black eye is called a bilateral perorbital hematoma.

Blue eyes have less pigment in them than brown eyes.

In 2005, about 177 million out of the estimated 287 million U.S. population are expected to need vision correction.

Forty-five million baby boomers age 35 to 49 wear spectacles or contact lenses.

Almost half of Americans would consider wearing glasses as a fashion accessory, even if they didn't need them.

About a third of the human race has 20/20 vision.

If you go blind in one eye, you'll only lose about one fifth of your vision.

Why does your nose run when you cry? It's excess fluid from your eyes.

Humans are the only mammals that cry tears.

Two out of three adults in the United States will need glasses at some point in their lives.

In 1979 a South African boy was found to have a marigold seed growing from his left eye.

When you're looking at someone you love, your pupils dilate. When you're looking at someone you hate, they do the same thing.

Coffee, Anyone?

People who drink coffee are less likely to commit suicide than people who don't.

The average American drinks 3.4 cups of coffee a day.

Thirty-seven percent of U.S. coffee drinkers use milk and sugar. Twenty-one percent drink it black.

There are 1,000 different chemicals in a cup of coffee—26 of them have been tested to see if they cause cancer in laboratory rats, and 13 of them do.

In the 1820s a temperance movement tried to ban coffee—and nearly succeeded.

Coffee beans aren't beans, they're fruit pits, making coffee the most-consumed fruit in the United States.

Why isn't iron added to milk? Iron-fortified milk turns coffee green.

When coffee first arrived in Europe, it was known as Arabian Wine.

The French writer Voltaire drank 70 cups of coffee a day.

In a 12-year study, it was found that coffee does not—as was previously believed—cause high blood pressure.

Been to a coffee-klatsch lately? The term is from the German *Kaffeeklatsch*, a combination of the words for "coffee" and "gossip."

One teaspoon of liquid nicotine or 1/2 ounce of pure caffeine are considered lethal doses for a 150-pound man.

Soda Pop

Africa's largest private-sector employer is Coca-Cola.

Coca-Cola was originally green.

Dr. Pepper is said to contain 23 fruit flavors. Can you taste them?

World's largest consumer of sugar: Coca-Cola Company. They also buy the most vanilla.

It costs the Coca-Cola Company more to buy the can than to make the cola.

Once America's most popular soft drink, root beer now accounts for less than 4 percent of the national market.

Diet Pepsi was originally called Patio Diet Cola.

In 1900 the average American drank 12 sodas a year. Today it's 600.

Coca-Cola was first marketed in 1885 as a remedy for hangovers and headaches.

Coca-Cola's CEO once told a British newspaper that he wouldn't be happy until people could turn on their taps and get Coke instead of water.

Original name for 7-Up: Bib-Label Lithiated Lemon-Lime Soda.

Root beer was an herbal tea before it was a soda; its creator, Charles Hires, added carbonated water to over 25 herbs, berries, and roots, and the rest is history.

Spice It Up

When Heinz ketchup leaves the bottle, it travels at a rate of 25 miles per year.

Most widely used herb in the world: parsley.

Hottest peppers: habaneros. Sweetest: bells.

Four tablespoons of ketchup contain as much nutrition as a medium-size tomato.

Piperine is the stuff in black pepper that makes you sneeze.

What part of the cinnamon tree is used to make cinnamon? The bark.

Vanilla comes from orchids.

The top-selling spice in the world? Pepper. Mustard comes in second.

When pizza became popular in the United States in the 1930s, sales of oregano shot up 5,200 percent.

Humans and Koshima Island monkeys are the only creatures that intentionally salt their food.

In the 1800s you could buy ketchup flavored with lobster, walnuts, oysters, or anchovies.

Pesto is most often made with basil, but variations can be made using parsley, spinach, or arugula instead.

* * *

WORD PLAY

I spent all of last **evening evening** out the pile.
That poor **invalid**, his insurance is **invalid**.
The bandage was **wound** around the **wound**.
They were much too **close** to the door to **close** it.
That buck sure **does** some odd things around the **does**.
The absentminded **sewer** fell down into the **sewer**.

For the Birds

Ostriches do not bury their heads in the sand.

Female canaries can't sing.

Vultures fly without flapping their wings.

The bones of a pigeon weigh less than its feathers.

Chickens are the only birds that have combs.

Crows don't fly in straight lines.

An ostrich's eyes are bigger than its brains.

There are 4.5 million wild turkeys in the United States.

Approximately 56,000 carrier pigeons "fought" in World War II.

When migrating birds fly in V formation, it increases their range by as much as 70 percent.

Penguins have an organ on their foreheads that desalinizes water.

Egg shells are 90 percent calcium carbonate—the same thing your teeth are made of.

Eagles can't hunt when it's raining.

Hummingbirds hold their nests together with spiderwebs.

In her entire lifetime, a female hummingbird will lay at most two eggs.

The pelican breathes through its mouth because it doesn't have nostrils.

Male birds in Australia have been observed mimicking the sound of a cell phone during courtship.

Sweet Tooth

It takes an estimated 2,893 licks to get to the center of a Tootsie Roll Pop.

Cracker Jack is the world's largest purchaser of popcorn.

The U.S. military specifications for fruitcake are 18 pages long.

In the year 2000, Italian pastry chefs built an edible Ferrari out of 40,000 cream pies.

Per capita, Alaskans eat twice as much ice cream as the rest of the nation.

What's the difference between jam and preserves? Jam has minced fruit; preserves have whole.

Remember tan-colored M&M's? They're gone. They were replaced by the blue ones in 1995.

According to experts, dark chocolate is the candy most likely to cause tooth decay.

Hostess Twinkies are 68 percent air.

Why is pound cake called pound cake? The original recipe called for a pound of butter.

Most popular Popsicle flavor: cherry.

World record for keeping a Lifesaver in the mouth with the hole intact: 7 hours, 10 minutes.

There are 24 flowers on every Oreo cookie.

America's most popular candy bar? Snickers.

It's estimated you'll eat some 35,000 cookies in your lifetime.

Getting Around

The three safest modes of transportation: ship, train, and commercial airplane (in that order).

When filled, the oil tanker *Jahre Viking* weighs 1.13 billion pounds.

Blackbeard's pirate ship was named *Queen Anne's Revenge*.

An American living in Japan in 1869 invented the rickshaw to transport his invalid wife.

The SS in a ship's name stands for "steamship."

In 1870 it took eight days to cross the United States by train.

The world's longest traffic jam was 84 miles long and took place in Japan in 1990.

In skywriting, the average letter is nearly two miles high.

In 1997 three times as many bikes as cars were manufactured.

The 10.1 mile tunnel in Saint Gotthard, Switzerland, is the longest vehicular tunnel in the world.

It is generally agreed that new cars are kept an average of at least five years.

One escalator carries as many people as 13 elevators.

An astronaut can reach the moon in less time than it took a stagecoach to travel the length of Great Britain in the 19th century.

The diesel cruise liner *Queen Elizabeth II* gets six inches to the gallon.

The term *hell on wheels* originally applied to the Union Pacific Railroad's saloon railcars.

How long will a person wait for an elevator without fidgeting? About 40 seconds.

It is estimated that you'll walk more than 65,000 miles in your lifetime.

Modern Symbols

THE PLAYBOY BUNNY
When Hugh Hefner was little, one of his prized possessions was "a blanket with bunnies all over it." Apparently, he never outgrew it—when he started *Playboy* magazine, he used the same bunny as his symbol.

THE JOLLY GREEN GIANT
In the early 1920s the Minnesota Valley Canning Company introduced a large variety of peas to the American market. They called the peas "green giants," and—because the law required it to protect their trademark—they put a picture of a green giant on the label. Oddly enough, the original giant (lifted from a volume of Grimm's Fairy Tales) was white, not green; he looked like a dwarf, not a giant; and he wasn't jolly—he was scowling. His image eventually softened, and he became such a powerful symbol that the company changed its name to the Green Giant Company.

BETTY CROCKER
The Washburn Crosby Company, a Minneapolis flour maker, got so many letters asking for baking advice that, in 1921, they made up a character to write back to consumers. They picked *Betty* because it sounded "warm and friendly," and *Crocker* was picked to honor a former company director. To come up with a signature for Betty (so she could sign "her" letters), the company held a contest for its women employees. The winner—still used today—was submitted by a secretary.

THE PILLSBURY DOUGHBOY
In 1965 Rudy Pera was trying to design an advertising campaign for Pillsbury's new refrigerated dough product . . . but he couldn't think of anything that would make the brand stand out. One day he began playfully pounding on a container of the dough, hoping to drum up ideas. "I imagined what could pop out," he recalls. "A dough man? A dough baker? A dough boy!"

RONALD MCDONALD

Willard Scott, weatherman on NBC's *Today Show*, was the first McClown. Here's the story he tells:

"The folks at the NBC television station in Washington—WRC-TV—had signed on a national kiddie show [called "Bozo the Clown"], and they tapped me to star in the thing . . . I did a lot of personal appearances as Bozo—at shopping malls, local fairs, that sort of thing. After a while a local McDonald's asked me to appear at an opening, and before too long my Bozo was a regular fixture at area franchises. When WRC dropped [the show], McDonald's didn't like the idea of having to drop a successful promotion. They were hooked on clown. And so—you guessed it—Ronald McDonald was born. He was almost christened Donald McDonald, but Ronald sounded just a touch more natural, so we went with that."

THE QUAKER OATS MAN

In 1891 seven oatmeal millers combined to form the American Cereal Company. One of the seven was Quaker Mill of Ravenna, Ohio, which had trademarked the Quaker man 14 years earlier. In 1901 the American Cereal Company changed its name to Quaker Oats, and the Quaker man was revived as its symbol. The real Quakers weren't too happy about this. They tried unsuccessfully to get Congress to prohibit manufacturers from using religious names on products.

* * *

THE COST OF THINGS: 1956

8 1/2-oz. box of Rice Crispies: 25¢.

Pound of steak: 43¢

Avis Rental Car: $5 a day, plus 8¢ a mile

RCA color TV: $795–$895

Median income for men: $3,400

For women: $1,100

The Detroit Tigers major league baseball team:
$5.5 million (a record at the time)

Brainiac

Your brain operates on the same amount of power that would light up a 10-watt lightbulb.

There are about as many nerve cells in your brain as there are stars in the galaxy.

Gesturing with your hands while speaking improves your memory.

Living brain cells are bright pink, not gray. They're about the color of cotton candy.

A newborn baby's brain weighs only three ounces. The average adult's brain weighs three pounds.

Your brain uses 40 percent of the oxygen that enters your bloodstream.

Brain waves have been used to run an electric train.

Your brain is only 2 percent of your body's weight, but uses 20 percent of your energy.

The brain can record about 86 million bits of information each day.

Brain cells are the only human cells that don't reproduce.

Every second, 100,000 chemical reactions occur in your brain.

Every second, your senses send about 100 million different messages to your brain.

It takes about 8/1000 of a second for a human nerve impulse to reach the brain.

The human brain can hold 500 times the information found in a set of *Encyclopaedia Britannica*.

In Vogue

Most types of lipstick contain fish scales as an ingredient.

The heel of a sock is called the "gore."

The first watches (portable clocks) were known as Nürnberg eggs.

In the 1600s in Europe, "fashion" wigs were often made of plaster of paris.

Watches get their name because they were originally worn by night watchmen.

Sneakers get their name because they don't squeak like leather shoes do.

How did Levi's 501 jeans get their name? The new denim's lot number was 501.

Americans spent approximately $250 billion on fashion, apparel, shoes, and accessories in 2000.

The G in G-string stands for "groin."

Clothing is the third most popular item purchased at yard sales.

The trial of O.J. Simpson revealed that there were only 299 pairs of size 12 Bruno Magli shoes ever sold.

The average ten-gallon hat can hold only three quarts of water.

A bolt of cloth is 120 feet long.

It takes between 35 and 60 minks to make a single coat.

Some people in Siberia make clothes out of halibut skins.

The average bra is designed to last for only 180 days of use.

It takes four hours to weave a hula skirt from 60 ti plants. The skirt will only last about five days.

According to a garment industry study, 75 percent of women wear the wrong size bra.

What's in a Name?

Most common first name in the world: Muhammad. Most common last name: Li. About 108 million people have it.

The five most common American surnames: Smith, Johnson, Williams, Jones, Brown.

Twenty-eight percent of Southerners refer to their mothers as Mama. Nine percent of non-Southerners do.

More than 1,000 people belong to the Society of Jim Smiths. All of them are named Jim Smith.

Three percent of all English surnames are derived from animal names.

The name Ann is used as a middle name 10 times more often than as a first name.

When pronounced correctly, Chinese surnames never have more than one syllable.

The most common name for male dogs and cats in the United States is Max.

The most popular names for American children born in 1970 and 1980 were Michael and Jennifer. By 2005 Michael had dropped to 12th place, and Jennifer didn't even make it into the top 100.

The name of the city we call Bangkok is 155 letters long in the Thai language and the longest place name in the world. The people of Thailand shorten it to Krungthep for everyday use.

The most common street name in America is Second Street.

Silly Putty

Binney & Smith, makers of Crayola, own the rights to Silly Putty and produce about 500 pounds of it every day.

Silly Putty comes in 16 different colors including glow-in-the-dark, glitter, and hot fluorescent colors. There's even Silly Putty that changes color depending on the temperature of your hands.

One of the original Silly Putty eggs is on display at the Smithsonian Institution's National Museum of American History.

Over 300 million eggs have been sold since its inception in 1950—enough to form a ball of Silly Putty the size of a Goodyear blimp.

In 1968 *Apollo 8* astronauts used a new adhesive to fasten down tools during their voyage into weightlessness: Silly Putty.

In 1989 a grad student at Alfred University wanted to find out what would happen to a ball of Silly Putty dropped from a roof. He dropped a 100-pound ball from the top of a three-story building. The ball first bounced about eight feet into the air, but it shattered into pieces on the second bounce.

In 2000 Binney & Smith sponsored a "Silliest Uses for Silly Putty Contest." The winner: Replace your stockbroker by throwing a ball of Silly Putty at the stock page in the newspaper and investing in whatever stock it lifts from the newsprint. (Second place went to the woman who suggested it could be used to form a fake swollen gland to get out of an unwanted date.)

In 2001 Silly Putty was inducted into the National Toy Hall of Fame, taking its place beside such classics as G.I. Joe, Lincoln Logs, and Monopoly.

Where in the World?

If you're west of the Ural Mountains, you're in Europe; east of them, you're in Asia.

Damascus, Syria, is the oldest continuously occupied city in the world.

India has an estimated 550 million voters.

At its peak, the Persian empire was roughly two-thirds the size of the United States.

Siberia contains more than 25 percent of the world's forests.

World's highest city: Lhasa, Tibet, at 12,087 feet above sea level.

Mississippi Bay is off the coast of Yokohama, Japan.

The only four countries on earth with one-syllable English names: Chad, France, Greece, and Spain.

China has a longer border than any other country in the world: 13,700 miles.

Twice as many people live in Shanghai, China, as in New York City.

Mongolia is the only country in the world where horses outnumber people.

Most visited mountain on earth: Mount Fuji, in Japan.

Russia's Lake Baikal is deep enough to hold four Empire State Buildings stacked atop each other.

The Pacific Ocean is twice as large as the Atlantic—and larger than all the continents combined.

There are more English speakers in China than in the United States.

For Word Nerds

What's a hooker? An Irish fishing boat with a single mast.

The abbreviation for pound, *lb.*, comes from the astrological sign Libra.

An erythrophobe is someone who blushes easily.

A gnomon is the thing that casts a shadow on a sundial.

In some parts of England garbage collectors are known as swill solicitors.

An exocannibal is a cannibal who eats only enemies. An indocannibal eats only friends.

According to one expert, the most frequently used English noun is *way*.

Illegible handwriting is known as griffonage.

A singulthus is a hiccup.

A gozzard is a person who owns geese.

Mediterranean means "middle of the world." That's what people used to think it was.

Dividing something into squares is known as graticulation.

The handle of a bucket or a kettle is called the bail.

An algologist studies seaweed.

What does genitofemoral neuropathy mean? "Jeans are too tight."

Another word for the crater caused by a meteor: astrobleme.

Siberia means "sleeping land."

Literally translated, hors d'oeuvre means "outside of work."

E Pluribus Unum means "from many, one."

A pulicologist studies fleas.

Bimonthly can mean every other month or twice a month.

I Do

In ancient Greece, tossing an apple to a girl was a marriage proposal. Catching it meant yes.

In ancient Rome, wedding guests wished a bride good luck by breaking the cake over her head.

At Old English weddings, guests threw shoes at the groom.

In the Middle Ages, you were supposed to throw eggs at the bride and groom.

The parents of the groom pay for weddings in Thailand.

Moroccan brides keep their eyes closed during a wedding to avoid the "evil eye."

According to *Brides* magazine, an average wedding costs nearly $19,000.

Impotence is grounds for divorce in 24 states.

The United States is the only western country with restrictions of marriage between cousins. Twenty-four states do not allow first cousins to marry each other.

Five percent of Americans never get married.

Forty percent of Americans say they believe in love at first sight.

Fifty-two percent of soon-to-be grooms and 39 percent of future brides say they'll include the phrase "to honor and obey" in their wedding vows.

Average age of a first-time American bride in 1970: 20.8. In 2003: 27.

States with the three highest divorce rates: Nevada, Arkansas, and Wyoming, in that order.

Myth-Spoken

Line: "That government is best which governs least."
Supposedly Said By: Thomas Jefferson (1743–1826)
Actually: William F. Buckley used this quote in a 1987 newspaper column. He probably took it from Henry David Thoreau, who used it in his 1849 essay "Civil Disobedience." But Thoreau didn't attribute it to anyone in particular. Why did Buckley attribute it to Jefferson? Who knows. Anyway, it was first said by the early American pamphleteer, Thomas Paine.

Line: "Here I stand—warts and all."
Supposedly Said By: Abraham Lincoln (1809–1865)
Actually: Vice President George Bush "quoted" this line in a 1988 campaign speech, but Lincoln never said it. When the *New York Times* called Bush headquarters to question the reference, one of Bush's speechwriters admitted having made up the quote.

Line: "Build a better mousetrap, and the world will beat a path to your door."
Supposedly Said By: Ralph Waldo Emerson (1803–1882), American essayist, philosopher, and poet
Actually: Sarah Yule, a writer, took it from an Emerson lecture and included it in her 1889 book, *Borrowings*, but she got it wrong. What Emerson actually said: "If a man has good corn, or wood, or boards, or pigs to sell, or can make better chairs, or knives, crucibles or church organs, than anybody else, you will find a broad, hard-beaten road to his house, though it be in the woods."

Line: "I can answer you in two words, 'im-possible.'"
Supposedly Said By: Sam Goldwyn (1882–1974), movie mogul
Actually: This is often quoted as one of his famous "Goldwynisms," but he didn't say it. Charlie Chaplin did.

Line: "I wish I'd studied Latin at school so I could talk to you in your own language."
Supposedly Said By: Vice President Dan Quayle to a group of schoolchildren, on a tour of Latin American countries
Actually: It was invented by Democratic congresswoman Pat Schroeder as an attack on Quayle. Even though she publicly apologized to the former VP for the remark, it lives on as a "genuine quote" in popular mythology.

Line: "Everyone talks about the weather, but nobody does anything about it."
Supposedly Said By: Mark Twain (1835–1910)
Actually: Twain was so prolific and so clever that a lot of good quotes are mistakenly attributed to him. But journalist Charles Dudley Warner was the real author of this line. To his credit, Twain never claimed it as his own.

Line: "You can't be too rich or too thin."
Supposedly Said By: The Duchess of Windsor, Wallis Simpson (1896–1986)
Actually: Aside from the fact that the king of England abdicated his throne in order to marry her, this is the only thing the duchess is remembered for. Too bad she didn't say it. Truman Capote said it in 1950 on David Susskind's TV talk show.

* * *

RODENTS

Rats can live longer without water than camels can.

A squirrel can fall as much as 600 feet
to the ground without injuring itself.

The harvest rat spends 22 hours a day looking for food.

Hibernating, a woodchuck breathes 10 times
per hour. Awake, 2,100 times per hour.

Moles are able to tunnel through 300 feet of earth in a day.

On the Small Screen

The Merv Griffin Show's director was Dick Carson, Johnny Carson's brother.

Paul Anka wrote Johnny Carson's *The Tonight Show* theme song.

Big Bird's address: 123 1/2 Sesame Street (zip code unknown).

Gilligan's first name on *Gilligan's Island* was Willy. The skipper's name was Jonas Grumby.

The average *Jeopardy!* winner takes home $11,500 per show.

Sixty percent of the U.S. television viewing audience watched the last episode of M*A*S*H in 1983.

As of 2005 Steve Martin has hosted *Saturday Night Live* the most times: 13.

Jay North, star of TV's *Dennis the Menace*, was also the voice of Bam-Bam Rubble.

The TV show *The Love Boat* was based on a novel.

Nancy Reagan appeared in *Diff'rent Strokes* to tell kids to "Just Say No."

In Arabic countries, *Sesame Street* is known as *Iftah Ya Simsim*.

In 1986, in the very last scene of *Search for Tomorrow*, after 35 years on the air, Stu asks Jo what she is searching for. "Tomorrow," she replies.

* * *

TOO MUCH TV?

According to the A.C. Nielsen Co., the average American watches more than four hours of television each day (that's 28 hours per week, or 2 months of nonstop TV-watching per year). In a 65-year life, that person will have spent nine years glued to the tube.

9 to 5

Seventy-five percent of industrial accidents happen to people who skipped breakfast that morning.

Corporate double-talk for layoff: "career-change opportunity" and "schedule readjustment."

Eighty percent of Americans will be fired from a job at least once in their lives.

Business travelers gain an average of five pounds every year they're on the road.

The top six reasons for being late to work: traffic, oversleeping, procrastination, household chores, car problems, having sex.

Odds that an American worker won't tell his or her spouse after they receive a raise: 36 percent.

One in three companies monitor the e-mails of at least some employees.

Word Origins

£ or lb.
Meaning: Pound
Origin: The abbreviation originates with the Latin phrase *libra pondo*, which means "a unit of measurement by weight." The Romans shortened the phrase to *pondo*, which ultimately became *pound* in English, but the abbreviation of the first word—*lb.*, for *libra*—endured. The symbol for British currency is a stylized *L*, or £, which comes from the same source. The value of the British pound was originally equal to one pound of silver.

V.I.P.
Meaning: Very important person
Origin: This frequently used abbreviation was created during World War II by a British officer in charge of organizing flights for important military leaders. In order to conceal the names from enemy spies, each of these were referred to as a V.I.P. in the flight plan.

Mrs.
Meaning: A married woman
Origin: Originally, *Mrs.* was a shortened version of *mistress*, a word that used to mean "wife" but has since acquired a very different meaning. Strictly speaking, because the word it once abbreviated has changed its meaning, *Mrs.* is no longer an abbreviation—unlike *Mr.*, its male counterpart, which can be spelled out as *Mister*.

K
Meaning: A strikeout in baseball
Origin: In the 1860s when a batter struck out, it was proper to say that he "struck." It was during this era that a newspaperman named Henry Chadwick created symbols for use with his new invention—the box score. He gave each play a letter: *S* for *sacrifice*, *E* for *error*, and so on. Since *S* was already taken, he used the last letter of *struck* instead of the first to abbreviate it: *K*.

Rx
Meaning: A drug prescription
Origin: Actually, there is no *x* in *Rx*. In medieval Latin the first word in medicinal prescriptions directing one to take a specific quantity of a concoction was *recipe*, meaning "take" or "receive." This was later symbolized as an *R* with a slash across its leg. The spelling *Rx* is an attempt to represent this symbol in English letters.

B.O.
Meaning: Body odor
Origin: In 1933 the Lifebuoy Health Soap Company ran a series of radio advertisements containing their new slogan: "Lifebuoy stops B--- O---." A heavy two-note foghorn warning was synchronized with the B.O., giving the phrase a negative spin it has retained ever since.

D-day
Meaning: June 6, 1944, the day Allied forces invaded France during WWII
Origin: The *D* in *D-day* does not stand for *designated* or *defeat*, as many believe, but simply for *day*. D-day actually means "day day." The redundancy comes from the common practice in army correspondence of referring to a top secret time as H-hour or D-day.

XXX
Meaning: Marking on bottles in cartoons to indicate that they contain alcohol
Origin: According to one theory, during the 19th century, breweries in Britain marked their bottles X, XX, or XXX as a sign of alcohol content. The number of Xs corresponded to the potency of the drink.

* * *

THE PEPPER

What's the botanical difference between green peppers, yellow peppers, and red peppers? Only the difference in age. They start out green, then turn yellow, then red, then purple, then brown. As they mature, they get progressively sweeter (until they spoil).

Penny Wise

The first U.S. cent, which was the size of today's 50-cent piece, was coined in 1793. In 1856 the mint produced the first penny of today's size.

Abraham Lincoln was the first president to be depicted on a U.S. coin, a penny issued in 1909. The penny is the only U.S. coin where the person faces right instead of left.

The 1921 Alabama Centennial half-dollar was the first U.S. coin designed by a woman, Laura Gardin Fraser.

When the Citizens Bank of Tenino, Washington, closed on December 5, 1931, the town was without ready cash to do business, so denominations of 25¢, 50¢, and $1 were printed on three-ply Sitka spruce wood, the first wooden money issued as legal tender in the United States.

In 1932 Congress issued a commemorative coin—the Washington quarter—to celebrate the 200th birthday of George Washington. The quarter was intended to be used for only one year, but it was so popular that it was continued as a regular-issue coin from 1934 on.

Booker T. Washington was the first African American to be depicted on a U.S. coin, a half-dollar issued in 1946.

During World War II, the United States minted pennies made of steel, to conserve copper for making artillery shells.

Until 1965, pennies were legal tender only up to 25¢. A creditor couldn't be forced to accept more than 25 pennies in payment of a debt. Silver coins were legal tender for amounts not exceeding $10 in any one payment.

If You...

IF YOU are brushing your hair, it's best to stop after about the 25th stroke. That's the right number for the best distribution of your hair's natural oils. Much more brushing than that can cause damage.

IF YOU have hair growing out of your armpit, you've got hirci. That's the fancy word for armpit hair.

IF YOU are stuck in the grip of a crocodile's jaw, jam your thumbs in its eyeballs. (Good luck.)

IF YOU get a "mustache" from drinking grape or cherry juice, you can quickly wipe it off with a bit of toothpaste dabbed on a washcloth.

IF YOU are an average American, your butt is 15 inches long.

IF YOU sneeze your most powerful sneeze, it'll come flying out of your face at a little more than 100 mph.

IF YOU have to choose between total lack of sleep or food for the next 10 days, go with lack of food. You'll die from total lack of sleep sooner (in about 10 days) than from starvation (a few weeks).

IF YOU are the electrician in charge of the lighting on a movie or TV set, you're a gaffer. If you're an assistant to the gaffer, you're known as the "best boy."

IF YOU weigh 120 pounds on earth, you'd weigh about 20 pounds on the moon.

IF YOU listen to a cricket chirp, you can figure out the temperature. Count the number of chirps per 15 seconds and add 40. That'll give you the temperature (Fahrenheit).

IF YOU are trying to find a tiny object on the floor, put a bare light at floor level. The light will cause the object to cast a shadow, making it easier to spot.

Looney Laws

Swedish law prohibits trained seals from balancing balls on their noses.

In Athens, Greece, you can lose your driver's license for being "poorly dressed" or "unbathed."

Penalty for stealing a rabbit in 19th-century England: seven years in prison.

It's OK to duel in Paraguay as long as you're a registered blood donor.

It's against French law to reveal the true identity of a member of the French Foreign Legion.

It's against the law to slam your car door in Switzerland.

Wearing a necktie in some parts of Iran can get you thrown in jail.

Paris law forbids spinning tops on sidewalks . . . and staring at the mayor.

Nineteenth-century Scottish law required brides to be pregnant on their wedding day.

In England it's against the law to sue the queen—or to name your daughter Princess without the queen's permission.

The law in Teruel, Spain, forbids taking hot baths on Sunday. (Cold baths are OK.)

In Reykjavík, Iceland, it's illegal to keep a dog as a pet.

If you curse within earshot of a woman in Egypt, the law says you forfeit two days' pay.

In Equatorial Guinea, it's illegal to name your child Monica.

Busy as a Bee

Honeybees are not native to North America. They were introduced from Europe in the 1600s by the Puritans.

Bees have different dialects. A German bee cannot understand an Italian bee.

Honey never spoils. In fact, honey placed in tombs in Southampton, England, over 400 years ago, was still good when the tombs were opened.

Bees use ultraviolet vision to see which flowers have the largest amounts of nectar.

A typical American consumes about a pound of honey per year.

A typical worker bee lives for one month and in that time collects enough nectar to make about 1/12 teaspoon of honey.

Honey comes in different colors and flavors—there are more than 300 unique kinds of honey in the United States alone. Why? Honey is made from diverse flower sources—clover, eucalyptus, or orange blossom, for example—and soil chemistry and honeycomb quality also influence how it tastes and looks.

An experiment: Will bees feed from water that's been artificially sweetened with Sweet'N Low? No.

* * *

WHY DO WE FLY FLAGS AT HALF-MAST?

In the days of sailing ships, when someone died on board or a national leader died, ships slackened their rigging, which gave the ship a disheveled look that was supposed to symbolize mourning, "the nautical equivalent of walking around in sackcloth and ashes." Lowering flags partway down the mast was another part of the practice, the only part that survives to this day.

The Lighthouse

No one knows for sure when or where the first lighthouse was built. Early lighthouses were too simple to be recorded; some were little more than candles placed in the windows of tall buildings at night. Others were hilltop structures on which large fires could be built. The earliest known lighthouses were built on the Mediterranean Sea in the 7th century B.C.

The Great Lighthouse at Alexandria, Egypt, was one of the Seven Wonders of the Ancient World. Completed around 280 B.C., it stood about 450 feet high on the island of Pharos in the Alexandria harbor. Still in operation as late as 1115, it was destroyed by earthquakes in the 1300s.

The oldest working lighthouse in the world is Spain's Tower of Hercules, built by the Romans in 20 B.C.

The oldest American lighthouse is the Boston Light, in Boston's outer harbor. Built in 1716 on Little Brewster Island, it was destroyed by the British during the American Revolution. It was rebuilt in 1783 and still stands today.

Before electricity, lighthouses provided light via wood or coal fires, or even candles. These were replaced by whale-oil lanterns, which gave way to kerosene lanterns in the 1800s. Keeping such a light continually lit wasn't easy. In the United States, most lighthouses had a full-time keeper (nicknamed Wickies because they kept the lantern wicks trimmed), who lived at the lighthouse and made sure it stayed lit.

First American lighthouse to use electricity: the Statue of Liberty, which served as a lighthouse in New York Harbor until 1902.

Every working lighthouse in the United States is automated. The last manned lighthouse, Maine's Goat Island Light, became automated in 1990.

No Sweat

In an average day, Americans sweat enough moisture to provide the city of Pittsburgh with a 24-hour supply of water.

When you exercise strenuously in hot weather, you can sweat away as much as two quarts of water in an hour, enough to cause your weight to drop during the workout. But this weight loss is only temporary. Since the weight you lose is all water, you gain it back as soon as you drink liquids and your fluid levels return to normal. Note: Many serious athletes measure their weight immediately before and after their workouts to determine how much water they need to drink to rehydrate themselves. It's about one pint per pound of weight loss.

On average, women can tolerate a body temperature of 1°F higher than men before they break into a sweat. But once they start to perspire, women produce just as much sweat as men do.

Where on your body you sweat the most depends on the reason why you're sweating: Are you hot or nervous? Cooling sweat shows up most on your forehead, upper lip, neck, and chest; nervous sweat appears most in your palms, feet, and armpits.

What is it like to sweat in the weightlessness of space? It's pretty gross . . . at least according to Rhea Seddon, a NASA doctor and astronaut who has flown on the space shuttle *Columbia*. "It pools on your skin and balls up into large, fist-size globules of sweat that sort of land on you. It's kind of yucky."

A Dog Says...

DOG
English: Bow-wow
Swedish: Voff Voff
Hebrew: Hav Hav
Chinese: Wang-wang
Japanese: Won-won
Swahili: Hu Hu Hu Huuu

CAT
English: Meow
Hebrew: Miyau
German: Miau
French: Miaou
Spanish (and Portuguese
and German): Miau

ROOSTER
English: Cock-a-doodle-doo
Arabic: Ku-ku-ku-ku
Russian: Ku-ka-rzhi-ku
Japanese: Ko-ki-koko
Greek: Ki-ki-ri-koo
Hebrew: Ku-ku-ri-ku

DUCK
English: Quack Quack
Swedish: Kvack Kvack
Arabic: Kack-kack-kack
Chinese: Ga-ga
French: Quahn Quahn

OWL
English: Who-whoo
Japanese: Ho-ho
German: Koh-koh-a-oh
Russian: Ookh

FROG
English: Croak
Spanish: Croack
German: Quak-quak
Swedish: Kouack
Russian: Kva-kva

GOOSE
English: Honk Honk
Arabic: WackWack
German: Schnatter-Schnatter
Japanese: Boo Boo

CHICKEN
English: Cluck-cluck
French: Cot-cot-cot-codet
German: Gak-gak
Hebrew: Pak-pak-pak
Arabic: Kakakakakakakakaka

PIG
English: Oink Oink
Russian: Kroo
French: Groin Groin
German: Grunz

U.S. Cities

Detroit has more "registered" bowlers than any other American city.

Fort Worth, Texas, was never a fort.

The U.S. census defines a place with 2,500 people as a town. If it has 2,501 or more, it's a city.

There are over 15,000 miles of neon lights in the signs along the Las Vegas strip.

Ropesville, Lariat, and Loop are all towns in Texas.

The 13th step of the state capitol in Denver, Colorado, is exactly one mile above sea level.

There's a town in Texas called Ding Dong.

The population of Washington, D.C., is greater than the population of Wyoming.

City with the largest Polish population on earth: Warsaw. Second largest Polish population: Chicago.

Florida's Disney World is larger than the entire city of Buffalo, New York.

City with the highest number zip code in the United States: Ketchikan, Alaska—99950.

Most of New York City's Broadway was once known as Bloomingdale Road.

At last count, 167 different languages are spoken in New York City.

Los Angeles is two centimeters closer to San Francisco than it was a year ago.

Future Imperfect

Alepouomancy: Draw a grid in the dirt outside your village. Each square represents a different question. Sprinkle the grid with peanuts, wait for a fox to eat them, then study the fox's footprints to see how the questions are answered.

Alphitomancy: Feed a special cake to an alleged wrongdoer. An innocent person will be able to eat and digest the cake; a guilty person will gag on the cake or become ill.

Bibliomancy: Open the Bible and read the first passage you see to learn your fortune. (In some Christian denominations, this is grounds for excommunication.)

Dilitiriomancy: Feed African benge poison to a chicken. Ask the gods a question, being careful to end the question with, "if the chicken dies, the answer is yes," or "if the chicken dies, the answer is no." Then wait to see if the chicken dies.

Haruspication: Study the guts of an animal, preferably a sacred one.

Hepatoscopy: Study only the animal's liver; ignore the rest of the guts.

Pynchonomancy: Throw darts at a paperback copy of *Gravity's Rainbow,* by Thomas Pynchon, then read the sentence on the deepest page penetrated by the dart.

Scarpomancy: Predict someone's future by studying their old shoes.

Scatomancy: Predict your future by studying your own poop. (Not to be confused with spatulamancy, the study of "skin, bones, and excrement.")

Stichomancy: Read the first passage of any book you see.

Tiromancy: Study the shape, holes, mold, and other features on a piece of cheese to determine your future.

Uromancy: Predict someone's future by studying their urine.

Music Notes

In the 1960s the Rolling Stones began calling themselves the World's Greatest Rock and Roll Band.

Mick Jagger runs the equivalent of five miles on stage during each Rolling Stones concert.

The duo Air Supply ("All Out of Love") played a gig at the Karl Marx Theater in Cuba in July 2005.

Country star Lyle Lovett is afraid of cows.

Loretta Lynn became country music's first millionairess in 1965.

The first female rock singer to be recognized by one name: Annette Funicello. Fans knew her as Annette from *The Mickey Mouse Club* (1955–1959).

The most recent U.S. Air Guitar Championships were held at the Key Club in Los Angeles. The winner: Fatima "Rockness Monster" Hoang.

Willie Nelson's first gig: playing guitar in a polka band.

Most-performed rock song in history: "You've Lost That Lovin' Feeling."

Colonial America

What did all the passengers of the *Mayflower* have in common? None of them had middle names.

Total combined population of the North American colonies in 1610: 350.

Before the American Revolution, there wasn't a single bank in America.

The founding fathers called the American Revolution "The War With Britain."

Twenty-five percent of U.S. territory originally belonged to Mexico.

The city of New Amsterdam changed hands three times between the Dutch and British until finally becoming New York.

Nathan Hale was only 21 when the British hanged him as a spy in 1776.

While America was fighting for its independence, King Kamehameha the Great was conquering and uniting the Hawaiian Islands.

Legend has it that on July 4, 1776, King George III of England noted in his diary: "Nothing of importance happened today." News of America's independence took a few weeks to reach him.

At Valley Forge, Washington's army didn't starve because there was no food. Local farmers preferred to sell it to the British because they had the cash to pay for it.

Say Ahh-h-h .

Human lips don't sweat.

A human jaw can open 30 degrees. A snake jaw can open 130 degrees.

Hardest substance in your body: the enamel in your teeth.

The tongue is the only muscle attached at just one end.

Orthodontic braces were invented in 1728.

The most sensitive part of the tongue is in the back.

Your tongue has 9,000 taste buds.

The enamel on a human tooth is only 1/1,000 of an inch thick.

It takes around 200,000 frowns to create a permanent brow line.

Right-handed people tend to chew their food on the right side; lefties tend to chew on the left.

The two lines that connect the bottom of your nose to your lip are called the philtrum.

Children have more taste buds than adults do.

Seventy-three percent of Americans would rather go grocery shopping than floss.

The Tooth Fairy is paying around $2 per tooth these days.

Forty percent of Americans have never visited the dentist.

In the United States, 5 million teeth are knocked out annually.

Your mouth produces a quart of saliva every day.

All-American Teen

Twenty-two percent of U.S. teenagers can't name the country the United States declared its independence from.

The average U.S. teenage girl owns seven pairs of jeans.

The typical U.S. 18-year-old has spent 11,000 hours in school and 18,000 hours watching TV.

A 2005 survey found that the average American receives his or her first romantic kiss at age 14.

Thirty-eight percent of teenage girls in the United States say they "think about their weight constantly."

American mothers spend an average of 93 minutes with their teens per day. Fathers: 78 minutes.

Ninety-five percent of parents can't identify common chat room lingo that teens use to signify that their parents are watching. BTW, those phrases are POS (Parent Over Shoulder) and P911 (Parent Alert).

About 30 percent of teenage males consistently apply sun protection lotion when sunbathing, compared to 46 percent of female teens.

Teens who eat dinner with their families six or seven nights a week are about half as likely to abuse drugs and alcohol as those dining together twice or less.

Sixty-eight percent of teenage girls said if they could change one body part, it would be their stomach.

Alphabets

In virtually every language on earth, the word for *mother* begins with the letter *m*.

The five least frequently used letters in order: *k*, *j*, *x*, *z*, and *q*.

The five most frequently used letters of the alphabet, in order: *e*, *t*, *o*, *a*, and *n*.

The Phoenicians invented the world's first phonetic alphabet in 2000 B.C.

Chances are that 13 percent of the letters in this book are the letter *e*.

Quotation marks have only been around for 300 years. They're the youngest punctuation marks in the English language.

The oldest letter in the alphabet is *o*. It's more than 3,000 years old.

More words start with the letter *s* than any other letter.

Amharic, the language of Ethiopia, has an alphabet of 267 letters.

The Cambodian language has 72 letters in its alphabet, the most of any language.

J, the youngest letter in the English alphabet, was not added until the 1600s.

There are 12 letters in the Hawaiian alphabet.

There are more than 40,000 characters in Chinese script.

Q is the only letter of the alphabet that doesn't occur in the name of any state.

What five-letter word is pronounced the same when the last four letters are removed? Queue.

Quartzy is the highest-scoring Scrabble word.

So far, there's no official name for the @.

How En-Lightning

Every second there are 100 to 125 flashes of lightning somewhere on earth.

A lightning bolt can be anywhere between 200 feet and 20 miles long, but the average length, cloud-to-ground, is 2 to 10 miles.

Estimated diameter of a lightning channel: 1/2–1 inch.

The chances of being hit by lightning in your lifetime are about 1 in 600,000. Still, anywhere from 500 to 1,000 people are struck by lightning every year in the United States.

The temperature of a lightning strike can reach 50,000°F—hotter than the sun's surface.

Lightning bolts flicker. A flash is a series of strokes that follow the exact same path as the first one. The record number of strokes ever recorded in a single flash is 47.

When you see a lightning flash, count the seconds until you hear the bang of thunder. Divide by five—sound travels about one mile every five seconds—and this will give you an approximation of the storm's distance from you, in miles.

About a quarter of all lightning strikes occur in open fields. Thirty percent happen in July; 22 percent in August.

You can get struck by lightning while you're on the phone. It happens to about 2.5 percent of all lightning-strike victims. You're safer using a cell phone.

Trees are lightning bolts' favorite targets. Proof? Lightning is the largest cause of forest fires in the western United States.

Lightning speeds toward the earth at an average of 200,000 miles per hour.

Candy Origins

BUBBLE GUM
The first bubble gum was invented by Frank Fleer in 1906, but it never made it to market. It was so sticky that the only way to remove it from skin was with vigorous scrubbing and turpentine. It took Fleer more than 20 years to fix the recipe. In 1928 the "new, improved" gum was introduced as Dubble Bubble gum. Fleer made it pink because pink happened to be the only food coloring on the shelf the day the first commercial batch of Dubble Bubble was made. When his gum became the largest selling penny candy on the market, other manufacturers copied it, including the color. Now pink is the standard color for bubble gum.

POPSICLES
Eleven-year-old Frank Epperson accidentally left a mixture of powdered soda mix and water on his back porch one winter night in 1905. The next morning he found the stuff frozen, with the stirring stick standing straight up in the jar. He pulled it out, and had the first Epperson icicle—or Epsicle. He later renamed it Popsicle, since he'd made it with soda pop. It was patented 18 years later, in 1923.

LIFESAVERS
In 1912 Cleveland candy maker Clarence Crane decided to make a mint to sell in the summer. Until then most mints were imported from Europe; Crane figured he could cut the price by making them in the United States. He had the candy manufactured by a pill-maker—who discovered that his machinery would only work if it punched a hole in the middle of each candy. Crane called the mints Lifesavers.

PEZ
Invented in 1927 by Eduard Haas, an Austrian antismoking fanatic who marketed peppermint-flavored PEZ as a cigarette substitute. The candy gets its name from the German word for peppermint, *Pfefferminze*. Haas brought the candy to the United States in 1952.

It bombed, so he reintroduced it as a children's toy, complete with cartoon heads and fruity flavors. (One of the most secretive companies in the United States, PEZ won't even disclose who currently owns the company.)

M&Ms

In 1930 Chicago candy maker Frank Mars told his son Forrest to get out of the country and not come back. Forrest went to England with a few thousand dollars and the recipe for his father's Milky Ways. He set up shop and began selling his own versions of the candy bars. While in Spain, Forrest discovered Smarties, a candy-coated chocolate treat that was popular with the Brits. He bought the rights to market Smarties in America, where he went into partnership with a business associate named Bruce Murrie. The candies were called M&M's, short for Mars and Murtie. In 1964, after much family bickering, the American and British Mars companies merged.

HERSHEY'S

Milton Hershey, the inventor of the Hershey Bar, was an unusual man. As a child he was brought up in a strict Mennonite family. Unlike most entrepreneurs, he never sought the usual material wealth that accompanies success. In 1909 he took a large sum of the money he had earned making candy bars and opened the Milton Hershey School for orphaned boys. Nine years later he donated the candy company to a trust for the school. Today the Milton Hershey School and School Trust still own 56 percent of the Hershey Company.

KRAFT CARAMELS

During the Depression Joseph Kraft started making caramels. He didn't particularly like candy; he just needed another dairy product for cheese sales reps to carry on their routes. The product succeeded because grocers needed a summer substitute for chocolate, which melted in the heat.

THREE MUSKETEERS

Advertising in the 1950s and 1960s suggested that the Three Musketeers got its name because it was big enough for three people to share. The truth is, it was originally made of three separate nougat sections: vanilla, chocolate, and strawberry. Eventually the strawberry and vanilla nougat sections were eliminated, leaving only the chocolate nougat.

Waterworld

The Pacific Ocean covers more of the earth's surface than all the continents combined.

The level of the world's oceans is 500 feet higher than it was 25,000 years ago.

The Atlantic Ocean is saltier than the Pacific Ocean.

For every gallon of seawater, you get more than a quarter of a pound of salt.

There are freshwater springs in the ocean.

At its deepest point, the Pacific Ocean is 36,198 feet deep (about 6.85 miles).

There are as many molecules in one teaspoon of water as there are teaspoons of water in the Atlantic.

Ice covers about 15 percent of the earth's landmass.

Eleven percent of the earth—5.8 million square miles—is covered by glaciers.

Niagara Falls was created by a glacier.

Technically there's only one ocean in the world, since they're all connected.

Mount Irazú in Costa Rica is the only point in the Americas where you can see both the Atlantic and Pacific oceans.

There are more than 30,000 islands in the Pacific Ocean.

All the lakes in the world, fresh- and saltwater combined, equal only .01 percent of the earth's water resources.

Fill your bathtub with water 20,000 times. That much water falls over Niagara Falls every second.

America at War

U.S. military spending, about $276 billion, is the highest in the world—five times higher than China at number 2.

The United States has never lost a war in which mules were used.

Only 16 percent of able-bodied males in the American colonies participated in the Revolutionary War.

Cost per day of fighting the Revolutionary War: $20,411. World War II: $409.4 million.

There were 840 soldiers in the regular army when the U.S. War Department was established in 1789.

The Confederate flag had 13 stars, but there were only 11 Confederate states. The extra stars represent Kentucky and Missouri, whose efforts to secede were unsuccessful.

By the end of the Civil War, 33 percent of all U.S. paper currency in circulation was counterfeit.

The longest-surviving Civil War veteran died in 1959.

At the outbreak of World War I, the U.S. Air Force consisted of only 50 men.

The most expensive military aircraft in the world is the U.S. B-2 *Spirit* stealth bomber, priced at $1.3 billion.

In spring 2001 the United States lost seven members of an MIA search team in a helicopter crash in Vietnam.

As of January 1, 2006, the cost of the war in Iraq in dollars: $230 billion; in American lives: 2,178.

Just for Dentists

The patron saint of dentists: St. Apollonia. Why? She reportedly had her teeth pulled out in A.D. 249 by an anti-Christian mob.

Despite the popular myth, George Washington didn't have wooden teeth—his four sets of dentures were made of hippopotamus bone, elephant ivory, and eight human teeth from dead people, held together with gold palates and springs.

Thanks to fluoride and other preventives, baby boomers are probably the last generation to have a lot of cavities in their permanent teeth.

Fancy a tooth tattoo? Tiny gold hearts, butterflies, and other images have become popular among certain trendy groups. The downside is that from a distance of more than about three feet it just looks like you have food stuck in your teeth.

Getting dentures was once considered a natural step in aging, but no longer. In 1959, dentists performed 34 extractions for every 100 people; now it's half that rate.

Drugs can cause cavities. Antidepressants, antihypertensives, antihistamines, decongestants, and muscle relaxants all inhibit production of saliva, a natural bacteria destroyer.

Hard to believe, but Colgate claims Tooth Fairy as a registered trademark.

* * *

BRILLIANCE IN THE BATHROOM
Playwright Edmond Rostand (1868–1918) didn't like to be rude to his friends, but he didn't like to be interrupted when he was working, either. Rather than risk having to turn away any friends who might drop by to visit, "he took refuge in his bathtub and wrote there all day." His biggest bathroom success: *Cyrano de Bergerac*.

America Eats

Chance that a peanut grown in the United States will end up as peanut butter: 33 percent.

Only 6 percent of grocery coupons printed are ever redeemed.

On average, you'll spend about five years of your life eating.

The average American makes 3.4 trips to the grocery store each week. Most popular day: Friday.

On average, grocery shoppers spend eight minutes waiting in line at the supermarket.

Estimated number of people who could be fed for a year by the food Americans waste in one day: 240,183.

Most popular seafood in America: tuna. The average American eats 3.6 pounds a year.

The average New Englander eats twice as much ice cream per year as the average Southerner.

Americans eat 4 million pounds of bacon and 175 million eggs every day.

The average American eats four pounds of artificial flavorings, colorings, and preservatives each year.

Language Worldwide

Don't flash the thumbs-up sign to an Aussie. Down Under it means the same as our middle-finger signal. In a German beer garden, though, it will get you another beer.

If you want to signal "no" in Albania, nod. If you want to say "yes," shake your head. The same goes for Bulgaria, and parts of Greece, Turkey, Iran, Bengal, and the former Yugoslavia.

In some Middle Eastern countries, belching during meals is considered a compliment to the cook.

To us, pointing one finger toward the side of the head and making a circle means "you're crazy." In Argentina, it means you've got a phone call.

Hands up! The gesture can mean surrender or victory.

In Pandhurna, India, people celebrate the new moon by hurling stones at each other.

In Germany, making the *shhhh* sound means "hurry up."

Middle Easterners think a strong, firm handshake is a sign of aggression.

Some Eskimos still rub noses when they're feeling romantic; when the Maoris of New Zealand do it, they're just saying hello.

That Italian chin flick you've seen on *The Sopranos*? It means "Fuhgeddaboudit!" with a vengeance.

The most offensive signal in Ireland? Failing to buy a round of drinks when it's your turn. Turning down the offer of a drink is almost as bad.

The Earth Is Round?

In the Cherokee nation, people believed that mud rose from under the waters and formed an island with four corners—the earth. The sun went underneath the island at night, and rose again the next day.

Ancient Babylonians thought the earth was inside a hollow mountain, floating on a sea. Everything—the sun, moon, sky, stars, water—was inside this mountain.

Ancient Egyptians believed that the whole earth was part of their god, Keb. The stars were the jewels of a goddess in the sky and their god of air held her aloft.

Ancient Hindus thought the earth was in an upside-down bowl being carried by elephants. The elephants stood on the back of a turtle that was standing on top of a snake. They hadn't quite worked out what the snake stood on.

Polynesian creation stories set the earth in a basket with a lid. A hole cut in the top by a god lets in light. The woven grass at night lets light peek through in the form of stars.

* * *

SLIPPERY WHEN WET

Ice isn't slippery. What makes people and things slip on ice is water. A thin layer of ice melts when pressure is applied to it and it is this wet layer on top of the ice that is slippery.

Hello Kitty

Belgians once tried to deliver mail using cats. (It didn't work.)

A can of cat food contains as much meat as five adult mice.

Oldest cat ever: Ma, an English tabby, who was 37 when she died in 1957.

Cats sweat through their paws.

Three thousand out of every 3,001 calico kittens are female.

The average cat has 24 whiskers—12 on each side of its nose.

Feline experts estimate that 70 million feral cats live in the United States today.

Domestic cats have 18 claws.

Cats have two sets of vocal chords: one for purring and one for meowing.

Austrians are the world's number one cat lovers. Thirty percent of Austrian households have at least one cat.

Experts say cats watch more TV than dogs do. (Cats are more visual. Dogs rely more on smell.)

Hyenas are more closely related to cats than dogs.

Albert Einstein was convinced his cat suffered from depression.

Catnip can affect lions and cougars as well as house cats.

Siamese cats really are from Siam (now Thailand). In ancient days, they guarded the temple when a person of high rank died; the cat was considered a receptacle for the dead person's soul.

Tigers can be taught to use litter boxes. Big litter boxes.

The Cost of Things

Christopher Columbus's fee for "discovering" America: about $300.

Average wage for the workmen who dug the Erie canal: $1 and 1 quart of whiskey per day.

The Erie Canal was built for $7 million, equal in cost today to a few miles of interstate highway.

The United States bought Alaska from Russia in 1867 for 2¢ an acre.

Price of a Stradivarius copy advertised in the 1909 Sears, Roebuck & Co. catalog: $6.10.

It cost $3 million to build the *Titanic* and $100 million to make the movie.

A first-class ticket for the *Titanic* in 1912 cost more than a crew member would earn in 18 years.

A three-minute phone call from New York to San Francisco cost $20.70 in 1915.

In 1920 the average check at a diner was 28¢.

Price of a box of Girl Scout Cookies when they debuted in 1936: 25¢.

America's first minimum wage, in 1938, was 25¢ an hour.

Cellular phones sold for $4,195 in 1984.

Daily salary of a U.S. senator in 1789: $6. Daily salary in 2001: $627.

Babe Ruth's salary in 1932 was $80,000. In 2005 Sammy Sosa's salary was $17 million.

Cost of tickets to the last live Beatles concert in 1966: $4.50–$6.50. Cost of tickets to a U2 concert in 2005: $49.50–$160.

Pop Music

Ozzy Osbourne has said that when he's lonely, he talks to his knees.

Sonny and Cher originally called themselves Cleo and Caesar.

Sheryl Crow's two front teeth are fake—the real ones got knocked out when she tripped onstage.

The Rolling Stones made their American TV debut on *The Red Skelton Show.*

None of the Beatles knew how to read music. (Paul McCartney eventually taught himself.)

The first CD to sell 1 million copies: Dire Straits's *Brothers in Arms.*

The number of Grateful Dead concerts right-wing columnist Ann Coulter claims to have attended: 67

In July 2004 Colin Powell sang and danced to "YMCA" for foreign ministers at an Asian security summit in Indonesia.

A synesthete is a person whose senses are cross-wired; there's one in Switzerland who tastes music—and reports that Bach is creamy.

Under a 1996 UK copyright law, the London schoolchildren who sang on the Pink Floyd hit "Another Brick in the Wall" in 1979 became eligible for royalties. It's estimated that each student is owed around £500 (about $850).

THE COST OF THINGS: 1926
Pound of steak: 37¢
Dozen eggs: 45¢
New York to Philadelphia on the Pennsylvania Railroad: $3
RCA Radio: $150
Frigidaire Refrigerator: $395
1926 Chevrolet: $510
Grand piano: $625

Building Boom

There are about 10 million bricks in the Empire State Building.

The first skyscraper was the 10-story Home Insurance Building in Chicago. Built: 1885. Torn down: 1931.

It takes 6,000 gallons of paint, 60 people, and four months to paint the Eiffel Tower.

The George Washington Bridge, spanning the Hudson River in New York City, is almost 3 feet longer on the hottest day of summer than on the coldest day of winter.

Greek temples were originally painted in bright colors. Over time they have been bleached white.

The geodesic dome is the only structure that becomes stronger as it increases in size.

The Eiffel Tower (at 984 feet) is more than three times taller than the Statue of Liberty. (Lady Liberty is 305 feet tall.)

Metal shrinks when it gets cold. That's why the Eiffel Tower is six inches shorter in winter.

California's Golden Gate Bridge isn't golden—it's "International Orange."

Tallest monument in the world: the Gateway Arch in St. Louis, at 630 feet.

The temple of Siva in Madura, India, is adorned with 30 million separate carved idols.

The Great Wall of China is long enough to stretch from New York City to Houston.

Windmills originated in Iran.

Crime Time

Twenty thousand silver teaspoons are stolen from the Washington, D.C., Hilton each year.

Odds that someone caught shoplifting is a teenager: 50 percent.

U.S. shoplifters steal an estimated $2 billion worth of merchandise every year.

The retail industry loses more inventory to employee theft than it does to shoplifting.

Items most likely to be shoplifted from a supermarket: cigarettes, beauty aids, and batteries.

Al Capone's business card said he was a used furniture dealer.

Justice Department prediction: one in 20 babies born today will serve time in prison.

Half of all crimes are committed by people under the age of 18.

According to criminal law, only three people are necessary for a disturbance to be called a riot.

A 15-year-old burglar was charged with armed robbery after pointing his pet boa constrictor at a man and ordering him to hand over all his cash.

More Americans are arrested for drunk driving than for any other crime.

Russia has almost twice as many judges and magistrates as the United States; the United States has eight times as much crime.

Nearly 50 percent of all bank robberies take place on Friday.

When burglars break into a home, they usually go straight for the master bedroom.

Ransom paid for a kidnap victim can be tax-deductible.

Blame Canada

Canada has the longest national coastline in the world: 151,400 miles.

More than 50 percent of all the lakes in the world are in Canada.

Thirty-six percent of the Great Lakes lie within Canadian territory.

Forty percent of the world's newspapers are printed on paper that comes from Canadian forests.

Per capita, Canadians buy more diamonds than anyone on earth.

Both English and French are official languages of Canada.

The first North American YMCA opened in 1851 in Montreal, Quebec.

The name *Canada* is derived from the Huron-Iroquois kanata language and means a "village or settlement."

Per capita, the cities of Winnipeg and Calgary drink the most Slurpees in the world.

Canada has more doughnut shops per capita than any other country.

Canada has six time zones.

Canada is the largest importer of American automobiles.

Canadian citizens consume more Kraft Macaroni & Cheese per capita than any other nation.

In 2004 alone, UFO sightings in Canada increased by 31 percent.

Artfully Done

Roman statues were often made with heads that could be removed and replaced with other heads.

The actual title of Da Vinci's *Mona Lisa* is *La Gioconda*.

It took Leonardo da Vinci about five years to paint the *Mona Lisa*.

X-rays of the *Mona Lisa* show that there are three different versions underneath.

The *Mona Lisa* has no eyebrows. Shaved eyebrows were the fad when she was painted.

A pietà is any representation of the Virgin Mary mourning over the dead body of Christ, not just the famous one by Michelangelo.

It took Michelangelo four years to paint the ceiling of the Sistine Chapel.

Rembrandt was his first name; his last name was van Rijn.

Rembrandt painted more self-portraits than any other world-famous artist: 62.

Whistler's Mother (which James McNeill Whistler called *Arrangement in Grey and Black*) is in Paris at the Musée d'Orsay, a branch of the Louvre. The painting is about five feet by five feet.

Henri Rousseau, famous for his exotic jungle scenes, never left Paris. He would go to the park, lie down among the grass and weeds, and sketch the plants hundreds of times their size.

Matisse coined the term *cubism* in 1908 as an insult to another painter's work.

The most expensive painting ever auctioned: Pablo Picasso's *Garçon a la Pipe (Boy With a Pipe)*. It fetched $104 million in 2004.

Take This Job

Two most dangerous jobs in the United States: commercial fishing and logging.

The average computer worker types 90,000 keystrokes in an eight-hour shift.

One in six employees says they got so mad at a coworker last year that "they felt like hitting them, but didn't."

Fifty-three percent of Americans think they're paid "the right amount."

A cashier entering digits by hand will average one error for every 350 characters.

The Mirage Hotel in Las Vegas has 12 gardeners on its staff to care for artificial plants.

An estimated 12 percent of U.S. businessmen wear their ties so tight that they restrict the blood flow to their brain.

Six in ten Americans say they would continue to work if they won $10 million in the lottery.

Bathroom Break

The Pentagon uses up 666 rolls of toilet paper on an average day.

Most-requested care package item by U.S. troops in Iraq: toilet paper.

Buculets are those little bumpers on the underside of your toilet seat.

On average, Americans buy 1.5 toothbrushes a year.

If you took a shower today, you used about 30 gallons of water.

The average water temperature for showers in the United States is 105°F.

A doniker is circus slang for "toilet."

* * *

REMEMBER 1982?

First issue of USA *Today* hits stands
Graceland opens to the public (adults: $6.50; kids: $4.50)
First permanent artificial heart transplant performed
Time magazine man of the year: Pac-Man
Falklands War begins and ends
Late Night with David Letterman debuts on NBC
#1 movie: *E.T.: The Extra-Terrestrial*

South America

It is common in Brazil to take 3 or 4 showers a day; visitors may be asked if they would like to shower before a meal.

The Amazon River is visible from space.

The Andes are the longest mountain range in the world, stretching more than 4,000 miles through seven countries.

São Paulo, Brazil is the fifth-largest city in the world and the largest in South America.

Quibido, Colombia, receives more than 350 inches of rain annually.

According to tradition, Brazilian cats have seven lives, not nine.

Ninety percent of Brazilian women classify beauty products as an essential rather than a luxury.

Brazil produced a coffee-scented postage stamp in 2001.

Before the arrival of the Spanish, the Incan Empire covered 35,000 square miles, almost twice the size of California.

La Paz, Bolivia, is the highest capital city in the world.

The first settlers of Patagonia were Welsh.

The Amazon River basin is the largest contiguous tropical rain forest in the world.

Peru's Inca Indians were the first to cultivate potatoes, around 200 B.C.

The native people of the Andes Mountains have 2 to 3 more quarts of blood in their bodies than people who live at lower elevations.

Farm Fresh

In 1910 about 32 million Americans lived on farms. Today fewer than 5 million do.

Of the 1,000 varieties of cherries grown in the United States, only 10 are grown commercially.

A year's worth of sap from a full-grown sugar maple tree will make only 1/3 gallon of syrup.

It takes about 12 ears of corn to produce a single tablespoon of corn oil.

Benjamin Franklin invented crop insurance.

It takes seven to eight tons of sugarcane to produce a ton of sugar.

It takes 345 squirts from a cow's udder to get a gallon of milk.

* * *

7 NICKNAMES OF PRESIDENT GROVER CLEVELAND

1. Big Beefhead
2. The Buffalo Hangman
3. The Dumb Prophet
4. The Stuffed Prophet
5. The Pretender
6. His Accidency
7. Uncle Jumbo

Familiar Phrases

PUT ON YOUR THINKING CAP
Meaning: Carefully and thoughtfully consider something
Origin: In previous centuries, it was customary for judges to put a cap on before sentencing criminals. Because judges were respected thinkers, it was referred to as a "thinking cap." (*Gordon's Book of Familiar Phrases*)

PLAY FAST AND LOOSE
Meaning: Stretch the truth or meaning of words or rules, deceive or trifle with someone
Origin: This term dates from the 16th century. It comes from a game called "fast and loose," which was played at fairs. Operators rolled up a strap and left a loop hanging over the edge of a table. To win, a player had to catch the loop with a stick before the strap was unrolled. But they never won. Cheating operators rolled it up in such a way that the feat was impossible. (*Have a Nice Day—No Problem!*, by Christine Ammer)

GET OFF SCOT-FREE
Meaning: Escape punishment
Origin: "In the thirteenth century, scot was the word for money you would pay at a tavern for food and drink, or when they passed the hat to pay the entertainer. Later, it came to mean a local tax that paid the sheriff's expenses. To go scot-free literally meant to be exempted from paying this tax." (*How Does Olive Oil Lose Its Virginity?*, by Bruce Tindall and Mark Watson)

SLUSH FUND
Meaning: A hidden cache of money used for illegal or corrupt political purposes
Origin: "Derived from Scandinavian words meaning 'slops,' this phrase is derived from the nineteenth-century shipboard practice of

boiling up large pots of pork and other fatty meats. The fat that rose to the top of the kettles was stored in vats and then sold to soap and candle makers. The money received from the sale of the 'slush' was used for the crew's comfort and entertainment." (*Eatioms*, by John D. Jacobson)

TOUCH AND GO
Meaning: A risky, precarious situation
Origin: "Dates back to the days of stagecoaches, whose drivers were often intensely competitive, seeking to charge past one another, on narrow roads, at grave danger to life and limb. If the vehicle's wheels became entangled, both would be wrecked; if they were lucky, the wheels would only touch and the coaches could still go." (*Loose Cannons and Red Herrings*, by Robert Claiborne)

KNOCK OFF WORK
Meaning: Leave work for the day
Origin: "[This phrase] originated in the days of slave galleys. To keep the oarsmen rowing in unison, a drummer beat time rhythmically on a block of wood. When it was time to rest or change shifts, he would give a special knock, signifying that they could knock off." (*Dictionary of Word and Phrase Origins, Vol. 2*, by William and Mary Morris)

BEAT THE RAP
Meaning: Avoid punishment for a wrongdoing
Origin: "It is likely that this slang Americanism originated in another expression, take the rap, in which rap is slang for 'punishment,' facetiously, from a 'rap on the knuckles.' One who takes the rap for someone else stands in for the other's punishment. Beat the rap . . . often carries with it the connotation that the miscreant was actually guilty, though acquitted." (*The Whole Ball of Wax*, by Laurence Urdang)

BE ABOVEBOARD
Meaning: Be honest
Origin: Comes from card playing. "Board is an old word for table." To drop your hands below the table could, of course, be interpreted as trying to cheat—by swapping cards, for example. "But if all play was above board this was impossible." (*To Coin a Phrase*, by Edwin Radford and Alan Smith)

Modern Progress

The cigarette lighter was invented before the match.

Ettore Sceccone invented the window squeegee in 1936.

Benjamin Franklin "invented" daylight saving time.

Charles Darwin's cousin invented the IQ test.

Nobody remembers who invented eyeglasses.

Garrett Morgan's claims to fame: inventor of the traffic light and the gas mask.

NASA invented the DustBuster.

Stilts were invented by French shepherds who herded sheep in marshes near the Bay of Biscay.

Mark Twain invented a Trivial Pursuit–like game called Mark Twain's Memory-Builder.

In about 250 B.C., Archimedes invented the screw.

Leonardo da Vinci figured out that the rings of a tree reveal its age.

The filaments for the first electric lamp were made of bamboo.

The telephone was invented in 1876. The telephone booth was patented in 1883.

Carpenter's pencils are square so they don't roll off roofs.

The man who created the Thighmaster was a Buddhist monk.

The chair was invented in about 2500 B.C. Benjamin Franklin invented the rocking chair.

The first person to use an elevator: King Louis XV, whose "flying chair" went between floors at Versailles in 1743.

The typewriter was invented before the fountain pen.

Dollars & Cents

There are six pounds of pennies in the average American home.

It is estimated that 75 percent of all U.S. dollars contain traces of cocaine.

There are an estimated 140 billion U.S. pennies in circulation.

The one-ounce Platinum American Eagle has the highest denomination of any U.S. coin. Value: $100.

U.S. mints stamp out 19.5 million pennies, 3.8 million nickels, 7 million dimes, 7 million quarters, and 19,178 half-dollars in an average day.

Paper money doesn't disintegrate when it goes through the washing machine because it's made from cotton or linen rags; the fibers bond much more firmly than fibers in regular paper.

Highest denomination ever minted by the U.S. Treasury: $100,000 bill. Lowest: $.05 bill.

A roll of coins wrapped in paper is called rouleau.

Odds that a piece of paper money printed by the U.S. Treasury is a one-dollar bill: 45 percent.

There are an estimated three hundred $10,000 bills in circulation in the United States.

Because of the weight of its face, a penny is slightly more likely to land "heads" than "tails."

Baseball

Average life span of a major league baseball: five pitches.

First baseball team to pay its players: Cincinnati Red Stockings.

Mickey Mantle is credited with the longest home run ever: 643 feet.

Babe Ruth wore a cabbage leaf under his baseball cap to keep cool during games.

In pro baseball, you can't replace an umpire unless he's injured or sick.

Number of baseball gloves that can be made from a single cowhide: five.

Babe Ruth's bat was nick-named Black Betsy.

The name of Los Angeles's professional baseball team in 1900 was the Tourists.

First baseball player to be named Rookie of the Year: Jackie Robinson, in 1947.

Fernando Tatis of the Cardinals is the only major leaguer to hit two grand slams in one inning.

At the first professional baseball game, the umpire was fined 6¢ for swearing.

Four baseball promotions that ended in riots: Beer Night, Scrap Metal Night, Wet T-Shirt Night, and Disco Demolition Night.

The Dodgers' original name was the Bridegrooms. Reason: lots of newlyweds on the team.

Since 1876, 91 pro baseball players have hit a home run their first time at bat. Nineteen of them have never hit another.

Space Junk

S ince 1957 the United States and the former Soviet Union have carried out approximately 4,000 space launches. Those launches account for the vast majority of the 10,000 large objects and the millions of smaller pieces of debris that orbit aimlessly above the earth. Most of the little stuff is too small to see on radar, but it's big enough to cause serious injury if it collided with a spacecraft. With every new space launch—an average of one every four days—the problem gets worse.

WHAT'S THE DAMAGE?

A small piece of space junk, say two to three inches across, would rip a five-inch hole in the wall of a pressurized spacecraft. And because objects in orbit move about six miles per second (more than 20,000 mph), the collision would liquefy both the piece of debris and the wall of the craft. With a flash of heat and blinding light, molten metal would splatter the inside of the cabin. Air would stream out of the hole, leaving any surviving astronauts just a few moments to escape. If the piece of debris were larger, the craft could "unzip," that is, its exterior would come away from the frame like the peel off a banana, and the contents of the craft would spew out. And, incidentally, add to the space junk tally. Here's the short list of what's up there:

- Used-up satellites

- The rockets that carried the satellites up in the first place

- Discarded fuel tanks

- Equipment from scientific experiments

- Your basic nuts and bolts

- Lens caps

- Thermal blankets

- The coolant from Soviet spy satellites, which is congealing into balls about an inch in diameter

- The 400 million tiny and long-obsolete antennae the air force released into orbit in 1963 to see if radio waves would bounce off them

First Americans

Most American Indians prefer to be called just that, not Native American.

For thousands of years the preferred method of killing buffalo on the plains was to chase them off a cliff.

Sitting Bull was not an Indian chief. He was a medicine man.

The word *Illinois* is Algonquin for "tribe of superior men."

Sacagawea was 16 years old and a new mother when her trek with Lewis and Clark began.

Jay Silverheels, who played Tonto on TV's *The Lone Ranger,* was a Canadian Mohawk.

A Hopi reservation in Arizona lies entirely within the boundaries of a much larger Navajo reservation.

Pensacola means "place of the bearded people" in some Seminole languages.

The Sioux confederacy consists of the Lakota, the Dakota, and the Nakota.

American Indians and Alaskan natives account for less than two percent of federal employees.

Alaska is most likely derived from the Aleut for "the great country" or "mainland."

The Hawaiians are considered "indigenous" but not "Native American." Neither are the Inuits of Alaska.

The Indian hero Geronimo joined the Dutch Reformed Church, but was kicked out for gambling.

Itsy Bitsy Spider

A black widow's poison is 15 times more powerful than rattlesnake venom.

A spider's blood is transparent.

There are about 37,500 known species of spider.

Spiders can eat their own weight in one meal.

Some small spiders don't build webs of their own; they live near webs and eat the leftovers.

Spiders live on all continents except Antarctica.

Young spiders can regenerate a leg if it's lost.

Spiders have been known to lay up to 300 eggs in a single egg sac.

Spiders have 48 "knees": eight legs with six joints on each.

Little Miss Muffet of the nursery rhyme really existed. She was the daughter of 16th-century physician Dr. Thomas Mouffet, who believed spiders had healing powers and forced his daughter to eat them.

The weight of insects eaten by spiders every year is greater than the total weight of the entire human population.

Spiders can go for long periods without food, some even up to a year.

A jumping spider can jump up to 25 times its own body length.

Black widows like warm, dark places, and in pre-indoor plumbing days, were "fond of hiding in outhouses, where they often spin webs across toilet seats."

Ask the Experts

Q: DO I REALLY HAVE TO SHAMPOO TWICE?
A: Of course not. Soaps are really efficient; one washing removes about 99 percent of the oil. But initially, that dirt and oil prevent the shampoo from forming the nice firm bubbles, which together make up lather. In fact, the only point of reapplying shampoo is that it's psychologically pleasing. (*Why Things Are, Vol. II,* by Joel Achenbach)

Q: HOW DID *LEFT* AND *RIGHT* COME TO REPRESENT THE ENDS OF THE POLITICAL SPECTRUM?
A: According to the Oxford English Dictionary: This use originated in the French National Assembly of 1789, in which the nobles as a body took the position of honor on the president's right, and the Third Estate sat on his left. The significance of these positions, which was at first merely ceremonial, soon became political. (*Return of the Straight Dope,* by Cecil Adams)

Q: WHAT'S THE DIFFERENCE BETWEEN HORNS AND ANTLERS?
A: The horns of antelopes and the antlers of deer, although comparable in function, differ considerably in structure. Horns, usually possessed by both sexes, are permanent features that continue to grow throughout the animal's life. They are bony projections from the skull, covered with keratin, which is tougher than bone. Antlers, by contrast, are pure bone and are formed and shed every year. They are normally grown only by male deer, with the exception of reindeer and caribou, whose females have them as well. (*Can Elephants Swim?,* by Robert M. Jones)

Q: WHAT IS THAT "NEW CAR SMELL"?
A: There's nothing quite like it, and all attempts to reproduce it artificially for colognes and air fresheners have fallen short. It is a

combination of scents from things one wouldn't normally smell voluntarily, condensed in intensity by the size of the relatively airtight passenger compartment. The odor components that go into it include fresh primer and paint, plastic, leather, vinyl, rubber, glues, sealers, and carpeting. The smell fades with time, as residual solvents leech away from exposure to light, heat, and air. (*Just Curious, Jeeves*, by Jack Mingo and Erin Barrett)

Q: WHY DO EYES COME OUT RED IN PHOTOGRAPHS?

A: The flash from the camera is being reflected on the rear of the eyeball, which is red from all the blood vessels. The solution: "Use a flash at a distance from the camera, or get your subjects to look somewhere else. Another trick is to turn up the lights in the room, making them as bright as possible, which causes the subject's pupil to contract and admit less of the light from the subsequent flash. (*Why Things Are*, by Joel Aschenbach)

Q: HOW CAN YOU COOL OFF YOUR MOUTH AFTER EATING HOT PEPPERS?

A: Drink milk, says Dr. Robert Henkin, director of the Taste and Smell Clinic in Washington, D.C. Casein, the main protein in milk, acts like a detergent, washing away capsaicin, the substance in hot peppers responsible for their "fire." (*Parade* magazine, November 14, 1993)

Q: DO INSECTS SLEEP?

A: Let's put it this way. They get quiet and curl up and look like they're sleeping. But what's really going on inside those molecule-sized brains nobody knows. The one sure way to know if an animal is sleeping is to hook it up to a machine that measures electrical patterns in the brain. That's how we know that birds and mammals—animals like dogs, cats, cows, and pigs—actually sleep. The problem with bugs is they don't have enough brains to hook the wires to. So we don't really know what they're doing. (*Know It All!*, by Ed Zotti)

U.S. Cities

Difficult, Tennessee, gets its name because its residents couldn't agree on a name for the town.

Smallest town in the United States: Hove Mobile Park City, North Dakota, with a population of two.

If New York City were as densely populated as Alaska, 14 people would live in Manhattan.

New York's Times Square was originally known as Long Acre Square.

Largest private landowner in New York City: the Catholic Church. Second: Columbia University.

Dallas was named after George Mifflin Dallas, vice president of the United States from 1845 to 1849.

Greater Los Angeles is bigger than Rhode Island and Delaware combined.

Two nations in the world are smaller than New York's Central Park: Monaco and Vatican City.

Southernmost state capital in the continental United States: Austin, Texas.

Birmingham, Alabama, has 22 more miles of canals than Venice, Italy.

321

Bottoms Up!

The average American consumes 22 gallons of beer a year.

The beer-drinkingest state: Nevada, at 35 gallons per capita. Least beer-imbibing state: Utah, at 13 gallons per person each year.

Italy consumes more wine per capita than any other nation on earth.

Odds that a grain of rice grown in the United States will end up being brewed into beer: one in 10.

Most popular hard liquor in Scotland: vodka.

France produces 20 million bottles of wine a day.

Kentucky produces more whiskey than every other state combined.

In Bavaria, beer isn't just an alcoholic drink—it's considered a staple food, like bread or eggs.

The spiral-shaped part of a corkscrew is called a "worm."

Wine is mentioned in every book of the Bible except Jonah.

What do you call the dent in the bottom of a champagne bottle? A kick (or a punt).

Gin comes from the French genièvre, for "juniper." (Gin is made from juniper berries.)

Why six-packs? Breweries thought six beers were "the maximum a woman could safely carry."

By 3000 B.C. there were at least six different types of beer in Egypt.

During Prohibition, half of all federal prison inmates were in jail for violating liquor laws.

If you feed beer to a laboratory rat, it will live six times longer than a rat that drinks only water.

Familiar Phrases

TO BE WELL-HEELED
Meaning: To have plenty of money or be well-to-do
Origin: "It might be assumed that well-heeled originally alluded to the condition of a rich person's shoes. But that is not the case. In the 18th century, it was a fighting cock that was 'well-heeled,' that is, fitted with an artificial spur before facing an opponent in the pit. From that, men began to 'heel' themselves, to carry a gun, before entering a trouble zone. Perhaps because most troubles can be alleviated by money, the expression took on its present financial aspect." (*Heavens to Betsy!*, by Charles Earle Funk)

TO HAVE SOMEONE OVER A BARREL
Meaning: To have the upper hand
Origin: "In the days before mouth-to-mouth resuscitation, lifeguards placed drowning victims over a barrel, which was rolled back and forth while the lifeguard tried to revive them. The person 'over the barrel' is in the other person's power or at his mercy." (*The Facts on File Encyclopedia of Word and Phrase Origins*, by Robert Hendrickson)

TO BE A BASKET CASE
Meaning: An overly anxious or stressed person who can't function normally
Origin: "First appeared as a slang term in WWI meaning 'a quadruple amputee.' Soldiers who had lost all their limbs actually were carried in baskets, because if they were carried on stretchers, they'd be too likely to fall out." (*Jesse's Word of the Day*, by Jesse Sheidlower)

PULL THE WOOL OVER SOMEONE'S EYES
Meaning: Fool someone
Origin: "Goes back to the days when all gentlemen wore powdered wigs like the ones still worn by the judges in British courts. The word

wool was then a popular, joking term for hair . . . The expression 'pull the wool over his eyes' came from the practice of tilting a man's wig over his eyes, so he couldn't see what was going on."

LET THE CAT OUT OF THE BAG
Meaning: Reveal the truth
Origin: Refers to a con game practiced at country fairs in old England. A trickster tried to sell a cat in a burlap bag to an unwary bumpkin, saying it was a pig. If the victim figured out the trick and insisted on seeing the animal, the cat had to be let out of the bag.

CHEW THE FAT
Meaning: Chat; engage in idle conversation
Origin: Originally a sailor's term. Before refrigeration, ships carried food that wouldn't spoil. One of them was salted pork skin, a practically inedible morsel that consisted largely of fat. Sailors would only eat it when all the other food was gone . . . and they often complained as they did. This (and other) idle chatter eventually became known as "chewing the fat."

HAVE A SCREW LOOSE
Meaning: Something is wrong with a person or mechanism
Origin: The phrase comes from the cotton industry and dates back as far as the 1780s, when the Industrial Revolution made mass production of textiles possible for the first time. Huge mills sprang up to take advantage of the new technology (and the cheap labor), but it was difficult to keep all the machines running properly; any machine that broke down or produced defective cloth was said to have "a screw loose" somewhere.

IN THE NICK OF TIME
Meaning: Without a second to spare
Origin: Even into the 18th century some businessmen still kept track of transactions and time by carving notches—or nicks—on a "tally stick." Someone arriving just before the next nick was carved would arrive in time to save the next day's interest—in the nick of time.

Measurements

THE INCH. In its earliest form, the inch was the width of a grown man's thumb. In the 14th century, King Edward II of England decreed that "the length of an inch shall be equal to three grains of barley, dry and round, placed end to end lengthwise." This evolved into today's standard measurement.

THE FOOT. Originally the length of a person's foot, the foot was later standardized in English-speaking countries to be 12 inches long. In other parts of the world, however, it could be anywhere from 11 to 14 inches in length.

THE YARD. Originally the standard length of the belt that Anglo-Saxons wore. In the early 1100s, King Henry I of England decreed that a yard would be the distance from his nose to the thumb of his outstretched arm, which came to about 36 inches.

THE MILE. A descendant of the ancient Roman measure called the *mille passuum*, which meant "a thousand paces." Each pace was the equivalent of 5 Roman feet, which meant there were 5,000 feet to the mile. Today there are 5,280 feet to the mile. Why the extra feet? Because when the English incorporated the mile into their system of measurement, they wanted it to be equal to 8 furlongs. A furlong—originally defined as the distance a horse could pull a plow without resting—was exactly 660 feet long, so the English multiplied 660 by 8 to get 5,280. (Why didn't they just knock some feet off the furlong and keep the mile a tidy 5,000 feet long? Because property was measured in furlongs—and changing the furlong would have screwed up every property holding in the kingdom.)

Royal Gossip

While performing her duties as queen, Cleopatra sometimes wore a fake beard.

In her entire life, Queen Berengaria of England never once visited England.

By the time the king of Siam died in 1910, he had fathered 370 children.

King George I of England (1714–1727) was German. He couldn't speak a word of English.

Queen Victoria's first act as queen: moving out of her mother's room.

Napoléon Bonaparte, a Frenchman, designed the flag of Italy.

King Henry VIII owned tennis shoes.

Queen Anne of England (1665–1714) had 17 children. They all died before her.

Anne Boleyn, second wife of Henry VIII, had six fingers on her left hand.

Louis XIV owned 413 beds.

England's Prince Charles won the Alfred E. Neuman Look-Alike Contest in 1992.

Mary Stuart became Queen of Scotland when she was only six days old.

In her entire lifetime, Spain's Queen Isabella (1451–1504) bathed twice. King Louis XIV bathed three times.

* * *

REMEMBER 1984?
First photos of missing children on milk cartons
Soviet Union boycotted summer Olympics in L.A.
Newsweek magazine dubbed 1984 the "Year of the Yuppie"
#1 movie: *Ghostbusters*

Word Origins

NAMBY-PAMBY
Meaning: Weak, wishy-washy
Origin: "Derived from the name of Ambrose Philips, a little-known poet whose verse incurred the ridicule of two other 18th-century poets, Alexander Pope and Henry Carey. In poking fun at Philips, Carey used the nickname Namby Pamby: Amby came from Ambrose; Pamby repeated the sound and form, but added the initial of Philips's surname. After being popularized by Pope in *The Dunciad*, namby-pamby went on to be used for people or things that are insipid, sentimental, or weak." (*Word Mysteries & Histories*, by the Editors of The American Heritage Dictionaries)

KALEIDOSCOPE
Meaning: A tubular optical toy; a constantly changing set of colors
Origin: "In 1817 Dr. David Breuster invented a toy which he called a kaleidoscope. He selected three Greek words that when combined had a literal meaning of 'observer of beautiful forms.' The words were kalos ('beautiful'), eidos ('form'), and skopos ('watcher'). The term has come into prominent use in its figurative sense; namely, a changing scene—that which subtly shifts color, shape, or mood." (*The Story Behind the Word*, by Morton S. Freeman)

MONEY
Meaning: Currency; a medium of exchange in the form of coins and banknotes
Origin: "Hera, queen of the Greek gods, kept her name out of the vulgate [common speech] until she moved to Rome and became Juno. As Juno Moneta (Juno the Monitress), she presided over a Roman temple where gold was coined. Moneta became the eponym of money, and Moneta's temple a mint." (*Thou Improper, Thou Uncommon Noun*, by Willard Espy)

COOKIE
Meaning: A small sweet cake, typically round, flat, and crisp
Origin: "The word was borrowed from the Dutch *koekje*, 'little cake,' which is the diminutive of Dutch *koek*, 'cake.' *Cookie* came into American English from the Dutch settlers of New York. It first appears in 1703 in the statement that 'at a funeral, 800 cockies . . . were furnished.' This early English spelling of the word differs from our modern spelling, but several other spellings also arose, such as *cookey* and *cooky*. The spelling *cookie* may have won out because the word is very common in the plural, spelled *cookies*." (*Word Mysteries and Histories*, by the Editors of The American Heritage Dictionaries)

DRAB
Meaning: Lacking brightness, dull
Origin: "In the 16th century, drab was a word for a kind of cloth, coming into English from French *drap*, 'cloth.' From this, the word came to mean the common color of such cloth, which was its natural undyed color of dull brown or gray. Hence the fairly general meaning 'dull,' whether of an object's color (where it usually is brown or gray still, as 'drab' walls) or in a figurative sense, as a 'drab' day or someone's 'drab' existence." (*Dunces, Gourmands & Petticoats*, by Adrian Room)

SALARY
Meaning: A regular payment made by an employer to an employee
Origin: "A salary, during the great days of the Romans, was called a *salarium*, 'salt-money.' The ancients regarded salt as such an essential to good diet (and before refrigeration it was the only chemical that preserved meat) that they made a special allowance in the wages of soldiers to buy *sal* (Latin for 'salt'). With time any stipend came to be called a salarium, from which English acquired the word *salary*." (*Hue and Cry and Humble Pie*, by Morton S. Freeman)

BLINDFOLD
Meaning: A piece of cloth tied around the head to cover the eyes
Origin: "The name of the folded piece of cloth has only a coincidental resemblance to the way the material is doubled over. *Blindfold* actually comes from the Middle English *blindfeld*, 'to be struck blind.' Walter Tyndale used *blyndfolded* in his English translation of the Bible (1526), and if he was not the first to make the mistake, he was certainly the most influential." (*Devious Derivations*, by Hugh Rawson)

Medicine Cabinet

Before World War I, Aspirin was a registered trademark of the German company Bayer. When Germany lost the war, Bayer gave the trademark to the Allies as a reparation in the Treaty of Versailles.

Why do men wear fragrances? Thanks to some clever marketing during World War II, Old Spice aftershave became part of the soldier's standard-issue toiletry kit and "changed the smell of things."

Hate taking care of your contact lenses? It could be worse. Early contacts were made from wax molds (wax was poured over the eyes). The lenses, made of glass, cut off tear flow and severely irritated the eyes. In fact, the whole ordeal was so painful that scientists recommended an anesthetic solution of cocaine.

On average, each person uses 54 feet of dental floss every year. That may sound like a lot, but dentists recommend the use of one and a half feet of dental floss each day. That's equal to 548 feet a year.

In the late 1940s aerosol hair spray was a growing fad among American women. The only problem was that it was water insoluble, which made it hard to wash out. Why? The earliest fixative was shellac, more commonly used to preserve wood.

Ancient Chinese, Roman, and German societies frequently used urine as mouthwash. Surprisingly, the ammonia in urine is a good cleanser. (Ancient cultures had no way of knowing that.)

Average American

Number of ice cubes the average American puts in a glass: 3.2.

About 77 million babies were part of the baby boom generation. Four percent of them walk to work.

Four percent of Americans are allergic to hamsters.

More Americans claim German ancestry (46.5 percent) than any other. Irish ancestry is number two, at 33 percent.

Fifty percent of Americans believe humans lived at the same time as dinosaurs.

Ninety percent of Americans thought income taxes were fair in 1944. Only 51 percent agreed in 2005.

When asked to name the odor that best defines America, 39 percent of Americans said "barbecue."

Forty-nine percent of Americans say they pray to God for financial advice.

Most adults believe we will make "first contact" with alien life by the year 2100.

The Time It Takes

Fifty-eight seconds for the elevator
in Toronto's CN Tower to reach
the top (1,815 feet)

One minute for a newborn baby's
brain to grow 1.5 mg

Forty-five minutes to reach an
actual person when calling the IRS
during tax time

Four hours, 30 minutes to cook a
20-pound turkey at 325°F

Ninety-two hours to read both the
Old and New Testaments aloud

Ninety-six hours to completely
recover from jet lag

Seven days for a newborn baby to
wet or soil 80 diapers

Nineteen days until baby cardinals
make their first flight

Twenty-five days for Handel to
compose *The Messiah*

Thirty days for a human hair to
grow half an inch

Extended Sitting Section

Here's a small selection of our favorite conspiracy theories, unexplained deaths, and other thought-provoking topics.

What do you think: Is it fact or fiction?

Elvis Lives!

*Plenty of people really believe Elvis is still alive. As
RCA Records used to ask: Can millions of Elvis
fans be wrong? You be the judge.*

Early in the morning of August 16, 1977, Elvis Presley and his
girlfriend, Ginger Alden, returned to Graceland from a late-
night dentist appointment. The two stayed up until about
7 a.m., when Alden went to bed. But, according to one source,
"because he had taken some 'uppers,' Elvis was still not sleepy." So
the King retired to his bathroom to read a book. (Sound familiar?)
That was the last time anyone saw him alive.

THE OFFICIAL STORY
When Alden woke up at 2:00 in the afternoon, she noticed that
Elvis was still in his bathroom so she decided to check on him.

When she opened the door, she saw Elvis sprawled face forward on
the floor. "I thought at first he might have hit his head because he
had fallen," she recalls, "and his face was buried in the carpet. I
slapped him a few times and it was like he breathed once when I
turned his head. I lifted one eyelid and it was just blood red. But I
couldn't move him." The King was dead.

Elvis was rushed to Baptist Memorial Hospital in Memphis, but
doctors could not revive him. He was pronounced dead at 3:00 p.m.
The official cause of death: cardiac arrhythmia brought on by "strain-
ing at stool." (The actual cause of death: most likely a massive overdose of prescription drugs.) That is what is supposed to have happened. Nevertheless, Elvis aficionados across the country see a host
of mysterious circumstances that suggest the King may still be alive.

SUSPICIOUS FACTS
- The medical examiner's report stated that Elvis's body was found

in the bathroom in a rigor-mortised state. But the homicide report said that Elvis was found unconscious in the bedroom. In *The Elvis Files*, Gail Brewer-Giorgio notes, "Unconsciousness and rigor mortis are at opposite ends of the physical spectrum: rigor mortis is a stiffening condition that occurs after death; unconsciousness, a state in which a living body loses awareness. Bedroom and bathroom are two different places."

- The medical examiner's report lists Elvis's weight at the time of death as 170 pounds; he actually weighed about 250 pounds.

- Elvis's relatives can't agree on how Elvis died. His stepbrother Rick claims Elvis suffocated on the shag carpet; his stepbrother David thinks Elvis committed suicide. Larry Geller, Elvis's hairdresser and spiritual adviser, claims that Elvis's doctors told Vernon Presley (Elvis's father) that the King had leukemia, which may have contributed to his death. Some theorists charge that the confusion surrounding Elvis's death proves that the star faked his death. If the King is really dead, why can't his loved ones get their stories straight?

UNANSWERED QUESTIONS

Did Elvis foresee—or fake—his death?

- Elvis didn't order any new jumpsuits—his trademark outfit—in all of 1977. Why not? Did he know he wasn't going to need any?

- On his last concert tour, Elvis was overheard saying, "I may not look good tonight, but I'll look good in my coffin."

- Was Elvis imitating his manager, Colonel Tom Parker? As a young man, Parker also faked his death. An illegal immigrant from Holland whose real name was Andreas Van Kujik, Parker left Holland without telling his relatives; they thought he was dead.

Was the corpse in Elvis's coffin really Elvis's?

- Country singer Tanya Tucker's sister LaCosta was at the King's funeral, and she was shocked at the body's appearance: "We went right up to his casket and stood there, and God, I couldn't believe it. He looked just like a piece of plastic laying there. He didn't look like him at all . . . he looked more like a dummy than a real person. You know a lot of people think it was a dummy. They don't think he was dead."

- Some observers said they thought the corpse's nose looked too "pugged" to be the King's. They speculated that even if the King had fallen forward and smashed his nose at the time of his death, it would have naturally returned to its original shape, or would at least have been fixed by the undertaker—if the body was really Elvis's. (*The Elvis Files*)

Was the corpse in Elvis's coffin a wax dummy?

- Some theorists believe that Elvis's coffin weighed more than it was supposed to. Brewer-Giorgio reports receiving a letter from an Elvis fan who claimed to have personally known the man who made the King's coffin. The coffin maker revealed that the casket was a rush order—and that there was no way the coffin could have weighed 900 pounds, as the press reported—even with the King in it. So what was in the coffin with Elvis that made it so heavy?

- According to Brewer-Giorgio, the discrepancy between the coffin's actual weight with Elvis in it and its weight at the funeral is about 250 to 275 pounds, "the weight of a small air-conditioner." "Was there an air-conditioner in the coffin?" Brewer-Giorgio asks, "Wax dummy? Something cool to keep the wax from beading up?"

- To many witnesses, Elvis's corpse appeared to be "sweating" at the funeral. Brewer-Giorgio says she asked Joe Esposito, Elvis's road manager, about TV reports that there were "beads of sweat" on Elvis's body. "He said that was true, that everyone was sweating because the air-conditioner had broken down. Except that dead bodies do not sweat." But wax melts.

Why were the mourners acting so strange at the funeral?

- Parker wore a loud Hawaiian shirt and a baseball cap to Elvis's funeral and never once approached the casket to say farewell to the King. Elvis's fans argue that if Elvis were really dead, Parker would probably have shown a little more respect.

- Elvis's hairdresser claims that he saw Esposito remove Elvis's TCB (Takin' Care of Business) ring from the corpse's finger during the funeral services. Why would he remove one of Elvis's favorite pieces of jewelry? Elvis would surely have wanted to have been buried with it—unless the corpse being buried wasn't the King's?

Is Elvis in the Federal Witness Protection Program?

- In 1970 Presley—a law enforcement buff—was made an honorary agent-at-large of the Drug Enforcement Administration by President Nixon, after a visit to the White House. According to some theorists, Presley became more than just an honorary agent—he actually got involved in undercover narcotics work.

- In addition to his DEA work, Elvis may have been an FBI agent. During the same trip to Washington, D.C., Elvis also wrote a letter to J. Edgar Hoover, volunteering his confidential services to the FBI. Hoover wrote back thanking Elvis for his offer, but there is no record of him ever taking it up. Still, Brewer-Giorgio and other theorists argue that the government may have been keeping the King's government service a secret.

- According to Brewer-Giorgio, Elvis was also "a bonded deputy with the Memphis Police and was known to don disguises and go out on narc busts."

- Elvis took his law enforcement role seriously. More than one biography details the time that the King ran out onto the runway of the Las Vegas airport, flagged down a taxiing commercial airliner, and searched it for a man whom he believed had stolen something from him. Elvis looked around, realized his quarry wasn't aboard, and gave the pilot permission to take off.

- Some theorists believe that Elvis's extensive work in law enforcement made him a target for drug dealers and the Mob—and that he entered the Federal Witness Protection Program out of fear for his life. According to Brewer-Giorgio, when Elvis supplied the information that sent a major drug dealer to prison, the King and his family received death threats.

Could Elvis Be in Hiding?

Hundreds of Elvis's loyal fans think they have spotted the King since his "death." He's been sighted at a Rolling Stones concert, working at a Burger King in Kalamazoo, buying gas in Tennessee, and shopping for old Monkees records in Michigan. One woman even claims that Elvis gave her a bologna sandwich and a bag of Cheetos during a 1987 visit to the Air Force Museum in Dayton, Ohio. Could so many people be lying or mistaken?

OTHER MYSTERIES COLLECTED BY ELVIS FANS

- Vernon Presley never went to the hospital the night Elvis "died." If Elvis were really dead, he probably would have.

- According to some reports, within hours of Presley's death, souvenir shops near Graceland began selling commemorative T-shirts of his death. How could they have made so many T-shirts in so little time—unless Graceland had let them know about the "death" in advance?

- Elvis's middle name, Aron, is misspelled "Aaron" on his tombstone. If he's really dead, why don't his relatives correct the mistake?

- Elvis is not buried next to his mother as he requested. Says Brewer-Giorgio: "'Elvis loved his mother very much and always said he would be buried beside her,' many fans have noted. 'So why is he buried between his father and grandmother?' they ask."

- On a number of occasions after the King's death, Priscilla Presley referred to Elvis as a living legend—strange words for a woman who believes that Elvis is dead.

- Before he died, Elvis took out a multimillion-dollar life insurance policy. To date, no one in his family has tried to claim it. If Elvis is really dead, why haven't they cashed in the policy?

THE MOURNERS

- The people who were in Elvis's home when he died insist that he really *did* die. Joe Esposito, Elvis's road manager for 17 years, was one of the first people to see the body. "Believe me, the man that I tried to revive was Elvis."

- Elvis may even have committed suicide. According to his step-brother David Stanley, "Elvis was too intelligent to overdose [accidentally]. He knew the *Physician's Desk Reference* inside and out." Why would Elvis take his own life? He was getting old, and the strain of his stagnating career may have become too much to bear. The pressure showed: in the last years of his life, Elvis's weight ballooned to more than 250 pounds, and his addiction to prescription drugs had gotten out of control.

- The impending publication of a book chronicling the King's vices may have been the final straw. In August 1977, the month of his death, two of his former aides were about to publish a book revealing much of his bizarre personal life to the public for the first time. He was already depressed, and the imminent public exposure of his drug habit may have pushed him over the edge.

* * *

REDUNDANCIES

hoist up

free of charge

recur again

enclosed herewith

excessive overharvesting

swivel around

new recruits

fellow colleagues

first priority

invited guest

completely satisfied

sink down

Myths About Mars

*You've learned everything you know about Mars from old science
fiction books, half-heard reports on CNN, and those Warner Bros.
cartoons starring Marvin the Martian. Well, as it turns out, most
of what you know about Mars is probably a little off base. We're
here to provide you with the real facts behind the myths.*

MARS MYTH #1: Mars is the closest planet to Earth.
MARS REALITY #1: Sometimes it is, but on average, Venus is the
closest planet to Earth. Venus orbits the Sun at an average distance of
67.2 million miles (108.1 million km), while the Earth is parked at 93
million miles (149 million km) and Mars is out there at 141 million
miles (226 million km). Pull out your handy calculator, and you'll see
that at its closest approach, Venus is about 25 million miles (40 million km) from Earth, while Mars's closest approach is something like
48 million miles (77 million km). (Mars can actually get closer,
thanks to its highly eccentric orbit, but never as close as Venus.)
When Mars is on the far side of its orbit from Earth, it's so far away
that two planets are actually closer to us: Venus and tiny Mercury,
which orbits the Sun at a distance of a mere 36 million miles (58 million km).

MARS MYTH #2: Mars is the planet most like Earth.
MARS REALITY #2: This depends on what you mean by "most
like Earth." It's most like Earth in its surface features and weather, in
its annual temperature range, its axial tilt, and its length of day
(which is about 24 1/2 hours long). In terms of actual size, Venus is
closer to Earth's size than Mars. With a radius of 7,500 miles (12,070
km), Venus is just 400 miles (644 km) smaller in diameter than
Earth; Mars has a diameter of a mere 4,200 miles (6,759 km). Venus
is also closer in terms of gravitational pull—on Venus you'd weigh 91
percent of what you do on Earth, while on Mars you'd weigh just 38
percent as much. Saturn, Uranus, and Neptune also have similar

gravitational pulls to Earth. In terms of water, the planet that is most like Earth is Jupiter's moon Europa, which scientists think may have an ocean of liquid water hidden beneath a massive covering of ice. So while Mars is like Earth in some ways, in many other ways it's not.

MARS MYTH #3: Mars is habitable by humans.
MARS REALITY #3: If you want to know what living on Mars is like, move to Antarctica, because that's how cold it is on Mars: the average temperature is a nastily cold –85°F (–65°C). Now, once you've moved to Antarctica, remove 99 percent of the air from the atmosphere because Mars's atmospheric pressure at the surface is just 1 percent of what Earth's is. Not that you could use it anyway, since about 95 percent of Mars's atmosphere is carbon dioxide, which you can't breathe. Elton John got it right when he said, "Mars ain't the kind of place to raise your kids." He should know; he's the Rocket Man.

MARS MYTH #4: They've discovered water on Mars.
MARS REALITY #4: Not exactly. In 2002, NASA scientists discovered what they called a "whopping large" hydrogen signal underneath and surrounding the southern pole of Mars—a hydrogen signal that almost certainly means that there is water on Mars, trapped in the martian soil. This discovery is a good thing: Water is an important ingredient in life as we know it, boosting the chances for life on Mars, and it would make it easier for us to visit and even colonize one day. But it's not clear whether any of that water is liquid; given Mars's frigid temperatures, it's more likely that any underground martian water is frozen.

In June 2000, NASA announced that they had found evidence that water might have once flowed on the martian surface—evidence in the form of gullies that looked a great deal like water-formed gullies on Earth. However, a year later, scientists from the University of Arizona noted that these gullies could have also been created by frozen carbon dioxide—carbon dioxide being the main ingredient of the atmosphere, and frozen carbon dioxide also being present in Mars's ice caps.

MARS MYTH #5: Mars's surface is covered with canals.
MARS REALITY #5: Nope. The idea of martian canals got its start with American astronomer Percival Lowell, who in the late 19th century mistranslated comments from an Italian astronomer about

the possibility of huge *canali*, or "channels," on the surface of Mars. Lowell thought *canali* meant "canals"—artificial structures made by advanced, intelligent creatures—rather than naturally occurring channels, which was the original idea. The existence of the canals was hotly debated for decades, until a visit from a Mariner spacecraft in the 1960s proved without a doubt that no canals (or channels, for that matter), existed at all—and there was no other sign of intelligent life on Mars. So that was that.

However, the canals still pop up from time to time. They're featured in popular science fiction books by Ray Bradbury and Robert Heinlein (both wrote many of their books before the question was settled). They were even a minor plot point in the 1996 movie *Mars Attacks!* By 1996 the filmmakers should have known better, but then it was a movie about martians attacking Earth, so you can't beat on them for not being factually correct.

MARS MYTH #6: NASA spacecraft spotted a face on Mars.
MARS REALITY #6: The famous "face on Mars" was discovered in 1976 when NASA spacecraft *Viking I* snapped a picture of a mesa in the Cydonia region of Mars. The mesa looked disturbingly like an actual human face—a human face two miles (3 km) long, that is. Since then, "the face" has been a popular pop culture icon and was even featured in the really terrible 2000 flick *Mission to Mars* (in which it really was a face left there by old, dead martians).

In 2001 the *Mars Global Surveyor* took a finely detailed picture of the "face"—and this time it looked like . . . a big pile of rocks, which is exactly what it is. The "face" on the mesa is really nothing more than a combination of shadows and the poor imaging resolution of the camera attached to the *Viking I* spacecraft. There's also a crater called Galle on Mars that looks like a "happy face."

MARS MYTH #7: Scientists found microbes from Mars on Earth.
MARS REALITY #7: The martian microbes may or may not be real. What we've got here is a meteor named ALH 84001, found in Antarctica in 1984 and originally from Mars, in which scientists discovered some interesting things: little squiggles that looked similar to fossilized Earth bacteria, carbon (a primary ingredient of life), and some organic molecules. It was enough for NASA to announce in 1996 that there was a possibility of life once existing on Mars. Then

the skeptics weighed in: The "squiggles" were too small to have been bacteria, the "fossils" could have been created by chemical processes without the need for living things, and the organic materials in the rock could have come from Antarctica, where the rock has been, after all, for about 13,000 years—plenty of time for contamination. The current status of the "microbes"? Well, they could be life. Or they might not be.

MARS MYTH #8: The martians sabotaged our spacecrafts so we wouldn't find out about them.
MARS REALITY #8: The spacecrafts in question would be 1999's ill-fated *Mars Climate Orbiter* and *Polar Lander* spacecrafts, both of which bit the big one after arriving at Mars. As interesting as it would be to say that these spacecrafts were knocked out of the sky by Marvin the Martian and his pals taking a little target practice, the fact is that both missions failed because of screwups back on Earth. The former spacecraft burned up in Mars's atmosphere; the latter went plummeting to the surface.

* * *

REMEMBER THE 80s?

1985
Coca-Cola reintroduced "classic" Coke
Reagan met Gorbachev in first U.S./Soviet summit
Pete Rose broke Ty Cobb's record of 4,191 base hits
#1 movie: *Back to the Future*
Calvin and Hobbes comic strip premiered

1986
Space shuttle *Challenger* exploded
Martin Luther King Day became U.S. holiday
Soviet nuclear plant Chernobyl had major meltdown
Album of the Year: Paul Simon's *Graceland*
On TV: *Miami Vice, Cheers, Family Ties*

The Rest of the United States

Here are some of the smaller, uninhabited islands owned by the United States. (Well, they may have a few inhabitants, but no natives.)

WAKE ISLAND

LOCATION: North Pacific Ocean, between Hawaii and the Northern Mariana Islands

SIZE: Two and a half square miles

POPULATION: 300

BACKGROUND: Wake Island is an atoll made up of three islets around a shallow lagoon. It was discovered in 1796 by British sea captain William Wake. The United States annexed it in 1899 for a telegraph cable station. An airstrip and naval base were built in late 1940, but in December 1941 the island was captured by the Japanese and held until the end of World War II. Today the facilities are under the administration of the Federal Aviation Agency.

KINGMAN REEF

LOCATION: North Pacific Ocean, between Hawaii and American Samoa

SIZE: Less than one-half square mile

POPULATION: Uninhabited

BACKGROUND: The United States annexed this reef in 1922. There's no plant life on the reef (which is frequently under water) but it does support abundant and diverse marine life. In 2001 the waters surrounding the reef were designated a National Wildlife Refuge.

MIDWAY ISLANDS

LOCATION: North Pacific Ocean, north of Hawaii

SIZE: Less than two and a half square miles

POPULATION: 150 U.S. Fish and Wildlife Service personnel

BACKGROUND: Part of the Hawaiian island chain, Midway was first discovered by a Hawaiian sea captain in 1859. At the urging of the North Pacific Mail and Steamship Company, which was looking for a coal depot for its Asian mail run, the U.S. Navy claimed the atoll for the United States in 1867. Midway is best known as the site of a U.S. naval victory over the Japanese fleet in 1942, one of the turning points of World War II. The naval station closed in 1993. Today the island is a wildlife refuge open to ecotourists.

GUANO ISLANDS

What is guano? Bird droppings. Fish-eating birds have been dropping their poop in the same spots for thousands of years. The result: huge deposits of guano, rich in nitrogen and phosphorous and highly valued as an agricultural fertilizer.

The Guano Act was enacted by the U.S. government in 1856. It authorized Americans to take "peaceable possession" of any uninhabited, unclaimed islands for the purpose of mining the guano. Nearly 100 islands were claimed for the United States under the act, mostly in the South Pacific. The United States still owns a half dozen—the others were abandoned or given up to other countries that claimed them. They're not really anybody's idea of paradise, so don't expect to see any postcards from these tiny islands. But some of these poop-covered rocks have interesting histories.

NAVASSA ISLAND

LOCATION: Caribbean Sea, between Haiti and Jamaica
SIZE: Less than two and a half square miles
POPULATION: No permanent residents
BACKGROUND: The Baltimore-based Navassa Phosphate Company began mining guano in 1865, using convicts at first, then former slaves. In deplorable living conditions, the ex-slaves were forced to mine one and a half tons of guano per day for a daily wage of 50¢. In 1889 they revolted, killing 15 white overseers. Forty workers were taken to Baltimore for trial. Acknowledging the basis for the uprising, the court sentenced only one worker to death—the rest were given life imprisonment. The Navassa Phosphate Company continued to mine guano until 1898.

In 1998 a California entrepreneur named Bill Warren filed a claim under the Guano Act, obtained a deed from heirs of the Navassa

Phosphate Company, and claimed ownership of the island. Predictably, the U.S. government denied his claim.

There is also a dispute between the United States and Haiti, which maintains that the island lies within its territorial boundary.

HOWLAND ISLAND
LOCATION: North Pacific Ocean, between Hawaii and Australia
SIZE: A little more than one-half square mile
POPULATION: Uninhabited
BACKGROUND: Claimed by the American Guano Company in 1858. Its other claim to fame: In 1937 an airstrip was built on the island as a stopover for aviation pioneer Amelia Earhart on her round-the-world flight. Earhart and her navigator took off from Lae, New Guinea, but never reached Howland. (The unexplained disappearance still intrigues conspiracy buffs.) Today Howland Island is a National Wildlife Refuge.

BAKER ISLAND
LOCATION: North Pacific Ocean, between Hawaii and Australia
SIZE: One-half square mile
POPULATION: Uninhabited
BACKGROUND: Named by an American whaler, Michael Baker, who found the island in 1832. Presently it is a National Wildlife Refuge run by the U.S. Department of the Interior.

JOHNSTON ATOLL
LOCATION: North Pacific Ocean, 800 miles southwest of Hawaii
SIZE: One square mile of dry land; 50 square miles of shallow water
POPULATION: 1,000 military and support personnel
BACKGROUND: The four tiny islands were discovered in 1796 by an American sea captain.

During World War II, the military used Johnston Island, the largest of the four outcroppings, as a refueling point for aircraft and submarines. A few days after the attack on Pearl Harbor, Japanese submarines fired on military facilities there but caused no casualties.

The U.S. Air Force took over in 1948 and used the site for high-altitude nuclear tests in the 1950s and 1960s. In 1964 a series of open-air biological weapons tests were conducted near the atoll using several barges loaded with rhesus monkeys. Chemical weapons have been stored on Johnston Island since 1971, but the U.S. Army began destroying them in 1981. Munitions destruction is reportedly complete, and the army plans to turn over the atoll to the U.S. Fish and Wildlife Service in 2003.

JARVIS ISLAND
LOCATION: South Pacific, between Hawaii and the Cook Islands
SIZE: Less than two square miles
POPULATION: Uninhabited
BACKGROUND: Discovered by the British in 1821; claimed by the American Guano Company in 1858; abandoned in 1879; annexed by Britain in 1889; abandoned soon after. Reclaimed by the United States in 1935. The island is currently a National Wildlife Refuge; a small group of buildings are occasionally occupied by scientists and weather researchers.

PALMYRA ATOLL
LOCATION: North Pacific Ocean, 1,000 miles south of Hawaii
SIZE: Four and a half square miles
POPULATION: Uninhabited
BACKGROUND: This group of 54 islets is known for its lush natural beauty and biological diversity.

The first to land on the atoll were sailors from the American ship *Palmyra*, which was blown ashore during a storm in 1852. Though the American Guano Company claimed the atoll, guano was never mined there. In 1862 King Kamehameha IV of Hawaii took possession of the atoll, which is actually a part of the Hawaiian archipelago. The United States included it when it annexed Hawaii in 1898, but when Hawaii became a state in 1959, Palmyra was excluded.

The 1974 murder of a yachting couple on Palmyra became the subject of a 1991 novel by Vincent Bugliosi (and a subsequent TV movie) entitled *And the Sea Will Tell*. Today the atoll is privately owned by the Nature Conservancy, which is managing it as a nature preserve.

Vitamins 101

*To impress upon you the importance of daily vitamin ingestion,
we'll now cheerfully terrify you with examples of all the diseases
and ailments you can get if you don't. Yes, that's right, nature
imposes penalties for not treating your body right. You probably
knew that. Now you're going to get it spelled out for you.
Let's take the vitamins in alphabetical order, shall we?*

VITAMIN A

What it does for you: Keeps your skin and your eyes healthy;
helps you heal your body.

What happens if I don't have it? Your night vision goes out the window, since vitamin A is a component of "visual purple," a protein that boosts your eyes' sensitivity in dim light. Your skin can become scaly and dry. The linings of your mucous membranes can lose their cilia, which will increase your susceptibility to bacterial infections. In severe cases of vitamin A deficiency, you get xerophthalmia, a totally disgusting disease in which your eyes become swollen, your tear ducts shut off, and your eyelids get all full of pus. Unsurprisingly, your corneas are more susceptible to infection and ulceration when your eyes are like this, and it's fairly likely you'll go blind.

I'm convinced. Vitamin A is in eggs, milk, liver, and green and yellow vegetables. But, be careful, too much vitamin A is not good either. Stick to the recommended daily allowance.

VITAMIN B1 (THIAMINE)

What it does for you: It helps your body break down carbohydrates and keeps your nervous system humming along nicely.

What happens if I don't have it? Then you get beriberi, which despite its mildly amusing name is really a righteously nasty little disease; the name of the disease is taken from a Sinhalese word meaning "extreme weakness." To start off, you lose your appetite and get all slackerlike; you experience digestive problems and numbness in your extremities. That numbness is just your body's way of saying, "Hey, moron, the long nerves in your arms and legs are beginning to atrophy!" From there, you have your choice: "dry" beriberi, in which those long nerves atrophy even more and you experience loss of muscle mass and motor control, or "wet" beriberi, in which you experience edema (i.e., fluid saturating your body), poor circulation, and cardiac failure. They both sound so good. It's really hard to choose. End results of severe beriberi: paralysis or death. Or both.

I'm convinced. Milk, liver, peanuts, and pork are all good sources of B1.

VITAMIN B2

What it does for you: A factor in your body's oxidization of carbohydrates and amino acids, and a key ingredient in some critical enzymes.

What happens if I don't have it? Your friends start to think you've become a vampire, because your eyes suddenly develop an increased sensitivity to light. They also wish you would, like, take a bath, because your skin is becoming all greasy and scaly. Your mouth is also in bad shape. Your lips redden and develop cracks at the corners (this is called cheliosis), and your tongue is inflamed and sore (glossitis). Basically a B2 deficiency makes you look all squinty and puffy, and where's the fun in that?

I'm convinced. Get your B2 from green vegetables, liver and other organ meats, and milk.

VITAMIN B3 (NIACIN)

What it does for you: Helps you metabolize carbohydrates and also oxidizes sugars.

What happens if I don't have it? You'll be introduced to pellagra, a perfectly charming disease that hits you with skin lesions that first look like sunburns (thanks to your skin's increased sensitivity to light) but later become crusty and scaly. Then constipation kicks in, alternating with diarrhea—what a lovely combination—and your mouth and tongue become inflamed and sore. Having fun yet? Just you wait, because later stages of pellagra bring dementia in a variety of fun flavors, like general nervousness, confusion, depression, apathy, and the ever-popular delirium. Also, since pellagra is mostly seen these days in drug addicts and severe alcoholics, guess what your friends will be thinking you've been doing in your spare time.

I'm convinced. Open up for peanuts, lean meats, fish, and bran.

VITAMIN B6

What it does for you: Helps in the formation and breakdown of amino acids, the breakdown of proteins and fats, and in the synthesis of important neurotransmitters.

What happens if I don't have it? Early on, you'll be sore, irritable, and weak. Later on, you'll experience anemia and possibly seizures. B6 deficiencies are not uncommon among chronic alcoholics—and, interestingly enough, some oral contraceptives can cause B6 deficiencies, as well.

I'm convinced. Chow down on whole-grain cereals, fish, legumes, and liver.

VITAMIN B12

What it does for you: It helps you make red blood cells and is important in digestion and the absorption of nutrients.

What happens if I don't have it? The first thing you might notice is that something's up with your tongue. A B12 deficiency keeps those little bumps on your tongue from forming, which means your tongue will be unusually smooth. Really kind of creepy if you think about it. More seriously, you'll experience pernicious anemia, defective function of your intestines, and you might even experience spinal cord degeneration, which is, as you might imagine, a very bad thing. Keep this up, and a vitamin B12 deficiency will kill you right dead. Vegetarians take note. Vitamin B12 is not available in vegetables. No, not a single one. No, it's not a conspiracy to get you to eat bacon. It's really a true fact.

I'm convinced. Eggs, milk, liver. Vegans, take that multivitamin and try not to think too hard about where that B12 might have come from. Hey, it could come from fungus or algae.

VITAMIN C

What it does for you: Keeps your connective tissue, cartilage, and bones healthy; keeps your metabolism chugging along.

What happens if I don't have it? Arrr, me matey! Ye'll get scurvy, me boy! Arrr! Yes, scurvy, the scourge of sailors, who didn't get enough fruit in their long sea voyages. (Fact: The British term limey comes from a lime juice ration provided to sailors to prevent scurvy.) Scurvy is genuinely unpleasant, with sore and bleeding gums, wobbly teeth (they'll spring right out of yer scurvy skull, matey!), stiff joints and extremities, internal bleeding, and let's not forget anemia, shall we? Ah, the life of a sea dog.

I'm convinced. Stock up on fresh citrus fruits, laddie! Oranges, lemons, limes, and so on. Also cabbage, bell peppers, and brussels sprouts.

VITAMIN D

What it does for you: Helps with calcium and phosphorus absorption in your body (these two compounds being essential for bones).

What happens if I don't have it? Well, if you're an adult, not too much. However, if your kids don't get enough vitamin D, they'll get rickets, in which bones soften and bend. This leads to bowed legs, knocked knees, and creepy-looking ribs, not to mention other developmental issues. As if your kids won't already have enough problems getting through junior high.

I'm convinced. Have some fortified milk and fish liver oil. Also, get some sun. Your body uses sunlight to create vitamin D internally. Yes, this will work for your kids, too, although a cup of milk here and there for them isn't a bad idea, either.

VITAMIN E

What it does for you: It's believed to help your body deal with free radicals, which may fool around with cellular structure if not watched closely.

What happens if I don't have it? You'll get clumsy, that's what. Vitamin E deficiency can lead to walking difficulties and inhibited reflexes, and may also cause your eye muscles to become paralyzed. How's that for freaky?

I'm convinced. Eggs, cereals, and beef liver are all fine sources of vitamin E.

VITAMIN K

What it does for you: Helps your blood clot.

What happens if I don't have it? Hope you like bruises, because you'll be getting a lot of them. And naturally, any cuts or scrapes you get will bleed that much longer because your body doesn't have what it needs to form effective clots. Stay inside. Eat all your food with a dull spoon.

I'm convinced. Leafy green vegetables are good. So is liver, which, come to think of it, seems to be the most vitamin-packed organ you can eat. If only it tasted like potato chips.

A Field Guide to Secret Societies

Are secret societies really responsible for the world's ills, as some people believe? Probably not, but on the other hand . . .

THE ILLUMINATI

Who They Are: This group was founded in 1776 by Adam Weishaupt, a Jesuit priest, in Bavaria. His mission: to advance the 18th-century ideals of revolution, social reform, and rational thought (the name means "the Enlightened Ones" in Latin). Weishaupt and his cronies were fiercely opposed by the monarchs of Europe and by the Catholic Church, which is why they had to meet and communicate in secret. German author Johann Goethe was a member. In the United States, both Benjamin Franklin and Thomas Jefferson were accused of being members and denied it, but both wrote favorably about Weishaupt and his efforts.

What They're Blamed For: This group has been associated with more conspiracy theories than any other. Considered the silent evil behind such paranoid bugaboos as One World Government and the New World Order, the Illuminati have been blamed for starting the French and Russian revolutions, as well as both world wars, and almost every global conflict in between. They are said to use bribery, blackmail, and murder to infiltrate every level of power in society—business, banking, and government—to achieve their ultimate goal: world domination.

BILDERBERG GROUP

Who They Are: Founded in 1952 by Prince Bernhard of Netherlands, the Bilderberg Group (named after the hotel in Oosterbeck, Holland, where the first meeting was held) was founded to promote cooperation and understanding between Western Europe and North America. To that end, leaders from both regions are invited to meet every year for off-the-record discussions on current issues. The list of attendees has included presidents (every one from Eisenhower to Clinton), British prime ministers (Lord Home, Lord Callaghan, Sir Edward Heath, Margaret Thatcher), captains of industry like Fiat's Giovanni Agnelli, and financiers like David Rockefeller. Invitees are members of the power elite in their countries, mostly rich and male. Meetings are closed. No resolutions are passed, no votes are taken, and no public statements are ever made.

What They're Blamed For: The fact that so many of the world's most powerful players refuse to disclose anything about the group's meetings strikes many outsiders as downright subversive. What are they doing? The group has been accused of handpicking Western leaders to be their puppets, pointing to circumstantial evidence like the fact that Bill Clinton was invited to attend a meeting before he became president, as was Britain's Tony Blair before he became prime minister. Conspiracy buffs have even accused the Bilderbergers of masterminding the global AIDS epidemic as a way of controlling world population to the benefit of the European/American elite.

SKULL & BONES SOCIETY

Who They Are: This society was founded at Yale University in 1833. Only 15 senior-year students are admitted annually; they meet twice a week in a grim, windowless building called the Tombs. Unlike most campus fraternities, Skull & Bones appears to focus on positioning its members for success after college. But no one knows for sure, because members are sworn to total secrecy for life. The names of past and current members include many of America's power elite: both George Bushes, William Howard Taft, as well as the descendants of such famous American families as the Pillsburys, Weyerhausers, Rockefellers, Vanderbilts, and Whitneys.

What They're Blamed For: What's wrong with a little good ol' boy networking? Nothing, perhaps, but Skull & Bones members have also been accused of practicing satanic rites within the walls of the Tombs. Initiation reportedly requires pledges to lie down in coffins, confess sordid details of their sex lives, and endure painful torture so that he may "die to the world, to be born again into the Order." Like the Illuminati, the Order (as it's called by its members) supposedly works to create a world controlled and ruled by the elite—members of Skull & Bones.

TRILATERAL COMMISSION

Who They Are: Founded in 1973 by David Rockefeller and former National Security Council chief Zbigniew Brzezinski, this organization is composed of 350 prominent private citizens (none currently hold government positions) from Europe, North America, and Japan (the trilateral global power triangle). Like the Bilderberg Group, their stated goal is to discuss global issues and to promote understanding and cooperation. Unlike other groups, this one is more visible: it publishes reports, and members are identified. It's also more diverse, with women and ethnic groups represented. However, membership is by invitation only, usually on the recommendation of serving members, making it one of the most exclusive private clubs in the world. There are no representatives from developing nations.

What They're Blamed For: Many conspiracy theorists view the Trilateral Commission as the "sunny" face of the evil machinations of international bankers and business moguls who are working to make the world their own little oyster, with one financial system, one defense system, one government, and one religion—which they will control. Again, all members are major players in business and government. Americans of note include Bill Clinton, Jimmy Carter, Henry Kissinger, and George Bush (the elder), former Federal Reserve Chairman Paul Volcker, former Speaker of the House Tom Foley, and former U.S. Trade Representative Carla Hills, to name a few. Since there is considerable crossover between the Trilateral Commission and the Bilderberg Group, the commission is thought by some to be under the control of the Illuminati. That it is completely private, with no direct role in government (read "no accountability"), only adds fuel to the fires of suspicious minds.

BOHEMIAN GROVE

Who They Are: Founded in 1872 by five *San Francisco Examiner* newsmen as a social boozing club, the Bohemian Grove has been called "one of the world's most prestigious summer camps" by *Newsweek*. Prospective members may wait up to 15 years to get in and then have to pony up a $2,500 membership fee. The grove itself is a 2,700-acre retreat set deep in a California redwood forest. Members' privacy is zealously guarded: no strangers are allowed near the site, and reporters are expressly forbidden entry. The Bohemian Grove motto is from Shakespeare: "Weaving spiders come not here," a reminder that all deal making is to be left at the gates. The members relax and entertain each other by putting on plays, lecturing on subjects of the day, and wining and dining lavishly.

So why does anyone care about the Bohemian Grove? Well, the membership is a virtual Who's Who of the most powerful people (mostly Republican) in American government and business. Members past and present include Dick Cheney, Donald Rumsfeld, Karl Rove, George W. Bush, Richard Nixon, Gerald Ford, Henry Kissinger, Caspar Weinberger, Stephen Bechtel, Joseph Coors, Alexander Haig, Ronald Reagan, and hundreds more. Critics claim there is no way men like these (no women are allowed) can hang out together and not make backroom deals.

What They're Blamed For: Conspiracy theorists claim that the Manhattan Project was set up at the Grove and that the decision to make Eisenhower the Republican presidential candidate for 1952 was hammered out between drinks on the lawn.

Darker charges have been made against the Grove as well. Members are purported to practice some odd rituals, such as wearing red hoods and marching in procession like ancient druids, chanting hymns to the Great Owl. Members say it's all in good fun, but outsiders wonder at the cultlike overtones. Outrageous rumors were rampant in the 1980s: sacrificial murders, drunken revels, even pedophilia, sodomy, kidnapping, and rape. Of course, none of this has ever been proven, but as limousines and private jets swoop into this secret enclave in the woods, the "big boys" continue to party and the rest of the world remains in the dark about just exactly what goes on.

* * *

MORE WAYS TO TELL A FORTUNE

Ailuromancy: Observe how a cat jumps.

Aleuromancy: Read messages in baked balls of dough.

Keriomancy: Study the flickering flame of a candle.

Oomancy: Crack an egg into a glass of water and study the shapes the egg white forms in the water.

Scrying: Study "crystals, mirrors, bowls of water, ink, blood, flames, or other shiny objects."

Moon Scam?

*Is nothing sacred? Those conspiracy nuts won't leave
anything alone. They attack our most sacred institutions.
(On the other hand, they could be right.)*

MOONSTRUCK

On July 20, 1969, millions of television viewers around the
world watched as Neil Armstrong stepped down from a
lunar landing module onto the surface of the moon and spoke the
now famous words, "That's one small step for man, one giant leap for
mankind."

In western Australia a woman named Una Ronald watched. She
saw the images of the moon landing in the early hours of the morning. But as the camera showed Armstrong's fellow astronaut Edwin
"Buzz" Aldrin demonstrating his moon walk technique, Ronald
swears she saw something else: a Coke bottle kicked into the picture
from the side. The scene was edited out of later broadcasts, she says.
Was this alleged "blooper" evidence of a giant hoax?

MISSION IMPOSSIBLE

If Una Ronald was the first to suspect the moon landing wasn't quite
what it appeared to be, she certainly isn't the last. And there is a lot
more than just the Coke bottle to excite skeptics.

Ten years before *Apollo 11* supposedly went to the moon, Bill
Kaysing was head of technical publications at Rocketdyne Systems, a
division of Boeing that still makes rocket engines for the space program. In his book *We Never Went to the Moon*, Kaysing says that in
1959 Rocketdyne estimated that there was about a 14 percent chance
we could safely send a man to the moon and back. According to
Kaysing, there is no way the space program could have advanced
enough in the following 10 years to send the three *Apollo 11* astronauts to the moon, followed by five more moon landings in the next
three years.

NASA experts recently admitted that they currently do not have the capability of sending manned missions to the moon. So how could they have done it more than 30 years ago? Even simulations these days require powerful computers, but the computer onboard the Columbia had a capacity smaller than many of today's handheld calculators. Kaysing and others think they know the answer, and they cite a number of anomalies that lead them to conclude that the Apollo missions were faked:

THE FLUTTERING FLAG: In 1990 a New Jersey man named Ralph Rene was reviewing old footage of the moon landing. As he watched the American flag fluttering in the airless atmosphere of the moon, it suddenly dawned on him: How can there be a breeze if there is no air? Rene's suspicions led him to research inconsistencies in the moon landing story, and to publish a book called *NASA Mooned America*. The fluttering flag was just the beginning.

PHONY PHOTOS: A close look at the thousands of excellent still photos from the moon landings reveal some very odd features. For one thing, they are a little too good. The astronauts seem to be well lit on all sides, regardless of where the sunlight is coming from, almost as if there were some artificial light source.

- Defenders claim that light was reflected from the lunar surface, bouncing back to light the shadow side of the astronauts. Oddly, that same reflective light does not illuminate the dark side of lunar rocks, which are even closer to the ground.

- Shadows seem to fall in different directions and look to be different lengths even for objects of a similar height, such as the two astronauts. This leads some to conclude that there were multiple light sources—possibly some man-made ones.

- Even when everything else is in shadow, the American flag and the words *United States* are always well lit, and sometimes seem to be in a spotlight. Was someone trying to squeeze extra PR value out of fake photos?

STARLIGHT, STAR BRIGHT: Some skeptics cite the absence of stars in photos of the lunar sky as evidence that they were not taken on the moon. After all, in the dark sky of the moon with no atmosphere, stars should be clearly visible.

- Experts agree—to the naked eye, stars in the sky of the moon should be magnificently clear. But, the experts say, stars wouldn't show up on film that was set to expose the much brighter lunar surface. On the other hand, why were there no pictures taken of the stars in the lunar sky? Surely how the stars look from the moon would have interested many people. Was it because astronomers could spot the fake photos too easily?

WHERE'S THE DUST? One of the most memorable images NASA released from *Apollo 11* was the imprint of Buzz Aldrin's boot in the lunar dust. But the lunar landing module apparently had less of an impact on the moon's surface.

- Moon photos show no visible disturbance from the high-powered thrust engines the *Eagle* landing module used to land, nor is there any dust in the landing pads.

- If the *Eagle* blew away all the dust, as some speculate, how did Aldrin make such a nice footprint?

DEADLY RADIATION: In a recent press conference, a NASA spokesman said that radiation is one of the biggest obstacles to space travel. Wouldn't it have been a problem 30 years ago?

- Two doughnut-shaped rings of charged particles, called the Van Allen Belts, encircle Earth. To get to the moon, astronauts would have had to pass through the belts, exposing themselves to deadly radiation unless they had a lot more protection than the thin shield the Apollo spacecraft provided.

- Once outside the radiation belts and Earth's protective atmosphere, astronauts would have been exposed to solar radiation. Expert opinions differ as to whether this exposure would have been life-threatening. But inexplicably, not one of the astronauts from the seven lunar missions got cancer, a well-known result of overexposure to radiation.

- Even more sensitive to radiation is photographic film. On all those beautiful moon photos there is absolutely no sign of radiation damage. Why not?

FOLLOW THE BOUNCING ASTRONAUT: What about the movie footage showing the astronauts demonstrating the moon's low gravity by bouncing around the surface? Skeptics say that could have easily been faked. In the moon's gravity—a sixth of Earth's—the astronauts should have been able to leap 10 feet in the air. But they didn't. In fact, in the movie footage they don't get any farther off the ground than they could on Earth.

And if it looks like they are moving in slow motion—that's because they are—half speed to be exact. Bill Wood, a scientist who worked for the NASA subcontractor responsible for recording Apollo signals and sending them to NASA headquarters in Houston, explains that the original film footage, shot at 30 frames per second, was transferred to video, which runs at 60 frames per second. If the film of the astronauts walking on the surface of the moon is viewed at regular speed their movements look remarkably normal.

MOON ROCKS: Besides the photos and film footage, the only physical evidence we have that astronauts actually went to the moon is lunar rocks.

- NASA points to the fact that scientists around the world have examined the rocks brought back by the Apollo missions and have no doubt that they originated on the moon. But the moon isn't the only place to find such rocks.

- In the ice of Antarctica, scientists have found remnants of lunar rocks blasted off the moon by meteoric impacts. Numerous expeditions have explored the continent for rock samples from the moon, Mars, and comets.

- In 1967, two years before the Apollo mission, such a group visited Antarctica, including ex-Nazi rocket scientist Wernher von Braun, by then working for NASA. Why would a rocket scientist be sent to look for rocks? Was he collecting fake evidence?

WHY FAKE IT?

These anomalies in the "information" given to the public about the Apollo moon missions have caused many to question whether we really did send anyone to the moon. But if the moon landings were faked, how was it done, and why?

The why is fairly easy to understand. The 1960s were the height of the cold war. The Space Race was on, and the Soviet Union had already beat the United States by launching the first satellite to orbit Earth, the first man—and woman—in space, and the first space walk, among other important achievements. The United States was clearly behind. In 1961 President Kennedy issued a challenge: "I believe this nation should commit itself to achieving a goal, before this decade is out, of sending a man to the moon and returning him safely to the Earth."

The Apollo program was born, and five months before the end of the decade, NASA displayed pictures of Americans on the moon, proof that we had beat the Russians to the most important prize. We won. Mission accomplished. But was it accomplished by actually sending men to the moon, or just making it look that way?

A FUNNY THING HAPPENED ON THE WAY TO THE MOON

Investigative journalist Bart Sibrel claims to have found a mislabeled NASA film showing multiple "takes" of a scene shown to the public as part of the "live" broadcast of the *Apollo 11* flight. In the footage the astronauts appear to be rehearsing the lines the public heard. Sibrel claims to have spent half a million dollars investigating the moon landings, and produced a video called *A Funny Thing Happened on the Way to the Moon*.

In 2002 Sibrel, backed by a Japanese film crew, confronted Buzz Aldrin outside a Beverly Hills hotel and challenged him to swear on a Bible that he had really gone to the moon. Aldrin responded by punching Sibrel in the face.

And what about those marvelous still photos? Many believe they were staged, perhaps in a secret location in Nevada, or even in a giant geodesic soundstage in Australia. Either way it would have been much easier to manipulate the lighting to get the results shown in the moon landing photos.

Would such a monstrous hoax have been easy to pull off? Certainly not. But to some people it seems more possible—and cheaper—than actually sending someone to the moon and back. Consider these statistics: Of the seven manned missions to the moon, only *Apollo 13* had trouble, which is an 86 percent success rate. In the years since, 25 unmanned crafts have been sent to Mars. Only seven have succeeded—a 28 percent success rate. Which figure seems more realistic?

JUST WHEN YOU THOUGHT IT WAS SAFE

Before you get too comfortable with the idea that the government created a huge hoax because we couldn't have possibly gone to the moon, keep in mind that there are also people who believe the film is fake, but that we actually did go to the moon. So why fake it? Maybe to cover up what we really found there. But that's another story.

* * *

ODD JOBS

Killer Bee Hunter. Your mission: Track down Africanized "killer" bees, which are migrating north from Central America, and destroy them before they can take up residence in North America.

Chicken Shooter. Fire dead chickens out of a cannon at aircraft to see what kind of damage occurs.

Mother Repairer. It's not what you think. It actually entails repairing metal phonograph record "mothers" (the master from which records are pressed) by removing dirt and nickel particles from the grooves.

Anthem Man. A unique profession: King Alfonso of Spain was tone deaf . . . he employed one man whose job was to alert him when the Spanish national anthem was playing (so he would know when to salute).

Worm Collector. Get ready to crawl through grass at night with a flashlight, to catch the best worms for fishing. Tip: Grab them in the middle to avoid bruising.

Pig Manure Sniffer. Workers try to recognize chemical markers in manure so researchers can determine which foods make pig manure so foul smelling. Women only, because estrogen increases sensitivity to smell.

Sewage Diver. Put on a diving suit and plunge into a sewage-containment vat.

Big Moments in Forensics

Who thought of identifying people with fingerprints?
When were blood types first discovered? When did Quincy
go on the air? Soon, you will know all.

Forensics is the science of whodunit. When a crime is committed, forensic scientists pore over physical evidence to discover
who did it, when it was done, and how it happened. It's just like
the board game Clue, except with more expensive detection equipment, and at the end, someone goes to prison. Like any good science,
the science and practice of forensics didn't happen overnight. While
the practice of forensics in crime-solving has exploded in recent
years, with everything from DNA typing to forensic accountants por-
ing over insider trades, some very basic forensic ideas have been kick-
ing around for years—long before CSI, Crossing Jordan, or even
Quincy. Come with us as we pursue the trail of forensics through history, from China to Los Angeles.

A.D. 700: The Chinese use fingerprints on documents and on clay
sculptures. Some time before this, ancient Babylonians were also
pressing thumbprints into clay documents for business transactions.
So at least a few civilizations out there are clued into the idea of fingerprints as identifying marks.

1248: We're in China again—this time for the publication of a book
entitled *Hsi Duan Yu (The Washing Away of Wrongs)*, which told its
readers how to tell the difference between someone who had been
strangled and someone who had been drowned. What makes this
such a big deal is that it offers medical reasoning instead of just saying something like "if they're floating in the water, there's a good
chance they've drowned." It's the first time anyone records the medical reasoning being used to solve crime.

1609: The first stirrings of forensic accounting occur when François Demelle of France publishes the first treatise on systematic document examination.

1784: In Lancaster, England, some guy named John Toms had a torn piece of newspaper in his pocket. The bad news for him was that the torn newspaper nicely fit another torn bit of newspaper found in a pistol that was used to commit a murder. The law puts them together—the first instance of physical matching—and Toms is convicted.

1810: Master criminal Eugène François Vidocq is on his way to the Big House when he has an idea. He'll use his criminal skills for the good of mankind instead! In addition to providing generations of comic book, movie, and TV show hacks a durable plot idea, he also forms the first detective force in the history of the world: the Sûreté of Paris. All of the detectives, like Vidocq, are former criminals. Among Vidocq's forensic innovations: making plaster casts of footprints and shoeprints, using ballistics, and competent record-keeping (on index cards, no less).

1813: Paris again, where Mathiew Orfila publishes the first treatise that systematically catalogs poisons and their effects. For this, he gets the title of Father of Modern Toxicology, although there probably wasn't an official ceremony. Orfila also was one of the first to develop forensic blood tests and to examine blood and semen with a microscope for forensic purposes.

1835: Scotland Yard investigator Henry Goddard determines that a butler had staged an attempted robbery when he traces a bullet back to a bullet mold owned by the butler. This is the first example of bullet matching, as well as one of the first actual recorded cases of "the butler did it."

1863: Is that blood or a spot of ketchup? A German scientist named Schönbein creates the first presumptive test for blood when he discovers that hemoglobin will oxidize hydrogen peroxide. Mixing peroxide and ketchup will simply give you inedible ketchup, although it's unclear if Schönbein made this observation.

1879: As police forces started keeping systematic records of crimes and criminals, they found themselves with more information than they could keep track of, especially in big cities. Alphone Bertillon, a clerk working for the Paris police, came up with a solution—measuring a lot of body parts on each criminal. He calculated that there was a one in four chance of two different criminals having one measurement match; by taking 11 measurements, he cut the odds to one in 4 million. A lot of criminals found policemen coming toward them with calipers in their hands and a gleam in their eyes. Police departments sorted their rogues galleries by the span of their outstretched arms and the length and breadth of their ears. This sounds pretty random, but so are fingerprints, which replaced bertillonage (aka the anthropometric method) in the early 20th century. Fingerprints were more random, which made them even less likely to be duplicated.

1880: Trouble in Tokyo! There's been a burglary, and an innocent man has been blamed for the heist! In steps Scottish physician and missionary Henry Faulds, who uses fingerprints not only to clear the accused, but also to help bring the actual criminal to justice. Faulds writes about using fingerprints for crime-solving in the science journal Nature, and then spends the next couple of decades in a nasty little letter-writing spat with one Sir William Herschel, about which of the two of them thought up the idea first. (Herschel—not to be confused with the other Sir William Herschel, the guy who discovered Uranus—concedes the point, finally, in 1917.)

1887: Everyone's favorite fictional master of forensics, Sherlock Holmes, makes his debut.

1892: Sir Francis Galton of Great Britain publishes *Fingerprints*, the first book to codify fingerprint patterns and show how to use them in solving crimes. Meanwhile, in Argentina, police investigator Juan Vucetich develops a fingerprinting classification system based on Galton's work and uses it to accuse a mother of murdering her two sons and then slitting her own throat to make it look like the work of someone else. Seems she left bloody fingerprints on a doorpost. That'll teach her.

1901: Human blood groups are identified and described by Austrian doctor Karl Landsteiner, who subsequently codified his discoveries into the blood types we know today. This discovery was useful in the field of forensics (to help identify criminals by the blood they might leave at the crime scene), as well as in medicine in general, and it lands Landsteiner a Nobel Prize in 1930.

1903: The first academic program for forensic science is created at University of Lausanne, Switzerland, by Professor R. A. Reiss.

1905: Teddy Roosevelt creates the FBI. He was president at the time. He could do that.

1910: Rosella Rousseau confesses to the murder of Germaine Bichon. Why? Because her hair is matched to hairs at the crime scene, a technique pioneered by Victor Balthazard, a professor of forensic medicine at the Sorbonne. The same year, another French professor of forensic medicine, Edmund Locard, helps to create the first police crime lab. The first U.S. crime lab was founded in 1925 by Los Angeles police chief August Vollmer.

1921: The portable polygraph (lie detector) is invented. In 1923 polygraph testimony is ruled inadmissible in U.S. courts.

1925: Blood's not the only bodily fluid you can type, suggested Japanese scientist K. I. Yosida, as he undertook studies to determine serological isoantibodies in other body fluids. He's right.

1960: An arsonist's job gets harder as gas chromatography is used for the first time in a lab to identify specific petroleum products.

1976: *Quincy, M.E.*, starring Jack Klugman as a feisty L.A. coroner, debuts and runs through 1983. The character of Quincy is allegedly based on real-life Los Angeles "Coroner to the Stars" Thomas Noguchi, who presided over the autopsies of Marilyn Monroe and Bobby Kennedy, and played a significant role in the investigation of the Manson family murders. The physical resemblance between Klugman and Noguchi is enigmatic at best.

1977: Japanese forensic scientist Fuseo Matsumur notices his fingerprints popping up as he prepares a slide for examination and tells his friend Masato Soba. Soba would use this information to help develop the first process to raise latent prints with cyanoacrylate, or, as it's more commonly known, superglue. Yes, superglue. Now you know why not to get it on your fingers.

1984: Yes, 1984. An ironic year for the first successful DNA profiling test, created by Great Britain's Sir Alec Jeffreys.

1986: Jeffreys uses his DNA profiling method to help convict the ominously named Colin Pitchfork for murder. Interestingly, in this same case DNA is used to clear another man accused of the crime.

1987: DNA profiling makes its debut in the United States and nails Tommy Lee Andrews for a number of sexual assaults in Orlando, Florida. However, in the same year, the admissibility of DNA profiling is challenged in another case, *New York v. Castro*, in which the defendant was accused of murder. This set the stage for many years of back and forth argument on the standards and practices of the labs that perform DNA profiling.

1991: *Silence of the Lambs* is released, starring Jodie Foster as an FBI investigator who uses forensic techniques to track down a serial killer, and Anthony Hopkins as the oddly genteel cannibal who helps her. Foster becomes the first actress to win an Oscar for playing an FBI agent; Hopkins becomes the first actor to win an Oscar for playing a character that has a good friend for lunch with fava beans and a nice Chianti.

1996: In Tennessee a fellow named Paul Ware is accused of murder, but the only physical evidence is a few hairs. Investigators use those hairs to extract DNA from mitochondria, a small structure within human cells. Mitochondrial DNA is different from DNA found in a cell's nucleus. Since there are quite a few mitochondria in every human cell, the amount of mitochondrial DNA to work with is larger. The mitochondrial DNA in the hairs is a match for Ware's. Ware is serving a life term in prison. It's the first use of mitochondrial DNA to convict someone of a crime.

2001: Not one but two shows about forensic scientists hit the TV: the redundantly titled *CSI: Crime Scene Investigation* and *Crossing Jordan*. None of the stars look remotely like Thomas Noguchi.

2005: There were at least a dozen new forensic TV shows, including the additions of *CSI: Miami* and *CSI: New York* based on the success of the original *Crime Scene Investigation*.

Castle Grande

Was it the world's most expensive private residence . . . or the world's biggest white elephant? Luckily, California's Hearst Castle is open for public tours. Pay it a visit and see for yourself.

OTHER PEOPLE'S MONEY

In 1894 William Randolph Hearst, age 31, a member of one of California's wealthiest families and the publisher of the *San Francisco Examiner*, commissioned an architect to build a mansion on a large tract of land in Pleasanton, California.

Somehow he never got around to telling the owner—his mother—he was building himself a house on her property. When she found out, she took it and kept it for herself. There wasn't much William could do about it—his mother, the widow of U.S. senator George Hearst, controlled the family's entire $20 million fortune. William hadn't inherited a penny of his father's estate and had nothing in his own name, not even the *Examiner*. His mother owned that, too.

Twenty-five years later, Hearst, now 56, wanted to build a hilltop house on the 60,000-acre ranch his mother owned in San Simeon, a small coastal whaling town halfway between San Francisco and Los Angeles. Hearst was fond of camping with his family and an entourage of as many as 50 guests and servants at the site, but wanted something "a little more comfortable."

A SLIGHT CHANGE IN PLANS

By now Hearst was well on his way to becoming one of the most powerful publishers in the country . . . but his mother still controlled the family fortune. He must have learned something from his 1894 experience, because he told his mother about the plan for San Simeon before he started construction, and he limited himself to a single tiny "Jappo-Swisso bungalow." Mrs. Hearst agreed to let him build, but insisted on keeping the property in her name because, she explained, "I'm afraid he might get carried away." She had good reason to worry.

Just a few months later, in April 1919, Hearst's mother died of influenza. William, her only son, inherited everything . . . and began rethinking his simple bungalow. He told architect Julia Morgan that he wanted something a little bigger.

"I don't think it was a month before we were going on a grand scale," Morgan's employee Walter Steilberg remembered. The bungalow quickly evolved into a large house . . . then a mansion . . . and finally one enormous mansion called Casa Grande, surrounded by three smaller "cottages"—Casa del Sol, Casa del Mar, and Casa del Monte—giving the hilltop retreat the appearance of an entire Mediterranean hill town.

Hearst called it La Cuesta Encantata, "The Enchanted Hill." To the public, it would become known as Hearst Castle.

AN UPHILL BATTLE

That was the plan, but as Julia Morgan explained to Hearst, bringing the large project to completion would not be easy or cheap. For one thing, there was no paved road and the rocky, barren spot where Hearst wanted to build was 1,600 feet up, which meant there was no easy way to get construction materials to the site. And with no topsoil, there was no way to plant the trees and gardens Hearst wanted, either. Furthermore, San Simeon was in the middle of nowhere, which meant that skilled workers would have to be brought in from hundreds of miles away and housed and fed on-site.

None of this mattered to Hearst. He'd loved San Simeon since childhood, and for the first time in his life he had the money to build his dream house. Nothing was going to get in his way. The dirt trail up the hill was paved; the pier in the town of San Simeon was enlarged to allow steamships to unload construction materials; dormitories were constructed for the workers; and tons of topsoil were hauled up to the site, enough to bury 50 acres of land under four feet of dirt. Construction began in 1919 . . . and was still underway more than 30 years later, when Hearst died in August 1951.

SALE OF THE CENTURY

While Morgan was working on the building plans, Hearst was hard at work indulging what his mother had once described as his "mania for antiquities"—he spent millions of dollars acquiring entire trainloads of antiques to furnish and decorate the 165 rooms—including 56 bedrooms and 19 sitting rooms—and the 61 bathrooms that made up his estate. His timing was perfect: cash-strapped European governments were instituting income and estate taxes to finance rebuilding in the aftermath of World War I. Once-wealthy families found themselves having to auction off artwork, antiques, and even entire castles, monasteries, and country estates to raise cash to pay their taxes. Hearst was their biggest customer.

RECYCLED MATERIALS
Hearst was especially fond of acquiring "architectural fragments"—floors, doorways, windows, mantles, chimneys, etc.—that could be carted off to San Simeon and set into the concrete walls of his estate. For more than 20 years, he compulsively bought just about everything that caught his eye and shipped it across the Atlantic to warehouses in the Bronx; from there most of it was sent by rail to warehouses in San Simeon.

Hearst peppered Julia Morgan with suggestions on which artifacts should go where, and none of these treasures were too sacred to be "improved" if need be. If something was too small, Morgan had it enlarged; if it was too big, she had it chopped down to size. "So far we have received from Hearst, to incorporate into the new buildings, some 12 or 13 railroad cars of antiques," Morgan wrote in 1920:

> They comprise vast quantities of tables, beds, armoires, secretaries, all kinds of cabinets, church statuary, columns, door frames, carved doors in all stages of repair and disrepair, over-altars, reliquaries, lanterns, iron grille doors, window grilles, votive candlesticks, torchères, all kinds of chairs in quantity, door trims, wooden carved ceilings . . . I don't see myself where we are ever going to use half suitably, but I find that the idea is to try things out and if they are not satisfactory, discard them for the next thing that comes that promises better.

THE COLLECTOR
Not all of this booty ended up at Hearst Castle—Hearst owned a castle in Wales, a beachfront mansion in Santa Monica, a 50,000-acre estate near Mt. Shasta in the northern part of California, and more. But he bought more antiques, artworks, and architectural

fragments than even these buildings could hold; to this day thousands of his purchases sit in their original packing crates in Hearst Corporation warehouses around the country.

COMPANY'S COMING
By the mid-1920s, enough of the construction had been completed at San Simeon to allow Hearst to begin entertaining guests as diverse as Winston Churchill, Charlie Chaplin, Calvin Coolidge, and George Bernard Shaw. He provided them with plenty to do: hiking, trout fishing, horseback riding, and tennis; there was also a billiard room, library, movie theater, and indoor and outdoor swimming pools. If guests wanted to play golf, there was even an airplane standing by to fly them to the nearest course. If they wanted to look at elephants, giraffes, or other exotic animals, that wasn't a problem either: Hearst's estate was also home to the largest privately owned zoo in the world.

A FEW SMALL PROBLEMS
When guests arrived at the estate, they quickly discovered that for all its grandeur, it wasn't very comfortable. Some guest rooms gave up so much space to antiques and art that there wasn't any room left for closets. The buildings could also be quite drafty, and the chimneys smoked terribly.

Hearst's peculiar quirks as host added to the discomfort. He didn't believe in serving his guests breakfast in bed, or even bringing them coffee. There were no kitchens in the guest houses, so anyone who wanted something to eat had to get dressed and come to Casa Grande.

The cocktail hour before dinner was another oddity. It could last as long as two hours or more, but Hearst served only one cocktail to each guest (two if you arrived early, drank quickly, and got lucky). Anyone caught smuggling their own liquor into San Simeon soon found their bags packed and set next to the car that was waiting to take them away.

Rationing his booze may have come back to haunt Hearst in ways he could never have imagined: one of his most ungrateful guests was a hard-drinking writer named Herman Mankiewicz, who went on to cowrite the screenplay for *Citizen Kane*, a film about a "fictional" newspaper baron who lives in an enormous castle called Xanadu, an obvious blast at Hearst.

Hearst was one of the wealthiest men in the country, but the Great Depression finally caught up with him in 1936; he found himself more than $100 million in debt at a time when newspaper circulation and advertising revenues were sharply off. At 74, he lost control of his business empire and was forced to sell off real estate, newspapers, and half of his art collection. He managed to hang on to San Simeon, but only by agreeing to halt construction and paying "rent" to his creditors until his financial situation improved.

HE'S BA-A-ACK

Hearst finally regained control in 1945 when he was 82, and immediately resumed construction at San Simeon. But Hearst's health was deteriorating, and in 1947 he was forced to move to Los Angeles to be closer to his doctors. He never returned to his castle, and died in August 1951 at the age of 88.

The Hearst Corporation directors were not nearly as infatuated with San Simeon as Hearst had been—they wanted to get rid of it. But nobody would buy it, because nobody could afford it.

The company offered it to the University of California free of charge . . . but the university refused to accept the "gift" unless it was accompanied by a huge endowment to cover operating costs. Finally in 1958, the corporation donated the buildings and the surrounding land to the state of California, which now operates it as a tourist attraction.

THE BIG QUESTION: HOW MUCH DID IT COST?

William Randolph Hearst spent so much money so quickly over so many years that it's difficult to calculate just how much he spent building and furnishing San Simeon. *Guinness World Records* estimates that he spent as much as $30 million (or about $277 million today). By contrast, Microsoft founder Bill Gates's mansion cost only $60 million.

That makes Hearst Castle easily the most expensive private residence ever built . . . and it's still unfinished.

* * *

"I do not seek, I find." —Picasso

The Adventures of Eggplant

Mix reality TV and Japanese game shows with the plot of the movie The Truman Show, *and you've got this unbelievable true story.*

MADE IN JAPAN

In January 1998 a struggling 23-year-old stand-up comedian known only by his stage name Nasubi (Eggplant) heard about an audition for a mysterious "show business–related job" and decided to try out for it.

The audition was the strangest one he'd ever been to. The producers of a popular Japanese TV show called *Susunu! Denpa Sho-Nen* (Don't Go for It, Electric Boy!) were looking for someone who was willing to be locked away in a one-bedroom apartment for however long it took to win 1 million yen (then the equivalent of about $10,000) worth of prizes in magazine contests.

Cameras would be set up in the apartment, and if the contestant was able to win the prizes, the footage would be edited into a segment called "Sweepstakes Boy." The contestant would be invited on the show to tell his story and, with any luck, the national TV exposure would give a boost to his career. That was it—that was the reward (along with the magazine prizes).

SUCH A DEAL

As if that wasn't a weak enough offer, there was a catch—the contestant would have to live off the prizes he won. The apartment would be completely empty, and the contestant wouldn't be allowed to bring anything with him—no clothes, no food, nothing. If he wanted to eat, he had to win food. If he wanted to wear clothes, he had to win those, too. Nasubi passed the audition and agreed to take the job.

On day one of the contest, the producers blindfolded him and took him to a tiny one-bedroom apartment in an undisclosed location somewhere in Tokyo. The apartment was furnished with a magazine rack and thousands of neatly stacked postcards (for entering the contests), as well as a table, a cushion to sit on, a telephone, notepads, and some pens. Other than that, it was completely empty.

Nasubi stripped naked and handed his clothes and other personal effects to the producers. He stepped into the apartment, the door was locked behind him, and his strange adventure began.

HOME ALONE

Nasubi spent his days entering magazine sweepstakes, filling out between 3,000 and 8,000 postcards a month. It took him two weeks to win his first prize—a jar of jelly. Two weeks later, he won a five-pound bag of rice.

But how could he cook it? He hadn't won any cooking utensils. He tried eating the rice raw, and when that failed he put some in a tin can, added some water, and put it next to a burner on the stove. Using this method, he cooked about half a cup of rice each day, and ate it using two of his pens for chopsticks. (The producers are believed to have given Nasubi some sort of food assistance, otherwise he would not have eaten anything for the first two weeks of the show. To this day it is unclear exactly how much assistance he received, but judging from the amount of weight he lost during the show, it wasn't much.)

SECRET ADMIRERS

Nasubi didn't know it at the time, but he was being watched. Sure, he knew about the cameras in the apartment, but the producers had told him that the footage would be used on *Susunu! Denpa Sho-Nen* after (and if) he completed his mission. And he had believed them.

But the producers had lied—he'd been on TV from the very beginning. Each Sunday night, edited highlights of the week's activities were broadcast in a one-hour show on NTV, one of Japan's national networks. The show was a big hit, and in the process Nasubi became a national celebrity, one of the hottest new stars in Japan. A naked star at that, albeit one whose private parts were kept continuously concealed by a cartoon eggplant that the producers superimposed on the screen.

NASUBI'S BOOTY

Viewers were there when Nasubi won each of his two vacuum cleaners, and they were there when he won each of his four bags of rice,
his watermelon, his automobile tires, his belt, and his ladies underwear (the only articles of clothing he won during months in captivity), his four tickets to a Spice Girls movie (which he could not leave
the apartment to see), his bike (which he could not ride outside),
and countless other items, including chocolates, stuffed animals,
headphones, videos, golf balls, a tent, a case of potato chips, a barbecue, and a shipment of duck meat.

Nasubi also won a TV, but the joy of winning it was shattered
when he discovered that his apartment had neither antenna nor
cable hookup. (The producers feared that if he watched TV, he'd find
out he was on TV.)

And he won a few rolls of toilet paper—10 months after his ordeal
began.

Nasubi sang a song and danced a victory dance every time a new
prize came in the mail; when he did, many viewers at home sang and
danced with him. When his food ran out, they gagged and sobbed
with him as he ate from the bag of dog food he won; when he prayed
for a new bag of rice, viewers prayed, too.

ROUND-THE-CLOCK EXPOSURE

Nasubi was such a media sensation that reporters tried to find out
where he was living. It took six months, but someone finally located
his apartment building in June 1998. Before they could make contact
with him, however, the producers whisked Nasubi off to a new apartment in the dead of night, telling him the move was intended "to
change his luck."

In July the producers set up a live Web site with a video feed and a
staff of more than 50 people (many of whom were there just to make
sure the moving digital dot stayed over Nasubi's private parts at all
times). Now people could watch Nasubi 24 hours a day.

Finally, in December 1998, one year after he was first locked into the
apartment, Nasubi won the prize—a bag of rice—that pushed his total
winnings over a million yen. So was he free? Not exactly: The show's
producers gave him his clothes, fed him a bowl of ramen noodles, and
then whisked him off to Korea, where he couldn't speak the language
and no one would recognize him. Then he was placed in another empty

apartment, where he had to win prizes to pay for his airfare back home.

When Nasubi finally accomplished that, he was flown back to Tokyo, taken to a building, and led into another empty room (it was really just a box, but he didn't know it).

INSTANT CELEBRITY

Out of habit, he stripped naked and waited for something to happen. Suddenly the roof lifted, the walls fell away, and Nasubi found himself, still naked, his hair uncut and his face unshaved for more than 15 months (he never did win clippers or a shaver), standing in an NTV broadcast studio in front of a live audience. Seventeen million more people were watching at home.

More than 15 months had passed since Nasubi had been locked into his apartment, and it was only now, as he held a cushion over his privates, that he learned he'd been on TV since day one. His weekly show had made him Japan's hottest new star, the producers explained to him. The diary he'd kept? It had already been published and was a best-selling book, one that had earned him millions of yen (tens of thousands of dollars) in royalties. That bowl of ramen soup the producers fed him the day he came out of isolation? The footage had been turned into a popular soup commercial. They told him about the Web site—it made money, too. All of this resulted in a lot of money for Nasubi.

It took quite a while for all of this information to sink in. "I'm so shocked," Nasubi finally said. "I can't express what I feel."

ONE OF A KIND

Today Nasubi is a happy, successful celebrity. Nevertheless, as crazy as Japanese game shows can be, it's unlikely that any other person will experience what he went through. Even if someone were crazy enough to agree to be locked in an apartment for such a long time, they would know from the beginning what was up.

But there's another reason: That much isolation just isn't healthy. Sure, he looked relatively happy on the show, and he certainly had moments of joy. But the footage had been edited to make Nasubi's experience seem better than it really was. In press interviews, he admitted there were times when he thought he was going to go nuts. "I thought of escaping several times," he told reporters later. "I was on edge, especially toward the end."

Who Killed Jimi Hendrix?

Jimi Hendrix had an astounding influence on pop culture. Yet few people of the 1960s were truly shocked when the musician died in 1970—he had a reputation for living hard and fast. Most people assumed he just burned out like a shooting star. But did he? Or was there more to it?

DEATH, DRUGS, AND ROCK 'N' ROLL

Hours before Jimi Hendrix died, he was working on a song entitled "The Story of Life." The last lines:

The story of life is quicker than the wink of an eye.
The story of love is hello and goodbye,
Until we meet again.

Perhaps no rock musician is more emblematic of the psychedelic 1960s than Hendrix. The flamboyant guitarist became famous not only for such onstage antics as lighting his guitar on fire, but also for the blistering performances that earned him recognition as a musical genius. Although only five albums were released during his lifetime, he was—and is—considered one of the greatest rock guitarists ever.

OVEREXPERIENCED

James Marshall Hendrix died in the squalid flat of a German girlfriend in London on September 18, 1970, after a long night of drinking and partying. After indulging in a smorgasbord of drugs and alcohol, he and his girlfriend returned to her apartment in the early hours of the morning where, according to the girlfriend, they both took some barbiturate pills to help them sleep.

A normal dose of the downers would have been just half a pill. The girlfriend claimed she took one pill. After Hendrix's death, an autopsy showed he had swallowed nine—18 times the recommended dosage. The autopsy also revealed "massive" quantities of red wine not only in his stomach, but also in his lungs. The quantity and combination of substances might well have been fatal if he hadn't first suffocated on the wine and his own vomit.

There is little mystery as to what killed Jimi Hendrix. The question is: How did it happen? Was it suicide, an accident . . . or murder? Ever since Hendrix's death, there have been those who believe there may have been more to the story than just another rock star done in by wretched excess. For some, things don't quite add up.

FATAL MISTAKE OR FOUL PLAY?

Friends of Hendrix rule out suicide. According to them, Hendrix believed the soul of a person who committed suicide would never rest. In spite of his many personal and professional problems, he would never take his own life.

Was it an accident? Hendrix was known for being able to take greater quantities of drugs than anyone else in his circle. He may have mistaken the potent barbiturates for regular sleeping pills and grabbed his usual handful. On the other hand, as experienced a drug-taker as Hendrix was, he was unlikely to make that kind of mistake. Besides, it was common knowledge that drinking alcohol with downers is asking for serious trouble.

But the quantity of wine found inside him, and around him on the bed where he died, raises an intriguing question: Did he drink that much or was it poured down his throat by someone else? How did so much get into his lungs? Oddly, the autopsy showed a relatively low blood-alcohol level in his body, leading some to speculate that Hendrix drowned in the wine before much of it was absorbed into his system.

But who would want Jimi Hendrix dead? It may be impossible to know now, more than 30 years after his death, but here are some compelling possibilities:

• **The Girlfriend.** According to the girlfriend, Monika Dannemann, she woke up the morning of the 18th, saw that Hendrix was sleeping normally, and went out for cigarettes. When she returned she saw that Hendrix had been sick and was having trouble breathing. She tried to wake him, and when she couldn't she began to panic and called musician Eric Burdon, with whom they had partied the night before. After first hanging up on her, Burdon called back and insisted Dannemann call an ambulance. Dannemann later told the press that Hendrix was alive when the ambulance arrived a few minutes later, about 11:30 a.m., and that she rode with him to the hospital. According to Dannemann, Hendrix was propped upright on the trip and suffocated on the way.

The ambulance attendants tell a different story. According to author James Rotondi, the two men arrived at the apartment to find it empty . . . except for Hendrix lying in a mess on the bed, already dead. They say they went through the motions of trying to revive Hendrix because that was standard procedure, but to no avail. They wrapped up the body, carried it to the ambulance, and drove to the hospital; Hendrix was pronounced dead on arrival. The autopsy cautiously concludes that the exact cause and time of death are unknown, but evidence points to a time of death much earlier—possibly several hours before the ambulance arrived.

Was Monika Dannemann trying to cover up something? If so, what and why? The world may never know—she committed suicide in 1996.

• **The Government.** Rock music has long been associated with rebellion, revolution, and social change, ideas that appeal to youthful fans but are a cause for concern for "the Establishment." It is well known that during the J. Edgar Hoover era, and perhaps even more recently, the FBI kept dossiers not only on political activists, but on actors, authors, and a wide variety of other potential "threats" as well. It is not surprising that influential musicians such as Jimi Hendrix would draw the interest of the U.S. government—but there may be more to it than that.

In his book *The Covert War Against Rock*, author Alex Constantine says Hendrix's FBI file, released in 1979 to a student newspaper in Santa Barbara, reveals that Hendrix was on a list of "subversives" to be placed in detainment camps in the event of national emergency. Hendrix was an icon of not only rock 'n' roll rebellion, but the Black Power and antiwar movements of the 1960s. Did U.S. intelligence agencies consider Hendrix not only subversive, but dangerous?

There are some conspiracy theorists who believe that Hendrix and other musicians, including Jim Morrison of The Doors, ex-Beatle John Lennon, and more recently, rappers Tupac Shakur and The Notorious B.I.G.—all of whom died under suspicious circumstances—may have been eliminated by the government. It would be remarkably easy to make the deaths look like accidents or murders committed by crazy fans—these musicians lived life close to the edge anyway. Paranoid fantasy? Or could there be some truth to these fears?

• **The Mob.** Government agents may not have been the only ones with an eye on Hendrix. Organized crime figures were involved with the music industry long before Hendrix was. To the Mob, the industry wasn't about music—it was about money and drugs. And there was plenty of both around Hendrix.

According to Constantine, Hendrix was muscled by the Mob after declining an invitation to play at the Salvation, a New York night club controlled by the Gambino crime family. Hendrix had been a regular at the club, but after the proprietor was murdered following an attempt to break free of Mob control, Hendrix evidently felt uncomfortable playing there. Shortly thereafter, Constantine says, a stranger approached Hendrix on the street and, while chatting, pulled out a .38 pistol and casually hit a target 25 feet away. Hendrix got the message and decided to play the club after all.

Another time, Hendrix was kidnapped from the Salvation by some thugs claiming to be part of the Mafia, Constantine claims. They took him to a Manhattan apartment and told him to call his manager, Michael Jeffery, and relay a demand to transfer his contract to the Mob . . . or else. Hendrix was rescued from the thugs by men sent by Jeffery, but later told people he thought Jeffery had arranged the whole thing.

So Hendrix may have had good reason not to trust his manager.

• **The Manager.** Those seeking to tie together the loose ends of government agencies, the Mob, and enormous amounts of money need look no further than Michael Jeffery. Jeffery served in British Intelligence in the 1950s and years later boasted of underworld connections. As Hendrix's manager, Jeffery had control of millions of dollars earned by Hendrix, much of which was diverted by Jeffery to offshore bank accounts.

Hendrix became increasingly aware that Jeffery was cheating him, and just before his death made arrangements to cancel his management contract. The manager understandably could have been upset at the prospect of losing such a lucrative client—but why kill Hendrix? The answer could lie in the rumor that Jeffery had taken out a million-dollar life insurance policy on the star. Additionally, Jeffery could have made much more from the dozens of Hendrix albums released after the musician's death. (There were many hours of unreleased music.)

Whatever involvement the former intelligence agent may have had in Hendrix's death would have had to have been indirect; he was vacationing in Spain when Hendrix died. To some, Jeffery was further implicated when he himself died under unusual circumstances less than three years later, in a plane crash.

FLY ON

A number of times in the weeks before his death the 27-year-old Hendrix asked friends, "Do you think I will live to be 28?" Did he have a premonition of what was coming? Friends say he was becoming increasingly paranoid . . . and perhaps with good reason. We may never know the truth about the death of Jimi Hendrix, but we do know that his life, as he wrote in his final song, was indeed "quicker than the wink of an eye."

* * *

A TALE OF TWO CHORDS

In July 2003, hard-rock band Metallica announced that they were suing the Canadian band Unfaith over their use of the guitar chords E and F. "We're not saying we own those two chords individually, that would be ridiculous," Metallica's Lars Ulrich was reported to have said. "We're just saying that in that specific order, people have grown to associate E and F with our music."

Unfaith's lead singer, Erik Ashley, responded, "I thought it was a prank at first. Now I'm not sure what to think." Actually, he knew exactly what to think. Why? Because he created the prank.

But that didn't stop the media from running with the story without contacting the parties involved. ABC talk show host Jimmy Kimmel reported it, as did MSNBC's Jeannette Walls.

So why did Ashley do it? "To gauge just how willing America was to buy a story as extraordinary—as outlandish—as Metallica claiming ownership of a two-chord progression." He added, "If this week was any indication, America is all too willing to believe it."

But after all of Metallica's well-publicized attempts to sue online music downloaders, was it really that hard to believe? Said one anonymous chat room attendant: "I'm not sure what's worse— that the story is a fake, or that it was actually conceivable that Metallica would do that."

What Happened at Roswell?

The "incident at Roswell" is probably the biggest UFO story in history. Was it a military balloon . . . or an alien spacecraft? You be the judge.

THE FIRST FLYING SAUCERS

In 1947 a U.S Forest Service pilot named Kenneth Arnold was flying over the Cascade Mountains in Washington State in search of a missing plane when he spotted what he claimed were nine "disc-shaped craft." He calculated them to be moving at speeds of 1,200 miles per hour, far faster than any human-built aircraft of the 1940s could manage.

When he talked to reporters after the flight, Arnold said the crafts moved "like a saucer skipping over water," and a newspaper editor, hearing the description, called the objects "flying saucers." Thus, the expression *flying saucer* entered the English language, and a UFO craze much like the one that followed Orson Welles's 1938 broadcast of *War of the Worlds* swept the country. "Almost instantly," Dava Sobel writes in his article "The Truth About Roswell," "believable witnesses from other states and several countries reported similar sightings, enlivening wire-service dispatches for days."

THE ROSWELL DISCOVERY

It was in this atmosphere that William "Mac" Brazel made an unusual discovery. On July 8, 1947, while riding across his ranch 26 miles outside of Roswell, New Mexico, he came across some mysterious wreckage—sticks, foil paper, tape, and other debris. Brazel had never seen anything like it, but UFOs were on his mind. He'd read about Arnold's sighting in the newspaper and had heard about a national contest offering $3,000 to anyone who recovered a flying saucer. He wondered if he'd stumbled across just the kind of evidence the contest organizers were looking for.

Brazel gathered a few pieces of the stuff and showed it to his

neighbors, Floyd and Loretta Proctor. The Proctors didn't know what it was, either. And neither did George Wilcox, the county sheriff. So Brazel contacted officials at the nearby Roswell Army Air Force base to see if they could help.

The next day, an army intelligence officer named Jesse Marcel went out to Brazel's ranch to have a look. He was as baffled as everyone else. "I saw . . . small bits of metal," he recalled to reporters years later, "but mostly we found some material that's hard to describe." Some of it "looked very much like parchment" and some of it consisted of square sticks as much as four feet long. Much was metallic.

The stuff was also surprisingly light—Brazel later estimated that all the scraps together didn't weigh more than five pounds. Marcel and his assistant had no trouble loading all the debris into their cars and driving it back to the Roswell base. The next day, Marcel took it to another base, in Fort Worth, Texas, where it was examined further.

SUSPICIOUS FACTS
Was the Wreckage from Outer Space?

- Brazel and the Proctors examined some of the debris before surrendering it to the military. Although it seemed flimsy at first, it was extremely resilient. "We tried to burn it, but it wouldn't ignite," Loretta recalls. "We tried to cut it and scrape at it, but a knife wouldn't touch it . . . It looked like wood or plastic, but back then we didn't have plastic. Back then, we figured it doesn't look like a weather balloon. I don't think it was something from this Earth."

THE MILITARY'S ABOUT-FACE

- The morning after the military took possession of the wreckage, the media relations officer at Roswell hand-delivered a news release to the two radio stations and newspapers in town. The release stated that the object found in Brazel's field was a "flying disc," which in the 1940s was synonymous with "flying saucer." It was the first time in history that the U.S. military had ever made such a claim.

- A few hours later, though, the military changed its story: It issued a new press release claiming that the wreckage was that of a weather balloon carrying a radar target, not a "flying disc." But it was too late—the newspaper deadline had already passed. They ran the first news release on the front page, under the headline

AIR FORCE CAPTURES FLYING SAUCER
ON RANCH IN ROSWELL REGION

Other newspapers picked up the story and ran it as well; within 24 hours, news of the military's "capture" spread around the globe.

- Interest in the story was so great that the next day, Brig. Gen. Roger Ramey, commander of the U.S. Eighth Air Force, had to hold a press conference in Fort Worth in which he again stated that the recovered object was only a weather balloon and a radar target that was suspended from it. He even displayed the wreckage for reporters and allowed them to photograph it.

MR. BRAZEL'S UNUSUAL BEHAVIOR

- Mac Brazel refused to talk about the incident for the rest of his life, even with members of his immediate family, except to say that "whatever the wreckage was, it wasn't any type of balloon." Why the silence? His son Bill explains, "The Air Force asked him to take an oath that he wouldn't tell anybody in detail about it. My dad was such a guy that he went to his grave and he never told anyone."

- Kevin Randle and Donald Schmitt, authors of *UFO Crash at Roswell*, claim that shortly after Brazel made his famous discovery, "His neighbors noticed a change in his lifestyle . . . He suddenly seemed to have more money . . . When he returned, he drove a new pickup truck . . . he also had the money to buy a new house in Tularosa, New Mexico, and a meat locker in Las Cruces." Randle and Schmitt believe the military may have paid Brazel for his silence.

TRUST ME
Today if the government announced it had captured a UFO—even if it was mistaken—and tried to change its story a few hours later by claiming it was really a weather balloon, nobody would buy it. But people were more trusting in the years just following World War II. Amazingly, the story died away. As Dava Sobel writes:

The Army's announcement of the "weather balloon" explanation ended the flying saucer excitement. All mention of the craft dropped from the newspapers, from military records, from the national consciousness, and even from the talk of the town in Roswell.

Even the *Roswell Daily Record*—which broke the story in the first place—was satisfied with the military's explanation. A few days later, it ran a headline that was even bigger than the first one:

GENERAL RAMEY EMPTIES ROSWELL SAUCER

And that was the end of it . . . or was it?

DÉJÀ VU

The Roswell story would probably have stayed dead if Stanton T. Friedman, a nuclear physicist, hadn't lost his job during the 1970s. UFOs were Friedman's hobby . . . until he got laid off; then they became his career. "In the 1970s, when the bottom fell out of the nuclear physics business," he explains, "I went full time as a lecturer." His favorite topic: "Flying Saucers ARE Real," a talk that he gave at more than 600 different college campuses and other venues around the country.

In his years on the lecture circuit, Friedman developed a nationwide reputation as a UFO expert, and people who'd seen UFOs began seeking him out. In 1978 he made contact with Jesse Marcel, the army intelligence officer (now retired) who'd retrieved the wreckage from Mac Brazel's ranch 31 years earlier.

At Friedman's urging, Marcel gave an interview to the *National Enquirer*. "I'd never seen anything like it," Marcel told the supermarket tabloid, "I didn't know what we were picking up. I still believe it was nothing that came from Earth. It came to Earth, but not from Earth."

BACK IN THE HEADLINES

The *Enquirer* interview couldn't have come at a more opportune time: It was 1979, and Steven Spielberg's film *Close Encounters of the Third Kind*, which had premiered several months earlier, had stoked the public's appetite for UFO stories. After lying dormant for more than 30 years, the Roswell story blew wide open all over again.

From there the story just kept growing. Dozens of new "witnesses" to the Roswell UFO began seeking out Friedman at his public appearances to tell him their stories. Soon the Roswell "cover-up" included humanoid alien beings. "Over the years," Joe Nickell writes in the *Skeptical Enquirer*, "numerous rumors, urban legends, and outright hoaxes have claimed that saucer wreckage and the remains of its humanoid occupants were stored at a secret facility—the (nonexistent) 'Hangar 18' at Wright Patterson Air Force Base. People swear that the small corpses were autopsied at that or another site."

For the record, neither Mac Brazel nor Jesse Marcel ever claimed to have seen aliens among the wreckage. No one went public with those claims until more than 30 years after the fact.

WHY BELIEVE IN ROSWELL?

Why are UFO conspiracy theories so popular? Anthropologists who study the "Roswell Myth" point to two psychological factors that help it endure:

- It appeals to a cynical public that lived through the Kennedy assassination, Watergate, Vietnam, and other government crises, and who believe in the government's proclivity for covering things up. As *Time* magazine reported on the 50th anniversary of the Roswell incident, "A state of mind develops which easily believes in cover-up. The fact that the military is known for 'covert' activities with foreign governments having to do with weapons which could wipe out humanity makes the idea of secret interactions with aliens seem possible. Once this state of mind is in place, anything which might prove the crash was terrestrial becomes a lie."

- UFO theories project a sense of order onto the chaos of the universe . . . and they can even serve as an ego boost to true believers, because they suggest that we are interesting enough that aliens with vastly superior intelligence actually bother to visit us. Believing in aliens, the argument goes, is much more satisfying than believing that aliens are out there but would never want to visit us.

WAS THERE A CONSPIRACY?

So is our government hiding evidence of an alien crash-landing on earth?

In 1993 Congressman Steven Schiff of New Mexico asked the U.S. government's General Accounting Office to look into whether the U.S. government had ever been involved in a space-alien cover-up, either in Roswell, New Mexico, or anyplace else. The GAO spent 18 months searching government archives dating back to the 1940s, including even the highly classified minutes of the National Security Council. Their research prompted the U.S. Air Force to launch its own investigation. It released its findings in September 1994; the GAO's report followed in November 1995; then a second air force report was released in 1997.

PROJECT MOGUL

All three reports arrived at the same conclusion: what the conspiracy theorists believe were UFO crashes were actually top secret research programs run by the U.S. military during the cold war.

Take Roswell: According to the reports, the object that crashed on Mac Brazel's farm was a balloon, but no ordinary weather balloon—it was part of Project Mogul, a defense program as top secret as the Manhattan Project itself. Unlike the Manhattan Project, however, Project Mogul wasn't geared toward creating nuclear weapons; it was geared toward detecting them if the Soviets exploded them.

In the late 1940s the United States had neither spy satellites nor high-altitude spy planes that it could send over the Soviet Union to see if Stalin's crash program to build nuclear weapons was succeeding. Instead, government scientists figured, "trains" of weather balloons fitted with special sensing equipment, if launched high enough into the atmosphere, might be able to detect the shock waves given off by nuclear explosions thousands of miles away.

UP, UP, AND AWAY

Project Mogul was just such a program, the reports explained, and the object that crashed on Mac Brazel's field in 1947 was Flight R-4, a Mogul balloon train that had been launched from Alamogordo Army Air Field—near the Roswell Base—in June 1947. The train of 20 balloons was tracked to within 17 miles of Mac Brazel's ranch; shortly afterwards, radar contact was lost and the balloons were never recovered . . . at least not by the folks at Alamogordo. The Roswell intelligence officers who recovered the wreckage didn't have high enough security clearance to know about Project Mogul, and thus they didn't know to inform Alamogordo of the discovery.

On the whole the program was successful—Project Mogul apparently did detect the first Soviet nuclear blasts. Even so, the project was discontinued when scientists discovered that such blasts could also be detected on the ground, making the balloonborne sensors unnecessary. The project was discontinued in the early 1950s.

OTHER PROJECTS

The air force's 1997 report suggested that a number of other military projects that took place in the 1940s and 1950s became part of the Roswell myth:

- In the 1950s the air force launched balloons as high as 19 miles into the atmosphere and dropped human dummies to test parachutes for pilots of the X-15 rocket plane and the U-2 spy plane. The dummies, the air force says, were sometimes mistaken for aliens . . . and because it didn't want the real purpose of the tests to be revealed, it did not debunk the alien theories.

- Some balloons also dropped mock interplanetary probes, which looked like flying saucers.

- In one 1959 balloon crash, a serviceman crashed a test balloon 10 miles northwest of Roswell and suffered an injury that caused his head to swell considerably. The man, Captain Dan D. Fulgham, was transferred to Wright Patterson in Ohio for treatment. The incident, the air force says, helped inspire the notion that aliens have large heads and that aliens or alien corpses are being held at Wright Patterson for study.

NEVER SURRENDER

Do the GAO and air force reports satisfy people who previously believed the object was a UFO? Not a chance. "It's a bunch of pap," says Walter G. Haut, who worked at the Roswell base and after World War II distributed the famous "flying saucer" news release in 1947, and is now president of the International UFO Museum and Research Center in Roswell. "All they've done is given us a different kind of balloon. Then it was weather, and now it's Mogul. Basically, I don't think anything has changed. Excuse my cynicism, but let's quit playing games."

Seer of the Century

*In 1900 John Watkins predicted the future—and got
a lot of it right. In an article written for the* Ladies' Home
Journal, *he looked a century into the future and foresaw
subways, air-conditioning, satellite TV, and lots more.
No one has ever come close to the feat—except
maybe Nostradamus. Here's a small excerpt.*

BACKGROUND

John Elspeth Watkins was a Philadelphia newspaperman whose predictions were recently rediscovered by two Indiana professors. They call him the Seer of the Century and note that he was lucky enough to see many of his predictions come true before dying in the 1940s.

What's amazing about these predictions? Remember what was going on in 1900: Production on primitive autos had just begun; they were still a novelty. People lived in squalor and ill health and died young. There was no such thing as an airplane. There was no radio; the first feature movie hadn't been made; the telephone had been invented a scant 25 years earlier. It was a whole different world—yet somehow, Watkins described ours in detail.

"These prophecies," he wrote in his introduction, "will seem strange, almost impossible." It's a fascinating measure of how things have changed to realize that our way of life seemed like science fiction to the average American of 1900.

EXCERPTS FROM WATKINS'S PREDICTIONS

"Man will see around the world. Persons and things of all kinds will be brought within focus of cameras connected electrically with screens at opposite ends of circuits, thousands of miles at a span. American audiences in their theatres will view upon huge curtains before them the coronations of kings in Europe or the progress of battles in the Orient. The instrument bringing these distant scenes to the very doors of people will be connected with a giant telephone apparatus transmitting each incidental sound into its appropriate place. Thus the guns of a distant battle will be heard to boom when seen to blaze, and thus the lips of a remote actor or singer will be heard to utter words or music when seen to move."

"The American will be taller by from one to two inches. His increase in stature will result from better health, due to vast reforms in medicine, sanitation, food, and athletics. He will live fifty years instead of thirty-five as at present—for he will reside in the suburbs."

"Hot and cold air from spigots. Hot or cold air will be turned on from spigots to regulate the temperature of a house as we now turn on hot or cold water from spigots to regulate the temperature of the bath . . . Rising early to build the furnace fire will be a task of the olden times. Homes will have no chimneys, because no smoke will be created within their walls."

"No mosquitoes nor flies. Boards of health will have destroyed all mosquito haunts and breeding grounds, drained all stagnant pools, filled in all swamp-lands, and chemically treated all still-water streams. The extermination of the horse and its stable will reduce the house-fly."

"Ready-cooked meals will be bought from establishments similar to our bakeries of today. Such wholesale cookery will be done in electric laboratories . . . equipped with electric stoves, and all sorts of electric devices, such as coffee-grinders, egg-beaters, stirrers, shakers, parers, meat-choppers, meat-saws, potato-mashers, lemon-squeezers, dish-washers, dish-dryers and the like. All such utensils will be washed in chemicals fatal to disease microbes."

"There will be no street cars in our large cities. All traffic will be below or high above ground when brought within city limits. In most cities it will be confined to broad subways or tunnels, well lighted and well ventilated, or to high trestles with "moving-sidewalk" stair-ways leading to the top. These underground or overhead streets will teem with automobile passenger coaches and freight wagons, with cushioned wheels. Subways or trestles will be reserved for express trains. Cities, therefore, will be free from all noises."

"Photographs will be telegraphed from any distance. If there be a battle in China a hundred years hence snapshots of its most striking events will be published in the newspapers an hour later. Even today photographs are being telegraphed over short distances. Photographs will reproduce all of Nature's colors."

"Automobiles will be cheaper than horses are today. Farmers will own automobile hay-wagons, plows, harrows, and hay-rakes. A one-pound motor in one of these vehicles will do the work of a pair of horses or more . . . Automobiles will have been substituted for every horse vehicle now known . . . The horse in harness will be as scarce, if, indeed, not scarcer, then as the yoked ox is today."

"Everybody will walk ten miles. Gymnastics will begin in the nursery, where toys and games will be designed to strengthen the muscles. Exercise will be compulsory in the schools. Every school, college and community will have a complete gymnasium . . . A man or woman unable to walk ten miles at a stretch will be regarded as a weakling."

"Submarine boats submerged for days will be capable of wiping a whole navy off the face of the deep."

"To England in two days. Fast electric ships, crossing the ocean at more than a mile a minute, will go from New York to Liverpool in two days. The bodies of these ships will be built above the waves. They will be supported upon runners, somewhat like those of the sleigh. These runners will be very buoyant. Upon their undersides will be apertures expelling jets of air. In this way a film of air will be kept between them and the water's surface. This film, together with the small surface of the runners, will reduce friction against the waves to the smallest possible degree."

"Telephones around the world. Wireless telephone and telegraph circuits will span the world. A husband in the middle of the Atlantic will be able to converse with his wife sitting in her boudoir in Chicago. We will be able to telephone to China quite as readily as we now talk from New York to Brooklyn. By an automatic signal they will connect with any circuit in their locality without the intervention of a 'hello girl.'"

"Automatic instruments reproducing original airs exactly will bring the best music to the families of the untalented. In great cities there will be public opera-houses whose singers and musicians are paid from funds endowed by philanthropists and by the government. The piano will be capable of changing its tone from cheerful to sad. Many devices will add to the emotional effect of music."

Index

Daniel, Jasper Newton, 161

Dannemann, Monica, 377–378

Danson, Ted, 101

Darwin, Charles, 73

Dassler Brothers Shoes, 22

Davidson, Elaine, 197

Davis, Jefferson, 229

days, 62, 77, 331

deadly sins, 77

decimal system, 20

deer, 319

Demelle, François, 362–363

denim, 195

Denmark, 230

Denny's, 156

dental floss, 9, 329

dentists, 126, 288, 296

dentures, 296

department stores, 103

deserts, 150

detectives, 363

Devil's Claw, 157

DeVito, Danny, 142

Dewar, Jimmy, 69

Dial soap, 22

diamonds, 31, 83

Diana, Princess, 211

diaper alarm, 63

Díaz, Andres, 63

dice, 7

Dickens, Charles, 106, 128

Dickin Medal for Valor, 216

Dickinson, Emily, 106

dictionaries, 93, 242

dieting, 182

Dietrich, Marlene, 21, 109, 127

Diff'rent Strokes, 273

dimension, fourth, 40

Dire Straits, 302

Disney World, 121, 231, 284

Disneyland, 121, 231

"Dixie," 38

Dixie Cups, 116

DNA profiling, 365–366

Dobbie, Scot Sandy, 197

dog years, 145

dogs, 15, 54, 59, 63, 66, 68, 201, 222, 283

dollar bills, 314

dollar sign, 46

dolls, 91

dolphins, 10, 96

dominoes, 7

doozy, 123

dope, 122

Double Bubble gum, 292

doughnuts, 69

Dow, Charles Henry, 161

Dow Chemical, 100

Dow Jones average, 161

Dr. Marten's, 161

Dr. Pepper, 175, 257

Dr. Seuss, 14, 106, 159

drab, 328

Draper, Kay, 99

dreaming, 236, 249

drinking, 322

drug testing, 47

drunk driving, 304

ducks, 283

Duesenberg, 123

dust, 88

dust storms, 234

E

eagles, 125, 259

Earhart, Amelia, 346

Earn Your Vacation, 101

ears, 48, 221

Earth, 66, 80, 81, 107, 162, 251

earthquakes, 251, 82

earthworms, 84, 198, 204

earwax, 48

Easter, 104

Eastman, George, 1

Eastwood, Clint, 142

Easy-Bake Ovens, 91

Edison, Thomas, 102, 224

Edward I, 132

Edward II, 325

eels, 71

egg rolls, 92

eggplant, 44

eggs, 143, 172, 297

eggshells, 135

Egypt (Egyptians), 8, 15, 68, 93, 150, 173, 206, 244, 299

Eiffel Tower, 197, 303

Einstein, Albert, 73, 211, 248, 300

Eisenhower, Dwight D., 200, 250

El Salvador, 42

electric blankets, 116

elements, 162, 36–37

elephants, 72, 107, 198, 203

Elizabeth I, 8, 181

e-mail, 240

Emerson, Ralph Waldo, 271

Emmett, Dan, 38
Empire State Building, 110, 166, 303
employees, 274, 307
energy, 118
English language, 189
eonite, 100
Epperson, Frank, 292
equal sign, 45
Erie Canal, 301
Erik the Red, 98
erotic, 178
Eskimo pies, 245
Esposito, Joe, 336, 338
Etch-A-Sketch, 91
evidence, criminal, 362–366
exclamation mark, 45
eyes, 255, 348

F
Fahrenheit, Gabriel Daniel, 161
Fairbanks, Douglas, 183
fairy tales, 128
falcons, 90
false teeth, 296
fantasy stories, 93
farms, 35, 143, 310
farting, 3, 33
fashion, 181, 265
fast and loose, 311
fast-food restaurants, 253
Father's Day, 104
Faulds, Henry, 364
FBI, 365, 378
feet, 61, 111, 135, 252
ferns, 212
ferrets, 105, 222
film industry. *See* motion pictures

fingernails, 67, 74, 187, 252
fingerprints, 362, 364, 365
fingers, 252
Finland, 98
fire beetles, 84
firecrackers, 8
fires, house, 25
fish, 10, 71, 145
flags, 280
flamingos, 125, 223
flavor, 154
fleas, 235
Fleer, Frank, 292
Fleischmann, Charles, 60
flies, 55, 84, 216, 235
Flipper, 101
floods, 9
flying fish, 90
flying saucers, 381–387
foam peanuts, 114
food poisoning, 113, 167
foods, hated, 215
foot (measurement), 325
football, 97
"For He's a Jolly Good Fellow," 38
Ford, Henry, 227, 228
Ford cars, 210
Ford Motor Company, 141
forensics, 362–366
forks, 27, 65
Fort Knox, 146
fortune cookies, 67
fortune telling, 285
Foster, Jodie, 366
Fox, Michael J., 127

fragrance (perfume), 181
France, 98
francium, 37
frankfurters, 21
Franklin, Benjamin, 30, 73, 142, 310, 313, 352
Fraser, Laura Gardin, 277
Fraze, Ermal Cleon, 27
freckles, 226
Freemasony, 85
french fries, 143, 172
French language, 189
Freud, Sigmund, 50, 73
Friday the 13th, 207
Friedman, Stanton T., 384
Frisbees, 75
frogs, 12, 283
fruit, 32, 131, 143, 192, 350–351
Fulgham, Dan D., 387
Funicello, Annette, 286
furlong, 325
furniture, 213
fuzz, 14

G
G. I. Joe, 91
Gable, Clark, 133
Galton, Francis, 364
gambling, 7, 100
game shows, 372–375
games, 7
Gandhi, Mahatma, 73
garbage, 9
Gardiner, Sandy, 155
Garfield, James, 163
Garland, Judy, 1

garlic, 44
garlic juice, 126
garnet, 31
gasoline, 210
Gateway Arch, 303
Gatorade, 175
geese, 283
gems, 31, 83
General Mills, 53
genuine, 179
George I, 326
George III, 287
George Washington Bridge, 303
German language, 189
Geronimo, 317
gestures, 298
ghost stories, 93
ghosts, 121
Gilligan's Island, 101, 273
gin, 322
Ginsberg's theorem, 139
giraffe, 72
Girl Scout cookies, 52
give someone "the bird," 57
glaciers, 294
glass, 80
Glinieckj, Al, 197
god, 146
Goddard, Henry, 363
Goethe, Johann, 352
gold, 31, 37, 80, 83, 126, 162
gold records, 99
gold rush, 31
Golden Gate Bridge, 303
goldfish, 10, 71
Goldilocks, 128
Goldwyn, Sam, 271

golf, 81, 116
golf ball, 90
gomer, 14
Gone With the Wind, 133, 147
goose bumps, 226
gorillas, 222
government, 47, 248
Graceland, 58, 95, 338
grams, 193
grandparents, 114
Grant, Ulysses S., 120
grapple tree, 157
grass, 212
grasshoppers, 235
Grateful Dead, 302
Grauman's, 183
Graves, Peter, 101
Grease, 133
Great Indian Hornbill, 138
Great Wall of China, 62, 303
Greece (Greeks), 19, 77, 303
Greek mythology, 31, 180
Green, Robert M., 245
green cards, 47
green onions, 131
Green's law, 139
Greenland, 98
greeting cards, 60
Gregorian calendar, 20
greyhounds, 107
Grigg, Charles L., 175
grocery shopping, 297
Guano Islands, 345
Guatemala, 42
Gummi Bears, 69
gun ownership, 9
gypsy, 23–24

H
Haas, Eduard, 292
hail, 184
hair, 67, 111, 112, 194, 214, 278, 319
hair spray, 329
Hale, Nathan, 287
Hales, Sarah Joseph, 38
Haley, Jack, Jr., 109
Haley, John, 64
half-mast, 280
Hall, Charles, 100
Hall, Joyce C., 60
Hallmark Cards, 60
Halloween, 104, 153
hamburgers, 196
Hamilton, Margaret, 142
Hamlet, 16
Hamlet, 147, 241
hammocks, 14
hamsters, 330
Handel, 331
hands, 252
handshakes, 298
hangnails, 24
Hanks, Tom, 127
"Happy Birthday," 38
Harding, Warren G., 186
"Hark! The Herald Angels Sing," 38
Harley-Davidson, 141
Harn Darn Jun, 93
Harrison, Benjamin, 185
Harrison, William Henry, 120
Harry, Deborah, 13
Hart, Dolores, 127
Harvard University, 239
Hasbro, 156

islands, owned by U.S.,
344–347
Issawi's law, 139
Italian language, 189
Italy, 98, 322

J

Jack Daniel Distillery,
161
jackpot, 122
Jackson, Andrew, 163
Jacob, Mary Phelps, 26
Jagger, Mick, 13, 286
jam, 260
James, Jesse, 191, 229
James, Richard, 170,
247
Japan (Japanese), 15,
77, 81, 372–375
Jarvis Island, 347
jaw, 288
Jaws, 147
Jazz Singer, The, 183
jeans, 265
Jeans, James, 118
Jefferson, Thomas, 163,
185, 271, 352
Jeffrey, Michael,
379–380
Jeffreys, Alec, 365
Jell-O, 69, 172
jellyfish, 10
Jeopardy!, 101, 273
Jerusalem artichokes,
131
jet lag, 331
jewelry, 83
jiffy, 20
"Jingle Bells," 17
Joan of Arc, 73
jobs, 199, 274, 307
Jockey shorts, 116
jockeys, 75

Joel, Billy, 142
Johnny Appleseed, 127
Johnson, Edward H.,
102
Johnson, Lyndon, 250
Johnson, Magic, 177
Johnson, Tom, 75
Johnston Atoll,
346–347
joke books, 93
Jolly Green Giant, 156,
262
Jones, Edward D., 161
Jones, James Earl, 109
Jordan, Michael, 177
jukeboxes, 19
jungle animals, 72
Jupiter, 174

K

K, 275
kaleidoscope, 327
karate, 49
kayaking, 49
Kaysing, Bill, 356
Keck Telescopes, 30
Keebler, Godfrey, 61
Keller, Helen, 73
Kelly, Gene, 183
Kenmuir, John, 108
Kennedy, John F., 250,
360
Kentucky Derby, 75
kerosene fungus, 51
Kerouac, Jack, 106
ketchup, 53, 201, 258
kidnapping, 304
kidneys, 225
kilograms, 193
kilts, 181
Kimmel, Jimmy, 380
King, Stephen, 106
King Henry VIII, 241

King of Kings, 183
King Tut's tomb, 126
Kingman Reef, 344
Kinko's, 61
kissing, 16, 65, 154,
192, 197, 289
kitchen utensils, 8, 65
kitty litter, 99–100
kiwifruit, 131
Klugman, Jack, 365
knights, 65
knock off work, 312
Krachie, Ed, 21
Kraft, Joseph, 293
Kraft Caramels, 293
Kraft Macaroni &
Cheese, 52, 305

L

L&M cigarettes, 156
Labric, Pierre, 197
lacrosse, 75
Lake Nicaragua, 42
Lake Titicaca, 42
lakes, 188, 294, 305
land ownership, 47
landfills, 88
Landsteiner, Karl, 364
languages, 189, 283,
298
lapis lazuli, 31
Las Vegas, 180, 284
Latham, Peter Mere,
366
laughing, 50, 70, 119,
221
Lauper, Cyndi, 1
Laurel, Stan, 109
Lavakan, 63
Lavassor, Madame, 102
Lawrence, Joseph, 61
laws, loony, 164, 279
lawsuits, 43

McEnroe, John, 75
McKinley, William, 120
McMahon, Ed, 101
measurements, 193, 325
meat, grades of, 66
Medicis, 103
medieval England, 8
men, 28, 50, 112, 119, 243
Mendelssohn, Felix, 38
mental health, 50
Mercedes-Benz, 210
mercury, 88
Mercury, 162
mesquite bushes, 148
Metallica, 380
metals, 77, 88
meteorites, 80
meteors, 174
metric system, 193
mice, 62
Michelangelo, 306
Michelin, Pierre, 1
Middle Ages, 8, 65
Midway Islands, 344–345
migraine headaches, 24
mile, 325
Miles, Sylvia, 4
military, 295
milk, 35, 143, 310
Mill Novelty Company, 100
Miller Brewing, 141
Miller, Glenn, 99
million, 20
Mills Brothers, 19
Milton Hershey School, 293
Mimosa pudica, 157
miniature golf, 116

Minnelli, Lisa, 109
Minuit, Peter, 208
Mir spacecraft, 30
mirrors, 30
Missio, Lino, 64
Mission Impossible, 101
Mix, Tom, 127
moles, 272
Mona Lisa, 306
money, paper, 314
money, 327
monkeys, 217
Monopoly, 7
Monroe, Marilyn, 127
Montana, Joe, 232
Montessori school, 239
mood, 50
moon, 62, 124, 162, 174, 248
moon landing, 356–360
moose, 105, 223
mopeds, 51
Morgan, Garrett, 313
Morgan, Julia, 368, 369
Morrison, Wade, 175
Morton Salt Co., 56
mosquitoes, 84, 394
Mother's Day, 104
moths, 217
motion pictures, 4, 103, 109, 127, 133, 147, 183
Mouffet, Thomas, 318
mountains, 76
mourning, 206
mouth, 288, 349
mouthwash, 329
movie posters, 133
movie theaters, 102
Mozart, Wolfgang, 19
Mr. Ed, 159

Mr. Potato Head, 156
Mrs., 275
Mt. Rushmore, 231
mucus, 33
murder, 34, 203
Murphy, Edward A., 218
Murphy's Law, 218–219
Murrie, Bruce, 293
muscles, 225, 351
mushrooms, 148, 212, 254
music videos, 13
Muslim heavens, 77
Mussolini, Benito, 73
My Fair Lady, 4
myths, 299

N
namby-pamby, 327
Nanook of the North, 183
narcotics, 122
NASA, 21, 51, 248, 313, 341, 342, 355–360
Nasubi, 372–375
National Cash Register Company, 27
national debt, 94
national parks, 231
Native Americans, 208, 317
Navassa Island, 345–346
Navassa Phosphate Company, 345
neckties, 181
Nelson, Christian, 245
Nelson, Willie, 286
Neptune, 162
Nero, 44